Learn Bosque Programming

Boost your productivity and software reliability with
Microsoft's new open-source programming language

Sebastian Kaczmarek

Joel Ibaceta

BIRMINGHAM—MUMBAI

Learn Bosque Programming

Group Product Manager: Aaron Lazar
Publishing Product Manager: Shweta Bairoliya
Senior Editor: Rohit Singh
Content Development Editor: Kinnari Chohan
Technical Editor: Pradeep Sahu
Copy Editor: Safis Editing
Project Coordinator: Francy Puthiry
Proofreader: Safis Editing
Indexer: Vinayak Purushotham
Production Designer: Joshua Misquitta

First published: April 2021

Production reference: 1280421

Published by Packt Publishing Ltd.
Livery Place
35 Livery Street
Birmingham
B3 2PB, UK.

ISBN 978-1-83921-197-3

www.packt.com

To my fiancée, Agata, for her support and indulgence during the writing of this book – thank you for giving me as much time as I wanted!

– Sebastian Kaczmarek

To my parents, who have supported me since the first day that I discovered the computers in my life.

– Joel Ibaceta

Contributors

About the authors

Sebastian Kaczmarek is an experienced programmer who specializes in web solutions. He holds an engineer's degree in information technology and is a certified Linux administrator. In the projects he has been a part of, he has worked with many technologies such as JavaScript, Node.js, MongoDB, PHP, MySQL, Java, Hadoop, HBase, and Angular.

Sebastian is passionate about JavaScript and Node.js and loves to share his knowledge on Stack Overflow, where he has reached over 177,000 people with his helpful posts.

Currently, he's working as a backend lead at a Polish software company where he is responsible for architecture design and the development of reliable solutions. In his free time, he likes reading books about astronomy and artificial intelligence.

*I want to thank the people who have been close to me and supported me,
especially my fiancée, Agata, my parents, and my siblings.*

Joel Ibaceta is an experienced software engineer who started writing code at an early age. Currently, he has more than 12 years of experience in the technology industry, building software and leading engineering teams throughout South America. He served as the technical leader of MercadoLibre, a Latin American unicorn, NASDAQ-100 company, and he currently works as co-founder and CTO of Kwema Inc., a US-based start-up that develops wearables for employees' safety.

He is a well-known speaker in LatAm technical communities and a hackathon enthusiast who has won some global prizes such as the Facebook Community Challenge.

*I want to thank all the people who have made this book possible and my
parents, who have supported me in my career development.*

About the reviewers

Federico Kereki is a Uruguayan systems engineer with an MSc in education, with 30+ years of experience as a consultant, system developer, university professor, and writer. He is a subject matter expert at Globant, where he gets to use a good mixture of development frameworks, programming tools, and operating systems.

He has taught at Universidad de la República, Universidad ORT Uruguay, and Universidad de la Empresa. He has written many articles for magazines and websites, and he's written three books on programming, and is currently at work on a new one on data structures and algorithms.

He has given many talks on programming-related topics, and his interests are in software quality and software engineering – with agile methodologies being his focus.

Harris Brakmic is a software engineer from Troisdorf, Germany. He mainly works with Angular, TypeScript, C#, and the Azure cloud, and sometimes develops apps for Android and iOS. Ranging from Java to C#, he has developed software in most major programming languages.

He mainly works as a full-stack developer, that is, everything from the backend (C# and the Azure cloud) to the frontend written in JavaScript or TypeScript and based on React, Angular, or Reactive.js. He is interested in working with Bosque and Idris 2.

Table of Contents

3

Bosque Key Features

Section 2: The Bosque Language Overview

4

Entrypoint Function

5

Types and Operators

6

Bosque Statements

7

Project: Bosque in the Cloud

Section 3: Practicing Bosque

8

Expressions in Bosque

9

Collections

10

Iterative Processing and Recursion

11

Project: AI Classifier

12
Namespaces, Concepts, and Entities

Section 4: Exploring Advanced Features

13
Testing in Bosque

14
Project Path Optimizer

Appendix A
Advanced Topics

Appendix B
What's Next in Bosque?

Other Books You May Enjoy

Index

Preface

Bosque is a new high-level programming language created by Mark Marron, inspired by the impact of structured programming in the 1970s. It adopts TypeScript syntax and ML semantics and is designed for writing code that is simple and easy to reason about for humans and machines. It aims to support high productivity and cloud-first development by removing sources of accidental complexity and introducing novel features.

Learn Bosque Programming covers the concept of a new paradigm called regularized programming and how it has been applied in Bosque. You will learn how to write programs and how to apply the key and unique features that make Bosque an attractive alternative for developers who are seeking improved productivity and who wish to think less about side effects.

The aim of this book is to provide a complete language reference for learning to program with Bosque, explain the regularized programming paradigm, and explore some real-life examples that reinforce the knowledge you will acquire. The book will also help you to dive into more advanced topics, such as the Bosque project structure, or contribute to the project.

Who this book is for

The book is targeted at experienced developers and early adopters who are interested in learning a new, mindset-changing programming language. If you know JavaScript or TypeScript and are willing to learn the advantages of Bosque compared to other programming languages, then this book is for you. You will also see how you can enhance your productivity and build better software using novel features and regularizations. The book assumes that you have experience with programming languages and that you are familiar with various programming paradigms, such as structured or functional programming.

What this book covers

Chapter 1, Exploring Bosque, provides some basic information about what the Bosque project is all about. Here, we will go through some of the theory and motivations behind this project. We will also learn the basics of code intermediate representations. We will learn what they are, why we need them, and what the Bosque approach is. Then, we will review the problem of accidental complexity and present the concept of regularized programming. Eventually, we will mention where Bosque can possibly be applied.

Chapter 2, Configuring the Bosque Environment, explains how to configure a development environment to start learning Bosque and become familiar with some of the tools for compiling scripts and testing our code. First, we will mention all the prerequisites and how they can be fulfilled. Next, we will go through the process of installing Bosque. Eventually, we will write our first Bosque "Hello, world" program.

Chapter 3, Bosque Key Features, provides a brief introduction to the most important features of the Bosque language. There are many features that Bosque offers, but we will focus just on the most interesting and innovative ones here. A detailed description of the remainder of the language syntax, operations, and semantics can be found in the chapters that follow.

Chapter 4, Entrypoint Function, explains the purpose of an entrypoint function in a Bosque script. We will also guide you in the process of writing your first function and later expand your knowledge by teaching you how to pass and receive arguments.

Chapter 5, Types and Operators, takes a tour of the Bosque type system, the primitive values, and the nominal and structural types. We will also review the operations we can apply to them. You will cover a number of useful examples designed to strengthen the knowledge acquired.

Chapter 6, Statements and Syntax, covers Bosque's set of statements and explains the various syntax elements. We will cover practical usage examples and comparisons with other languages. You will learn the language syntax and see how Bosque simplifies various use cases compared to other popular languages.

Chapter 7, Project: Bosque in the Cloud, shows how you can use the features learned and deploy your program in the cloud. We will demonstrate how to create an API using Bosque. Following this chapter, you will be able to create applications in Bosque and deploy them in the cloud.

Chapter 8, Expressions in Bosque, reviews a set of expressions in Bosque, starting with the most frequent expressions in other languages as arguments or scoped access until we reach the most specific Bosque expressions as typed projection or PCode constructors.

Chapter 9, Collections, covers the core collections that Bosque provides. We will go through concepts such as lists, maps, and sets and their useful methods. We will also cover the lesser-known concepts available in Bosque that are undocumented. Finally, we will also mention collections that are currently not fully implemented, such as DynamicMaps, DynamicSets, Stacks, and Queues.

Chapter 10, Iterative Processing and Recursion, explains what iterative processing and recursion looks like in Bosque. First, we will explain why there are no loops available and how we can solve various problems related to iteration without them. Next, we will take a closer look at recursion and restrictions that Bosque sets to simplify recursive calls in our programs. Also, we will cover the NSIterate namespace and its implemented methods.

Chapter 11, Project: AI Classifier, utilizes the features that we have learned so far, allowing you to build a simple AI project. The idea is to create a basic classifier that predicts an output based on two input values. In this example, we will try to train our intelligent model so that it will be able to guess which quadrant of the Cartesian coordinate system a point belongs to. Following this chapter, you will know how Bosque can be applied to simple AI solutions.

Chapter 12, Namespaces, Concepts, and Entities, reviews the definitions of the structural types of Bosque, with a focus on concepts and entities. We will also explore how Bosque implements some concepts known in object-oriented languages, such as inheritance, polymorphism, and static methods, and finally review the concept of namespaces to identify our code scripts.

Chapter 13, Testing in Bosque, covers the concept of symbolic testing to improve the quality of the code we write and prevent bugs without increasing the associated complexity. At the end, we will review some applied testing cases to have a better idea regarding asserts and good practices.

Chapter 14, Project: Path Optimizer, explains how to build an application that finds the shortest path between two points. We will make use of the features we have learned about so far and see how they can be applied to such a project. We will utilize common algorithms in order to perform this task. After reading this chapter, you will know how to apply Bosque in applications that use advanced algorithms.

Appendix A, *Advanced Topics*, shows what the project structure looks like, describes its internals, and how you can contribute to the Bosque project. Since the project is still under heavy development and lacks implementations, and also contains bugs and feature requests, everyone is welcome to improve the language by means of their own contributions.

Appendix B, *What's Next in Bosque*, reviews some useful features that are currently in the pipeline but have not yet been implemented, because this is still a language in development and an alpha version.

To get the most out of this book

You will need Git installed on your computer – any working version. All examples have been tested using Bosque v0.5.0-rc-1. All the necessary instructions in terms of how to get up and running with Bosque are presented in *Chapter 2, Configuring the Bosque Environment*.

Software/hardware covered in the book	OS requirements
Bosque	Windows, macOS X, or Linux
TypeScript	
ECMAScript 2020	
Clang	

If you are using the digital version of this book, we advise you to type the code yourself or access the code via the GitHub repository (link available in the next section). Doing so will help you avoid any potential errors related to the copying and pasting of code.

Download the example code files

You can download the example code files for this book from GitHub at `https://github.com/PacktPublishing/Learn-Bosque-Programming`. In case there's an update to the code, it will be updated on the existing GitHub repository.

We also have other code bundles from our rich catalog of books and videos available at `https://github.com/PacktPublishing/`. Check them out!

Download the color images

We also provide a PDF file that has color images of the screenshots/diagrams used in this book. You can download it here: `https://static.packt-cdn.com/downloads/9781839211973_ColorImages.pdf`.

Conventions used

There are a number of text conventions used throughout this book.

`Code in text`: Indicates code words in text, database table names, folder names, filenames, file extensions, pathnames, dummy URLs, user input, and Twitter handles. Here is an example: "We have the `ApplicationContext` entity, which holds two fields: `emailServiceEnabled` and `user`."

A block of code is set as follows:

```
let context = ApplicationContext@{
    emailServiceEnabled = false, user = user
};
```

When we wish to draw your attention to a particular part of a code block, the relevant lines or items are set in bold:

```
entrypoint function main(): String {
    let user = User@{ name = "John Doe", id = 1 };
    var context = ApplicationContext@{ emailServiceEnabled =
     false, user = user };

    context = enableEmailService(ref context);
    return sendEmail(context);
}
```

Any command-line input or output is written as follows:

```
$ symtest ai-classifier.bsq -e "NSMain::run"
```

Bold: Indicates a new term, an important word, or words that you see on screen. For example, words in menus or dialog boxes appear in the text like this. Here is an example: "If you don't have it in the first list, you can either create a new variable named `Path` using the **New…** button or you can find it in the **System variables** list."

> **Tips or important notes**
> Appear like this.

Get in touch

Feedback from our readers is always welcome.

General feedback: If you have questions about any aspect of this book, mention the book title in the subject of your message and email us at customercare@packtpub.com.

Errata: Although we have taken every care to ensure the accuracy of our content, mistakes do happen. If you have found a mistake in this book, we would be grateful if you would report this to us. Please visit www.packtpub.com/support/errata, selecting your book, clicking on the Errata Submission Form link, and entering the details.

Piracy: If you come across any illegal copies of our works in any form on the internet, we would be grateful if you would provide us with the location address or website name. Please contact us at copyright@packt.com with a link to the material.

If you are interested in becoming an author: If there is a topic that you have expertise in, and you are interested in either writing or contributing to a book, please visit authors.packtpub.com.

Reviews

Please leave a review. Once you have read and used this book, why not leave a review on the site that you purchased it from? Potential readers can then see and use your unbiased opinion to make purchase decisions, we at Packt can understand what you think about our products, and our authors can see your feedback on their book. Thank you!

For more information about Packt, please visit packt.com.

Section 1: Introduction

In this part, we introduce the Bosque project. After reading this section, you will understand its key concepts and how to start experimenting with it.

This section comprises the following chapters:

- *Chapter 1, Exploring Bosque*
- *Chapter 2, Configuring the Bosque Environment*
- *Chapter 3, Bosque Key Features*

1
Exploring Bosque

The Bosque project was born from Mark Marron's work, where he questioned the accidental complexity that exists in programming languages nowadays. He proposed a new programming language design that eliminated the factors of this complexity in terms of loops, recursion, mutable state, and reference equality, among others, thus resulting in a new paradigm called Regularized Programming.

Bosque has a syntax inspired by TypeScript and adopts semantics from **ML** and JavaScript, giving rise to a programming language that is easy
to write and read.

The simplicity of Bosque allows programmers who decide to adopt Bosque to focus on the core of the problem without worrying about the errors that are caused by the language's accidental complexity. Consequently, they will build more reliable, robust, and predictable programs that have been prepared, by design, to support new trends.

In this chapter, we will cover the basics of what the Bosque project is, as well as some of the theory and motivation behind this project. We will also learn the basics of code **intermediate representations (IR)**. We will learn what they are, why we need them, and what the Bosque approach is. We will also review the problem of accidental complexity and present the concept of regularized programming. Eventually, we will mention where Bosque can be applied.

We will cover the following topics:

- Identifying the need for another language
- Learning what intermediate representation is
- Discovering regularized programming
- Understanding accidental complexity
- How the experiment is going so far
- Bosque applications

By the end of this chapter, you will have knowledge about what Bosque really is and how it works.

Identifying the need for another language

Some of the most frequent questions programmers ask during their early learning years are "Why are there so many programming languages?," "Why don't we just use the same language for everything?," and "Why do we keep creating more programming languages?". A useful analogy to explain the diversity of the programming languages that exist today is to imagine programming languages as musical instruments. We have string, wind, and percussion instruments based on different physical principles; in the same way, programming languages are designed based on different architectures and paradigms. However, instruments or programming languages are often used to generate structured and ordered compositions.

We cannot objectively say that a guitar is not appropriate to play the fifth symphony by Beethoven, since we could only give an appreciation for this based on our personal tastes. In the same way, choosing a programming language might not represent preferring syntax or specific expertise.

But it is also true that interpreting some compositions without the appropriate instrument could be an arduous task, and it could mean sacrificing a big part of the piece due to the physical limitations of the instrument's design. A similar scenario unfolds when we're trying to use programming languages to do things that they were not designed to. Often, this could mean putting in a tremendous technical effort, or having to sacrifice performance, productivity, or stability.

In summary, *The Four Seasons* by Vivaldi can be beautifully played with a violin and maybe not with a drum; similarly, R rather than Lua could be much more suitable and efficient for statistically analyzing information, while Lua is better for extending Nginx servers instead of Ruby. Although we can use the same tools for everything, they will not always be the most appropriate.

Now that we have a better idea about the diversity of programming languages and their suitability for solving some specific types of problems, the following question arises: "Why was Bosque created?"

When it comes to developing high-level programming languages, one of the main objectives has always been to try to simplify the process of writing code so that it's as close to human language as possible. This allows us to simplify the process of giving instructions to machines using the potential of human reasoning.

But generally, each continuously evolving process implies an increase in complexity, and this complexity may cause mistakes, in the same way that programming languages have been acquiring characteristics that make them complex and prone to causing hard-to-identify errors. By learning from the past and questioning the actual complexity of programming languages, Bosque was born. To solve this and to learn from the past, as inspired by the impact generated by Structural Programming in its day, Bosque was born as a new programming language that eliminates accidental complexity.

As a result, we have a coding process that's more straightforward, predictable, and readable. This allows programmers to focus on the most important stuff or the main program logic, thus improving productivity and making software more reliable.

In the words of Bosque's creator (Mark Marron):

> *"The Bosque language demonstrates the feasibility of eliminating sources of accidental complexity while retaining the expressivity and performance needs for a practical language, as well as hinting at the opportunity for improved developer productivity and software quality."*

Now that we understand why Bosque exists, lets learn how it builds an executable program from high-level source code.

Learning what Intermediate Representation is

Nowadays, it's not unusual to find high-level programming languages that use one or more intermediate representations when they're translating source code into binary code or machine code. By doing this, the compilation process can be simplified without us losing the advantages of a high-level language. It opens the path to developing new programming languages and being friendlier with developers and closer to the process of human reasoning. Bosque is no exception.

Let's learn how intermediate representation works by looking at an example.

First, an abstract representation is usually modeled through a graph that describes the program we are compiling through a data structure. This can occur in different ways:

- An **abstract syntax tree (AST)**
- Lineal IR's three-way code or Postfix notation

Let's take a look at the following expression:

```
5 * a - b
```

This expression can be expressed using the following AST:

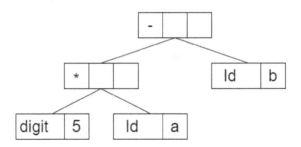

Figure 1.1 – AST graph representation

If we quickly inspect the graph, we can identify the code's intent through its structure. We could use this abstract representation to generate an intermediate code representation that is more agnostic to the architecture or execution environment. This code is usually a sequential representation of the syntactic tree. Generally, from this abstract representation, an intermediate code representation could be generated. Even though this is more similar to final object code, this code is usually a sequential representation of the syntactic tree, agnostic to the architecture or execution environment.

Here, we can observe the representation in the intermediate code of the previous structure:

```
t1 = 5 * a
t2 = b
t3 = t1 - t2
```

From this intermediate code, and by using a suitable compiler, a final executable binary can be generated, which would be the result of our source code's compilation. Let's look at a more complex example based on a C# snippet. This can be interpreted as follows:

```
while ( x > y ) {
    if ( x > 0 ) {
        x = x - y;
    }

}
```

The AST representation of the previous code is as follows:

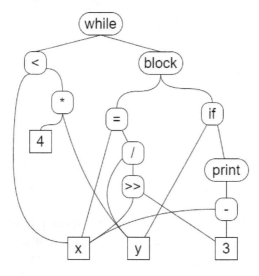

Figure 1.2 – AST graph representation

During its interpretation, the C# source code is converted into an intermediate code called IL, representing the original code's intention. However, in this case, it is less understandable at first glance, as shown here:

```
.locals init (
    [0] int32 x,
    [1] int32 y,
    [2] bool,
    [3] bool
)
IL_0001: ldc.i4.0
IL_0002: stloc.0
IL_0003: ldc.i4.0
IL_0004: stloc.1
// sequence point: hidden
IL_0005: br.s IL_0017
// loop start (head: IL_0017)
    IL_0007: nop
    IL_0008: ldloc.0
    IL_0009: ldc.i4.0
    IL_000a: cgt
    IL_000c: stloc.2
    // sequence point: hidden
    IL_000d: ldloc.2
    IL_000e: brfalse.s IL_0016
    IL_0010: nop
    IL_0011: ldloc.0
...
```

Later, this intermediate code will be converted into low-level code so that it can be interpreted by the virtual machine that will build the final executable – in this case, .NET Framework. Some additional examples of known intermediate languages are as follows:

- **GNU RTL**: This is an intermediate language that's used to support many of the programs in the programming languages found in the GNU Compiler Collection.

- **CIL**: This an intermediate language that's used by Microsoft .NET Framework's high-level languages. The final binary code is generated from this representation.

- **C**: Even though it wasn't designed as an intermediate language, it's often used as a layer of abstraction for the assembler language, which is why so many languages have adopted it as their intermediate representation.

The advantages of having an intermediate representation include being able to have an intermediate stage of interpretation from the high-level language. In this stage, we can optimize, analyze, or correct the code in the most appropriate way according to the language's design and objectives.

The process of transforming an intermediate representation into native code that results in an executable binary is also called **ahead-of-time** (**AOT**) compilation. This has many advantages over the **just-in-time** (**JIT**) compilation, generally resulting in a considerable reduction in execution time, resource savings, and shorter startup times.

This is why the Bosque compilation process uses a binary generation tool based on AOT compilation, called ExeGen, whose usage we will explore in more detail in the next chapter. Additionally, the Bosque project has an IR that's been explicitly designed to support the needs of the regularized programming paradigm. It explores how to build intermediate representations so that they include support for symbolic testing, enhanced fuzzing, GC compilation, and API auto-marshaling, among others.

Some of these characteristics that Bosque IR supports are part of the regularized programming paradigm, as we will see next.

Discovering regularized programming

One of the main paradigms that is used when stepping away from machine code and representing instructions in high-level expressions is structured programming, which is based on the theory proposed by Böhm-Jacopini during the 1960s, when it was proved that any computable function can be modeled using flow control structures, iteration, and subroutines. It was also asserted that the GO TO instruction could be exempted because its use could lead to the development of spaghetti code. One of the recognized promoters of this idea was E. Dijkstra, who covered it in his paper *Go To Statement Considered Harmful*.

Following this paradigm, we can design flow charts that represent our program's logic in a more readable fashion. This allows programs to be developed in a more efficient, trustworthy, and legible manner:

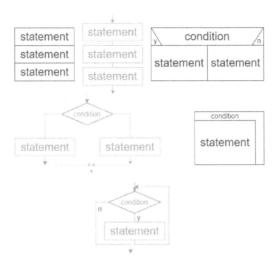

Figure 1.3 – Basic structures proposed by the structured programming paradigm

This paradigm was used by IBM investigator Harlan Mills to develop an indexation system for The New York Times investigation files. It was a great success and gave birth to other companies who had started to adopt the paradigm with enthusiasm.

A new age had arrived and code had become easier to write. The problems at hand could be reduced using a series of structures and diagrams.

Afterward, we saw the imminent arrival of structured design, modularity, and modular programming because of the use of structured programming in more complex settings, thus dividing the problem at hand into more straightforward, smaller problems, and these into other, simpler problems.

This happened in the middle of a golden age for programming that gave birth to more programming languages and more compilers, allowing us to abstract the complexity of the architecture where programs would be executed. IDEs and high-level tools were also that reduced the entry barriers for writing code, taking programs to the many industries that existed at the time.

In the next few years, we saw the uprising of new paradigms such as **object-oriented programming (OOP)**, which represented programs as systems containing entities with properties, behaviors, and states. It intended to apply mental models to problem solving since it was easier to represent the problem in terms of their objects, properties, interactions, and the effects of these interactions.

With OOP, not only mathematical or automation problems could be shaped, but more complex systems could be represented through software, allowing us to reuse mental models or knowledge about the industry and transfer it to an application. However, because of this, we had to worry about remembering and following the state changes of all the objects that had been created during the application's entire life cycle. This implies that even though it's easier to model a real-life system through entities and their interactions, we also have to deal with the language's technical complexity and abstraction issues.

Many years have passed since those days, and we've witnessed the appearance of many other paradigms, the fall of some models, and the revindication of others that seemed like they'd never come back. Technology has also changed – nowadays, problems are more complex, and the internet has taken great relevance in software development. Today, we need to write code much faster to comply with the pace of the changes that are being made, but we also live with what we've inherited from the predecessors of the first designs, architectures, and models, even though we also have many open problems from more than 30 years ago.

Bosque proposed that we go a step further and, just like structured programming, presented a new way to simplify the code writing process through regularized programming. This enhanced the legibility, productivity, and code analysis process, and also helped simplify existing models. This starts with throwing out the source of the mistakes that come with accidental complexity, making it easier to implement formal reasoning models to code. Bosque proposes that we rethink the way in which we build programming languages from a perspective similar to structured programming, with the goal of simplifying the code writing process, thus enhancing its legibility, reliability, and productivity.

This simplicity is a consequence of eliminating the sources of accidental complexity, avoiding the unexpected behavior of our programs, and providing a deterministic perspective for writing code. This new design favors translating formal reasoning models into source code. As a result, we have a new paradigm called "regularized programming."

In the next section, we will understand the advantages of eliminating complexity in programming languages

Understanding accidental complexity

Speaking about complexity implies that it's difficult to understand something through simple reasoning. For example, it's hard to predict the result of a program's execution or piece of code that uses various recursion instances, because it's hard to figure out what the result will be without doing a more detailed analysis of the process.

Often, this complexity is inherent to the problem we're trying to solve, which we call essential complexity since we cannot dispense it. A recurrent exercise in mathematics and physics, which has allowed us to make significant advances, is to simplify complex models by eliminating sources of complexity that aren't inherent to the phenomenon we're trying to describe. The problem in software development is that this complexity is an essential part of the problem that's being solved, and it's not so easy to simplify the problem.

Although this complexity is not unique to software, it can be harder to show. For example, if we're constructing a building, which is a structure with plenty of complexity, it's easier to show what part of the structure isn't correctly aligned, a dimension that doesn't comply with the blueprints, or rather that the omissions are pretty obvious. The invisible nature of software means that we need to put in more effort to try and identify the cause of an error in a complex system.

One of the most critical advances in the software industry has been the development of high-level languages that simplify many of the possible causes of error due to complexity. This was achieved by encapsulating problems in abstract structures, hierarchies, and modules, thus allowing programmers to improve their productivity and the comprehension of their written code. This also enabled them to focus on solving the core of the problem and not deal with disk access, memory registers, and precise details surrounding the architecture or the hardware.

The models these languages have been built on carry some sources of complexity that Mark Marron identified in his work, and that Bosque pretends to avoid from the design stage of the new programming language.

Now, let's understand each of these sources of complexity and how Bosque avoids them in its design.

Immutability

Mutability can be more intuitive at a higher level but harder to comprehend in detail, besides making analysis tools harder because it affects the application's state. On the other hand, it implies having to compute logical frames. This could be an arduous task for developers as they must remember the state changes for each entity in their applications.

Mutability is an object trait that allows them to be changed. This concept could be intuitive at first glance because we are used to thinking about transforming things through processes, especially if we have spent a lot of time programming with OOP.

However, this adds an extra level of complexity since we must be aware of all the changes our objects will undergo during the entire execution process.

Additionally, if we consider that our code uses methods and functions that have been provided by external libraries or language helpers, which can change our objects or entities' states, then all the events that modify an object's state become arduous. Consequently, we have less predictable programs.

Let's look at an example to understand this better.

Let's say we have the following code in JavaScript, which describes an object – `Charles`, in this case:

```
let person = {
    name: "Charles"
}
```

Now, let's create a function that assigns a new value to save this person's age:

```
function setAgeToPerson(person, age) {
    person.age = age;
}
```

Now we are able to add the age property to person, calling to the function `setAgeToPerson()`:

```
setAgeToPerson(person, 21);
```

So, if we query for the properties of `person`, we will have age and name.

However, let's imagine that a third-party library provides the `setAgeToPerson()` method. If we had previously assigned a value to age, we could incur an error that could be difficult to identify since we are changing a property with the same name from different places.

This can become a problem if we have many events throughout the code that alter the state or composition of an object, which is even more complex if we consider asynchronous executions or dynamic dispatching.

Due to this and the Bosque philosophy of eliminating sources of complexity, immutability is adopted for all the values throughout the language.

Contrary to mutability, immutability is the concept that objects cannot change state once they've been created. This concept may be familiar to you if you have had experience with functional languages.

Other than improving the predictability of the code and minimizing errors, immutability has many benefits when it's time to understand the code that's been written. The following are some other benefits of immutability:

- Easy-to-test code
- Thread-safe by design
- No invalid states
- Better encapsulation

In summary, immutability in Bosque allows our applications to be more predictable, secure, and stable, thus allowing us to clearly identify the state of our application through the code that's written. It doesn't let hidden code make unexpected changes.

Loop-free

Loops are part of many junior programmers' training, so it is common to think about them when we're solving problems. However, we may create errors when we use them, which could be avoided.

As we know, when we use loops, we must be careful and correctly use comparison operators such as <= instead of <. This is a frequent mistake, almost like forgetting the semicolon at the end of the line, so we also have to be careful when it comes to creating infinite loops.

On the other hand, loops usually involve an additional effort to try and understand their intent. This is because the programmer must do a mental process, similar to reverse engineering, to get a better idea of the result that will be obtained when they execute a piece of code that contains some nested loops.

Often, the primary intent in loops could be replaced by a higher-order function, which provides better clarity about its intent. Let's look at an example of this. Let's take an array of numbers using JavaScript:

```
const arrayOfNumbers = [17, -4, 3.2, 8.9, -1.3, 0, Math.PI];
```

To obtain the sum of all the values of the array in JavaScript, we could write something like this:

```
let sum = 0;
arrayOfNumbers.forEach((number) => {
    sum += number;
});
console.log(sum);
```

However, we could use the `reduce` function to avoid using loops and the need to use mutable data, whose final intention is easier to comprehend:

```
const sum = arrayOfNumbers.reduce((accumulator, number) =>
accumulator + number
);
console.log(sum);
```

In summary, loops could imply that additional effort is needed to read written code and reduce its predictability.

Loop-free coding makes our code declarative instead of imperative, thus simplifying it so that we have a better understanding of its purpose. This also allows us to apply generalized reasoning and better integration to immutable data.

Bosque encourages us to write loop-free code by providing a series of useful methods for working with collections and arrays through algebraic bulk operations.

Indeterminate behaviors

Sometimes, when we compile a program, we don't think we'll encounter any problems. However, when we do execute the code, the result is different from what we had expected. This is called an indeterminate behavior.

Although some algorithms are non-deterministic by design, this implies that, by using the same input, we could expect different results. This could increase the complexity of controlling possible error scenarios.

Some examples of this include attempting to assign values in a matrix beyond the established limits, an unexpected resulting from a math operation due to type inference, or concurrent code execution.

Bosque proposes programs with unique results for the same incoming parameters in order to simplify how the written code is understood. It also helps us avoid errors due to unforeseen execution flows or unexpected behavior.

To achieve this goal, it is necessary to eliminate indeterminate behavior sources such as uninitialized variable support, mutable data, unstable enumeration order, and so on.

Additionally, Bosque proposes eliminating environmental sources of indeterminism such as I/O, random numbers, UUID generation transferring this responsibility to the runtime host, and decoupling it from the language core. Due to this, the host will be responsible for managing the environment's interaction.

That is why Bosque programmers will never see intermittent production failures and will always have more stable and reliable code.

Data invariant violations

The invariance concept guarantees that a property or condition will always comply with predefined conditions, so assumptions can be made without incurring errors. This allows for design-by-contract implementation.

Within a loop, the invariant is represented as the necessary instructions to bring the precondition's value toward the postcondition's fulfillment. For example, if we want to have the sum of numbers in an array, the invariant would be the instructions to accumulate each value's sum. Most programming languages provide operators with access and update elements in arrays/tuples/objects, which changes the state of an object through an imperative multi-step process, making it difficult to track all the changes as a range of mistakes can be made.

Bosque proposes that we use algebraic bulk data operators, which help us focus on the overall intent of the code through algebraic reasoning instead of using individual steps. Let's look at some examples of bulk operations that have been written in Bosque.

We can get the elements located at positions 0 and 2 with the following code:

```
(@[7 , 8 , 9 ] ) @[0 , 2 ] ;          // @[7, 9]
```

Alternatively, we update the value of position 0 by 5 and assign position 3 the value of 1. Consequently, position 2 will be assigned none:

```
(@[7 , 8] <~(0=5, 3=1);               / @[5, 8, none, 1]
```

Then, we can add the value 5 at the end:

```
(@[7 , 8] <+(@[5]);                   // @[7, 8, 5]
```

Don't worry if you don't fully understand the previous code. We'll learn how to build bulk functions in more detail in *Chapter 3, Bosque Key features*.

Aliasing

At execution time, the same memory position can typically be accessed through different symbolic names. So, when we modify this value through one of these names, the value is changed for all the other names. We call this situation aliasing, which can generate unexpected behaviors and errors that will be difficult to identify.

A practical situation occurs in a buffer overflow scenario, as we know some programming languages allow manual memory management, so if the amount of data in the reserved area (buffer) is not adequately controlled, this additional data will be written in the adjacent area, thus overwriting the original content, which will produce unexpected behavior or a segmentation fault.

The programming languages that we use today having implementations based on particular hardware architectures, for example, how the information is stored in memory through different names or how pointer aliases work, because they could be different in some languages.

On the other hand, using aliases requires that we maintain a specific program execution order to obtain the expected behavior. Write access must be carried out in the same order in which it was written. This implies a big challenge for reordering optimizations.

The immutable nature of values in Bosque means that we only need to use read-only pointers, so analyzing aliases is not necessary, thus simplifying our problem.

How the experiment is going so far

Bosque was born from an investigation paper based on the idea of questioning the causes of accidental complexity and proposing a solution that tries to eliminate this from the design of a new language. This paper exposed an interesting setting about how we could improve productivity, have clearer, more legible code, and, in turn, have a smaller margin for committing errors during the development process – all of which can be done by eliminating the causes of complexity.

Later, the language was published as an open source project on GitHub, ready to receive support and community contributions. During this stage, Bosque ceased to be a prototype or experimental language for starting a roadmap to complete its development. It did this by implementing many of the basic characteristics, which turned it into a language for developing applications. However, at the time of writing this book, version 1.0 has not been released yet.

In this process, elements such as commentaries, core libraries, and tools were added that simplify the curve of its adoption by new developers. A series of characteristics were also added for its possible applications. If we're ready to sacrifice things that haven't been implemented yet to adopt regularized programming and to start to change our ways of thinking and solving problems, Bosque is a good choice.

What next?

According to the imminent implementations roadmap that should pop up in the next few months, the following will be coming next:

- Memoization and singleton pragmas
- Module/package support
- Improvements to the core collection libraries
- Earlier microframeworks, to simplify the development and adoption process
- N-API native modules so that we can use Bosque via Node.js
- Integration with the Morphir Project
- Multiple file compilation

Let's look at some cases where regularized programming and the Bosque approach might be more suitable than other languages.

Bosque applications

As we know, we can try to build a house with Lego, but this could be a much more difficult task than doing so with bricks, iron, and mortar. Although we can do something with different tools, some are more appropriate than others. That is why the following question always arises when we explore a new programming language: What are the applications where this language would be more appropriate over others that I already know about? We will try to answer this question by cover a few scenarios, although this does not imply that these are the only things we can do with Bosque.

Cloud-first development

One of the main challenges of new, trending technologies such as serverless applications, microservices architecture, and IoT is reaching interoperability with a minimum computational cost. Nowadays, we must deal with serializing and deserializing messages or the slow response times of cold services starting up.

Bosque includes features such as API types to simplify the development of APIs. Its initialization design allows a zero-cost load for cold startups, in addition to characteristics such as immutability and its deterministic nature, which will enable us to build high-performance and resilient applications for cloud environments.

Automatic verification

One of the advantages of a programming language that allows you to implement models based on formal reasoning is that this can be analyzed by tools that allow us to identify and eliminate errors through verification and validation processes. This improves the reliability of the execution's results. Some of the application settings could be as follows:

- Cryptographical protocols

- Implementation of finite state machines

- A network's mathematical models

Synthesis programming

The deterministic nature of Bosque makes it an ideal candidate for the application of AI for code synthesis from formal specifications. This has been an existing challenge since the first days of AI as a study branch, so this synergy could be fascinating.

Summary

Bosque is a new high-level programming language based on a new paradigm called regularized programming, which proposes eliminating accidental complexity sources.

Accidental complexity occurs during the evolutionary process of programming languages as they adapt to new contexts and implement various paradigms.

Eliminating complexity sources allows us to simplify how we write code, allowing developers to focus on the problem's core. This also enables us to write programs that are more predictable, readable, and reliable.

A simple, deterministic, and readable language is suitable for solving the challenges that new technologies bring, such as IoT development, serverless applications, and cloud-first solutions. So, Bosque could be an exciting language for your next project if you consider yourself an early adopter.

Now that you've read this chapter, we understand what the Bosque project is and what the regularized programming paradigm proposes. As a result, you have a better idea of the accidental complexity problem in the programming languages that are available today and are ready to consider Bosque as a new alternative for future projects.

In the next chapter, we will prepare our development environment so that we can start writing programs in Bosque.

Questions

1. What is the Bosque project?

2. What is the regularized programming paradigm?

3. What is accidental complexity?

4. Why should you choose Bosque for your next project?

Further reading

Here are some additional reference materials that you may wish to refer to regarding what was covered in this chapter:

*   Dijkstra, E. W. (1968). Go To Statement Considered Harmful. *Communications of the ACM*, 147-148.

*   Brooks, F. P. (1987). No Silver Bullet – Essence and Accident in Software Engineering. *Computer*, 10-19.

*   Marron, M. (2019). *Regularized Programming with the Bosque Language.* Microsoft Research.

*   Jonathan Goldstein, A. A. (2020). *A.M.B.R.O.S.I.A: providing performant virtual resiliency for distributed applications.* Proceedings of the VLDB Endowment.

*   Harper, R. (2011). *Programming in Standard ML.* Carnegie Mellon University.

2
Configuring the Bosque Environment

Now that we've learned what the Bosque project is and why it was developed, we are ready to see it in action.

In this chapter, we will learn how to configure a development environment to start experimenting with Bosque, and we will become familiar with the tools used to compile scripts and test our code. First, we will look at all the required prerequisites and how they can be fulfilled. Next, we will go through the installation process of Bosque itself. Eventually, we will write and compile our first Bosque "Hello, World" program.

Here is a list of the topics that we are going to cover:

- Prerequisites for Bosque
- Installing C++ compiler
- Installing Bosque
- Setting up the IDE for Bosque
- Writing a "Hello, World!" program
- ExeGen – Ahead-of-time Bosque compilation

By the end of this chapter, you will have a fully working Bosque environment, ready to write, compile, and run your own programs.

Technical requirements

All the specific requirements are mentioned and explained in the next section.

Prerequisites for Bosque

Before we can start using the Bosque language and experimenting with its features, we need to meet several requirements:

- A 64-bit operating system
- The LTS version of Node.js and NPM
- TypeScript
- A C++ compiler

At this point, you may wonder why we need Node.js and TypeScript in order to run Bosque programs. The answer is that the whole Bosque implementation is mostly written in TypeScript. The parser, type checker, interpreter, and command-line runner—all of these need to be built and transpiled into JavaScript before we can start using them.

Another thing that may seem a little bit confusing is the need for a C++ compiler to be installed on our system. The reason for this is that it is used for generating executable binaries from the Bosque source code. This is described in more detail in the next section. In this section, let's focus on the first three requirements.

64-bit operating system

This is something of a self-evident requirement, isn't it? At the same time, it's kind of strict—either you have 64-bit platform and you can run Bosque, or you don't and you can only see others playing with it. However, if you are in the group of those who have a 32-bit platform, there is still hope. It is possible that you have installed a 32-bit host OS, but your CPU is 64-bit. You can check this without installing any additional software. I will quickly show you how to do this on Windows, Linux, and macOS.

If you are certain that you are running a 64-bit operating system, you can skip this section and jump straight to *The LTS version of Node.js and NPM* section. The following description is intended for those who have installed a 32-bit OS, but are willing to check whether their CPU can handle 64-bit software, and if it does, then how to make use of it.

Windows

If you are using a Windows operating system, you need to open the Windows search box, type system information, and select the **System Information** option. On the right section of the window, look for the **System Type** element. If its value includes **x86**, this means that the CPU is 32-bit and unfortunately, there's not much you can do to run Bosque on your machine. However, if the value includes **x64**, then the CPU is 64-bit and there is a way for you to configure the Bosque environment.

Linux

For Linux users, the simplest way to check whether the CPU is 32-bit or 64-bit is to run the following command in the terminal:

```
$ lscpu
...
CPU op-mode(s):          32-bit, 64-bit
...
```

Look at the **CPU op-mode(s)** option. If the value includes **64-bit** (as shown in the preceding code), this means that your CPU is capable of running 64-bit software and you can also run Bosque.

MacOS

If you are using macOS, then there is a bit more work to do. First, click the Apple icon in the menu bar and select the **About This Mac** option. In the window that appears, look for the **More Info** option and click it. Now, open the **Hardware** section and find the **Processor Name** attribute. At this point, you need to copy the name and consult the internet as to whether it's a 32-bit or 64-bit processor. If it's the latter, you are the happy owner of a CPU that can handle the Bosque language.

Virtual machine

This section is for those of you who have confirmed that their CPU can handle 64-bit software, but whose host OS is 32 bit.

The solution for you is to use a virtual machine. There is plenty of software supporting virtualization regardless of what operating system you use. The most common ones are VirtualBox, VMware, or Hyper-V. It is up to you which software to choose. Personally, I prefer VirtualBox. Thanks to virtualization, you can run any operating system you want on your host machine. This means that if your CPU is 64-bit, you can install a 64-bit operating system on a virtual machine and proceed with the installation of Bosque on the VM.

You should pick the virtualization software and an operating system of your preference and install it according to the official instructions available on manufacturer's website. We will not cover the installation steps in this book; we will focus on the direct Bosque dependencies instead.

Docker

Another way to install all of the requirements is to use Docker. It is a very convenient way because it wraps all of the prerequisites inside a container, and you can keep your system clean. However, keep in mind that you still need to have 64-bit CPU in order to run Bosque—you can't overcome this.

If you are using Windows, the minimum version required to install and run Docker is Windows 10 Professional or Enterprise. For macOS users, it is version 10.14 or newer.

You need to install Docker Desktop and Visual Studio Code Remote Development Extension Pack, or you can manually use Docker image and run it. All of the required instructions can be found in the Bosque GitHub repository at `https://github.com/microsoft/BosqueLanguage/blob/master/docs/extras/docker.md`. As with the virtual machine method, we will not cover the Docker installation steps in this book, as we want to focus on the direct Bosque dependencies. However, if you decide to use Docker and succeed, you can skip the next few sections and jump straight into the *Setting up the IDE for Bosque* section.

The LTS version of Node.js and NPM

Now that we are sure that we have 64-bit operating system installed, we can focus on the next requirement, which is Node.js and NPM. As previously stated, the Bosque implementation is mostly written in TypeScript. In order to run it, we need the Node.js runtime.

You can check whether you have it installed on your system by opening your favorite terminal and typing the following commands:

```
$ node -v
$ npm -v
```

At the time of writing, the LTS version of Node.js is 14.16.1, which includes NPM 6.14.12. If any of these commands failed, it means that you don't have all the required software installed. In that case, you should continue reading this section. However, if you confirmed that you have installed Node.js and NPM by running these commands, you can skip this section.

Installing Node.js is pretty straightforward. The next sections will show you how to install Node.js and NPM on various operating systems.

Windows

In order to get Node.js and NPM on a Windows machine, go to the official website at `https://nodejs.org/` and download the LTS version that is recommended for most users. Once the installer is downloaded, run it and proceed with the instructions shown in the installer window. You will be asked to accept the license agreement and choose the destination folder and components that you wish to install. If you are not sure what to select, you can safely click on **Next** at each step and then click on **Install** at the end. After a while, you should see a dialog box stating that Node.js has been successfully installed. You just need to click on the **Finish** button and that's it—you have everything ready to proceed to the next section. The following screenshot shows the final window, showing a successful installation of Node.js:

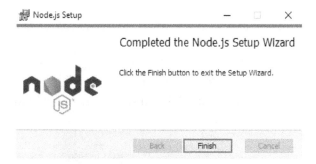

Figure 2.1 – Successfully installed Node.js

Linux and MacOS

The installation of Node.js on Linux or macOS machines is as simple as it is on Windows. You can go to the official website at `https://nodejs.org/` and download the installer file that will be automatically selected for your platform. However, I recommend a slightly different approach. There are situations where you need to use a different version of your runtime to test some features. For example, you might need to check whether your NPM module will work with some older versions of Node.js. Managing multiple versions of Node.js may be problematic when you have one global version installed and need to replace it with an older one for a short time. This is why we have tools such as **Node Version Manager** (**NVM**) available; it allows us to maintain multiple versions of Node.js simultaneously and switch between them at any time. I strongly recommend using it whenever possible.

To install NVM, you need to run the installation script. You can do it in a few ways, but I will only show you one. Open your favorite terminal and run the following command:

```
$ curl -o- https://raw.githubusercontent.com/nvm-sh/nvm/
v0.36.0/install.sh | bash
```

This will download the installation script and run it immediately. Once this is done, you need to close and reopen the terminal window. Note that the version in the link may vary depending on when you are reading this book. At the time of writing, the latest one is v0.36.0.

Now we can install the LTS version of Node.js by running the following command:

```
$ nvm install --lts
```

Once this command finishes, you should have all the required components installed. You can verify this by running these commands again:

```
$ node -v
v14.16.1
$ npm -v
6.14.12
```

You should see the versions of Node.js and NPM installed on your system respectively, as shown under the preceding commands.

TypeScript

We are halfway through. The next thing we need to do is to install TypeScript, which is the main language used to implement Bosque.

In order to verify whether you have already installed it, you can run the following command in any terminal regardless of your operating system:

```
$ tsc -v
Version 3.4.5
```

If the output shows a version number (as shown in the preceding code under the command), it means that you can skip this section; otherwise, you need to install TypeScript on your machine.

The installation of TypeScript is the same for Windows, Linux, and MacOS, and it comes down to running only one command:

```
$ npm install -g typescript
```

After the installation process completes, you will be able to use the `tsc` command. You can verify this by running the following command again:

```
$ tsc -v
```

You should see the version of TypeScript installed on your machine.

Installing a C++ compiler

After fulfilling the prerequisites, it is time to install a C++ compiler. This component is required for generating executable binaries from the Bosque source code. It is described in more detail later on in this chapter. By default, Bosque tools expect the **Clang** compiler on Windows, Linux, and macOS, but if you wish to use a different one, or if you already have a C++ compiler installed on your system, this is also fine. If this is the case, you can skip this section completely and jump straight into the *Installing Bosque* section.

> **Important note**
>
> If you choose not to use the default Clang compiler, you will have to add the `--compiler` option when compiling programs using the `exegen` command. It is described at the end of the chapter, in the *ExeGen – Ahead-of-time Bosque compilation* section.

In order to install the Clang compiler, you should install something called **LLVM**. This is a collection of components that are used to optimize and generate machine code. This library allows us to use any of its modules to build compilers or other software connected with programming languages. One of its components is Clang. This means that by installing LLVM, you automatically install Clang with all other required software.

I will quickly describe the installation process of Clang on various operating systems.

Before we start, it is worth checking whether you have already installed Clang on your machine. In order to do this, you need to run the following command in the terminal:

```
$ clang --help
```

If it fails, this means that installation is required. However, if this command outputs help information, then you can skip this section and jump straight into the *Installing Bosque* section.

Windows

Installation of LLVM on Windows is pretty simple. You need to visit the official download page at `https://llvm.org/builds/` and find the **Windows installer (64-bit)** link in the **Windows snapshot builds** section. Clicking on this link should start the download. After the installer is downloaded, you should run it and proceed with the instructions shown on the screen. At the end of the installation process, you should see the following screen:

Figure 2.2 – Successfully installed LLVM

This process should result in the Clang compiler being installed on your machine, ready to work. To verify whether everything went fine, you can run the previous command again and see whether you can see the help information.

Linux

There are a few ways to get Clang on Linux, depending on your distribution.

For Ubuntu or Debian distributions, you can visit the download page at `https://apt.llvm.org/` and follow the installation steps described there.

If you are using other Linux versions, you can visit a different download page at `https://releases.llvm.org/download.html` and select the correct installer depending on your distribution.

The last way requires a little bit more work. If the previous methods do not work for you, this one most likely will. You need to manually clone the LLVM project repository and build it. All of the required steps are described on the official website at `https://clang.llvm.org/get_started.html` in the *Building Clang* and *Working with the Code | On Unix-like Systems* section.

After completing all the steps, you should have the Clang compiler installed on your machine and verified.

MacOS

If you are a user of macOS, then you should be happy. The installation of LLVM on your operating system is very simple. The only thing you need to do is open the terminal and run the following command:

```
$ brew install llvm
```

This command will print a lot of output messages indicating the installation of all the dependencies. If no `error:`, `fatal:`, or `Error:` messages were shown, it means that the command succeeded, and once it's done, you should be able to use Clang on your system. Simple, isn't it?

This was the last component that Bosque needs to run properly. If you have persevered up to this point, you should be proud of yourself. The hardest part is done. All the requirements are met and we can jump straight to the key element of our journey—Bosque.

Installing Bosque

Finally, it is time to install the Bosque language itself. The source code of the Bosque language is available on GitHub. This is the place where we must download the source files from. We can do this in two ways:

- Downloading a ZIP file directly from the GitHub repo at `https://github.com/microsoft/BosqueLanguage/` and manually extracting the contents of the archive

- Cloning the repository on our local machine

Both ways are equally effective, so you can go with the one that suits you better. We, however, will focus on the second way as it is simpler and faster.

The first thing to do is to open any terminal in a location of your choice and run the following command:

```
$ git clone git@github.com:microsoft/BosqueLanguage.git
```

Keep in mind that the location that you have chosen is the one where the Bosque language is going to be installed.

Now, go into the `./BosqueLanguage/impl/` directory that was just created:

```
$ cd BosqueLanguage/impl/
```

This directory consists of the whole Bosque implementation. There are a lot of files and directories that define things such as parser, interpreter, type checker, and more. As you have probably guessed, some external libraries and modules have been used to implement all of these things. So let's install them by running the following command:

```
$ npm install
```

This command may take a while, depending on your internet connection speed:

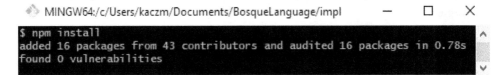

Figure 2.3 – Successfully installed Bosque dependencies

Once the dependencies are installed, you are ready to build the sources. In order to do this, you need to run the following command:

```
$ npm run build
```

In fact, this command is not necessary to run. This is because, at the time of writing, the next two commands are internally doing the same thing, plus some extra stuff, such as testing or creating an alias. However, I recommend running this command on its own because the definition of the `test` and `make-exe` scripts may change in the future, and running the build script may become necessary. Nonetheless, if you don't want to run this script, you can jump straight to the `test` or even `make-exe` scripts, as they will do the same thing.

Once the build process is over, it is a good idea to run tests so we can be sure that everything was installed correctly and works fine. You can do this by running the following:

```
$ npm test
```

This will take a few minutes to complete, so if you don't want to wait that long, you can skip this step. However, it is recommended that you do so, as you can ensure that Bosque was installed correctly, so you will be certain that potential future errors are not caused by failed installation. This command will throw a lot of output messages showing which test suite is currently in progress. If everything goes well, you should see a message similar to the following at the end:

```
All 6 test suites passed!
```

The last step is to run the following command:

```
$ npm run make-exe
```

This command will create an alias for compiling Bosque programs into executable binaries. If you see something like this at the end of the output, it means that the command succeeded:

```
[...]\npm\exegen -> [...]\npm\node_modules\bosque-reference-
implementation\bin\runtimes\exegen\exegen.js
```

```
[...]\npm\node_modules\bosque-reference-implementation ->
[...]\BosqueLanguage\impl
```

To verify that the alias is created, you can run the following command:

```
$ exegen --help
```

If you see some help information, this means that the alias has been created successfully.

At this point, you should have installed the Bosque language on your system. Congratulations!

In fact, you could start writing Bosque programs right away—which you can do, if you want—but I strongly recommend that you prepare yourself a bit better by installing an IDE that supports the Bosque syntax; it will make it a lot easier to write and understand the code.

Setting up the IDE for Bosque

This section covers the installation process of the **Visual Studio Code** (**VSC**) extension that supports the Bosque language. Because the language itself is very new, there are not many advanced solutions supporting it yet, so the existing extension to **VSC** comes directly from the Bosque creators and is currently limited to syntax and brace highlighting only. Nonetheless, it makes the code much more readable.

You probably know this IDE already; it's one of the most popular code editors out there. It's free to use and has a rich set of extensions that—when organized well—can create a really powerful IDE. The installation process is pretty straightforward, so we will not go through this step by step. If you don't have VSC installed yet, all you need to do is go to the official website at `https://code.visualstudio.com/download/`, download the installer, and run it.

After the installation completes, you can install the Bosque language extension. In order to do this, you need to copy the `./bosque-language-tools/` directory directly into the `./extensions/directory`. I'll show you how to achieve this depending on your OS.

Windows

The simplest way to install the extension on Windows is to open two Explorer windows. In one Explorer window, navigate to the directory in which you have installed the Bosque language. In the other, navigate to the location where VSC has been installed. The location path should look similar to this one:

`C:\Users\kaczm\AppData\Local\Programs\Microsoft VS Code\`

Once you have both of the windows opened in the right locations, you need to copy the `.\bosque-language-tools` directory from the first window (the one with the Bosque installation) to the `.\resources\app\extensions\` directory in the second window (the one with the VSC installation).

Now, you need to restart the VSC editor, if you have it opened already.

Linux and MacOS

If you are using Linux or macOS, you can do this by opening your favorite terminal in the location where you have installed the Bosque language and typing the following command:

```
$ cp -r ./bosque-language-tools ~/.vscode/extensions/
```

This will recursively copy the directory with all of the subdirectories in the desired target location.

After this, you need to restart the editor, if you have it running.

This is it: you have installed the VSC extension that supports the Bosque syntax. To test whether everything works fine, let's write our first Bosque program and see whether the syntax is highlighted properly and the program will compile without any errors.

Writing a "Hello, World!" program

First things first: let's create a folder for our first program. You can do this directly from VSC or by using your favorite terminal. Since we have just set up our IDE to play with Bosque, I recommend that you use it. First, click **File | New File**. A new tab named **Untitled-1** should appear—click **File | Save** (or press *Ctrl + S* on the keyboard) in order to rename it and save it at your desired location. Save the file under the name main.bsq. If you prefer to do this using a terminal, open it and type the following command:

```
$ mkdir first-project
$ cd first-project
```

Now, open VSC in the directory you have just created and create a file named main.bsq, as described earlier.

Once you have created the main.bsq file, fill it with the following content and save it:

```
namespace NSMain;
entrypoint function main(): String {
        return "Hello, world!";
}
```

I will explain this code in a second. For now, just write the preceding code and save the file.

After this, run the following command:

```
$ exegen main.bsq
```

This command runs the Bosque compiler, which creates an executable file. Depending on your OS, it will be a.exe or a.out. As you may already have guessed, the first one is created on Windows while the second one is on Linux and macOS.

Let's run it and see how it works. On Windows, you just need to run the following command:

```
$ .\a.exe
```

On Linux and macOS, the following command should work:

```
$ ./a.out
```

If you encounter an error with the permissions, saying bash: ./a.out: Permission denied, try to run the following command first:

```
$ chmod +x a.out
```

After running the executable file, you should see the **"Hello, world!"** text on your screen, as shown in the following screenshot:

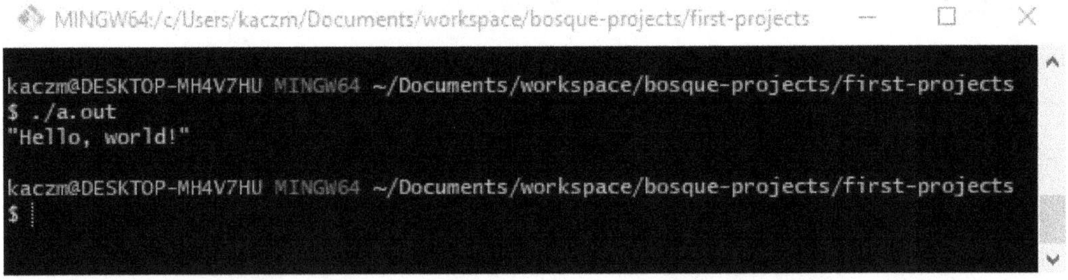

Figure 2.4 – Output of the "Hello, world!" program

You may have expected that the output would not contain enclosing quotes. In Bosque, strings are printed with quotes—it is an intentional implementation. We won't dive into the Bosque internals to show this because that wouldn't bring much benefit, so you must just trust me on that when I say this is how it's been implemented.

At this point, you have learned how to compile and run Bosque programs. It's a big step forward. Congratulations!

Now, let's get back to the code you have written and see what happens there in more detail.

Understanding the code

Let's break down this code line by line.

Look at the first line:

```
namespace NSMain;
```

If you are familiar with languages such as C++ or C#, then you probably know already what namespaces are. Nonetheless, let's remind ourselves what they are.

A namespace is kind of a bag for your functions, variables, and so on. Normally, you cannot have two functions with the same name defined in the same scope. Usually, it's treated as a compile-time error and your program won't be even compiled. A namespace allows us to wrap these two functions into different groups so that they won't collide anymore. Basically, they enable us to achieve a better code separation.

In Bosque, you must declare a namespace. Without any namespace declaration, the program won't even compile. NSMain is a default namespace, which the ExeGen tool is looking for during compilation. You can change it using the --entrypoint (-e) parameter, which I will talk about in the next section.

The second line looks like this:

```
entrypoint function main(): String {
```

Here, we have two main things to look at. The first one is the entrypoint keyword. As the name suggests, it tells Bosque that this is the main entry point of the program that the whole execution will start from. More on this is explained in *Chapter 4, Entrypoint Function*. At this point, it's important to know that you must have at least one entrypoint function in your program.

The second thing is the function main(): String part of the code. This line defines a function called main without any parameters and with the return type String. The syntax is very similar to TypeScript, where we define types after a colon. You must provide a return type for the entrypoint function, otherwise, you'll get an error.

The third line consists of the following code:

```
return "Hello, world!";
```

This simply states that the function should return the provided text. Since we have specified the return type of the main function as String, we must return a string. If you change this value to something else—for example, a number—then the program won't compile. One more important thing to notice is the semicolon at the end of the line. In Bosque, you must put semicolons at the ends of lines—they are required and work in the same way as they do in other popular programming languages, such as C++.

And that is it. Now, you understand the code of your first program and know what is going on. I strongly recommend that you play with this code a little bit. Try to return different types of values and see the output. This way, you will get used to the process of compilation and running the executables, and will familiarize yourself with the errors that are thrown in various scenarios.

ExeGen – Ahead-of-time Bosque compilation

I have mentioned the ExeGen tool a few times before. It's time to take a closer look at this in more detail to see how it works and how to use it.

Remember when you ran the following command during Bosque installation?

```
$ npm run make-exe
```

This command creates the exegen alias command, which runs the ExeGen tool with the provided parameters. We will go through the supported list of parameters with an explanation of what they do, but first, let's clarify what this program is and how it works.

Basically, ExeGen is a simple command-line tool that takes a .bsq file as an input and produces an executable binary as an output. Its internal logic is a bit more complex than it sounds, though. Roughly speaking, the tool first generates an assembly from an input .bsq file. Then, it emits a C++ code based on the preprocessed assembly. In the end, it runs a C++ compiler that produces an executable binary.

Such a compilation process has a few advantages. One of them is that it allows Bosque programs to start up really fast. Having an executable binary helps a lot, in this case. Another advantage is that during the C++ code emitting phase, you can optimize the code so that it will be even faster (for example, by precompiling some logic directly into constant values, speeding up the startup.

Parameters for ExeGen

The ExeGen tool takes a list of parameters. We will go through all of them, as the list is not very long:

- `-e, --entrypoint [entrypoint]`: When you were writing your first program, you created an `entrypoint` function. You named it `main` and everything was working fine. If you tried to change this name to something else and tried to compile your program, it wouldn't work. The same applies to the namespace you created—if you tried to change it to something else, the compiler would throw an error. This is because the default entry point that ExeGen is looking for is `NSMain::main`. In order to change this, you can pass the `-e` parameter to ExeGen and provide your entry point name. For example:

```
$ exegen main.bsq -e "NSCustom::start"
```

- `-o, --outfile [name]`: You have probably noticed that every time you used ExeGen so far, it has produced an `a.exe` or `a.out` file. Let's be honest—it's not the best name for your program executable, and changing it after every compilation can be frustrating. Fortunately, you can specify the name using the `-o` parameter. For example:

```
$ exegen main.bsq -o main.exe
```

This will produce a `main.exe` file instead of the `a.exe`.

- `-c, --compiler [compiler]`: Back in the *Installing C++ compiler* section, I said that by default, Bosque expects the Clang compiler, but you can install another one if you wish. And that's true. However, if you don't use the default compiler, you need to specify it when using ExeGen by using the `-c` option. For example, if you are using GCC compiler, you can specify it like this:

```
$ exegen main.bsq -c gcc
```

- `-l, --level [level]`: This option lets you specify the compiler build level. By default, it's set to **debug**, which means that all asserts/pre/post/invariant checks are enabled, debugging messages are produced, and no optimization is done. There are two more options: **test**, which enables only test and release checks, still produces debug messages, and performs light optimization; and **release**, which enables only release checks, disables all debug messages, and performs platform-specific optimization. You can change the compiler build level like this:

```
$ exegen main.bsq -l release
```

- -f, --flags [flags]: This option allows you to pass additional flags to the C++ compiler of your choice. For example, if you are using the GCC compiler and you wish to print all warning messages, you can pass an additional flag to the compiler:

```
$ exegen main.bsq -c gcc -f "-Wall"
```

At the time of writing, these are all the parameters that are supported by the ExeGen tool. Keep in mind that you can use multiple parameters at once. If you are using the default compiler and entrypoint function, generally, you will probably be using only the -o option, so the executables' names won't collide. For production builds, you'll want to use the -l option to set the compiler build level to release.

Alright, so in this section, you learned about what the ExeGen tool is, how it works, and how you can customize its behavior. This knowledge may become useful later on in this book, as well as in your own experiments.

Now it's time to summarize this chapter.

Summary

You've learned a lot so far. This chapter has taught you a lot of practical things that are crucial when getting started with Bosque. Let's do a short recap of what you've learned.

First, we talked about the software requirements to run Bosque. We covered the required OS architecture and what you can do if your host system does not meet the requirements. After that, you learned what additional software is mandatory in order to install and run Bosque.

Then, we covered the compiler—why it is needed and how to install it. You learned about the default Bosque compiler, which is used to generate executables, and how you can install it on Windows, Linux, and macOS.

You then installed the Bosque language itself, along with the tools such as ExeGen. You also learned what the recommended IDE for Bosque is, and how you can install the syntax highlighter so that writing Bosque programs is much easier.

The next big thing that you looked at was your first Bosque program. We wrote a simple "Hello, World!" program and compiled it. Then, we went through the code line by line and looked at what was going on there. You learned about the required namespace and the entrypoint function and what types of values it can return.

Finally, we took a closer look at the ExeGen tool, which is responsible for producing executable binaries from our Bosque programs. We talked a little bit about how the tool works internally and what's good about that. In the end, you learned what parameters are accepted by the tool and how you can customize its behavior.

Now you are ready to jump into the Bosque language features. In the next chapter, we will cover the key features of the language and what they do. We will also compare them to some popular languages so it will be easier to see the advantages of Bosque.

Questions

1. What is the default C++ compiler that Bosque uses?
2. Which tool generates executable binaries from the Bosque source code?
3. What is the keyword that must be added to the main function of the Bosque program?
4. Are semicolons a must in Bosque programs?
5. How can you change the default namespace and main function name and compile your programs without errors?
6. What would happen if you changed the main function name from `main()` to `Main()` and tried to compile the program again?

Further reading

Here are the links to some useful resources related to Bosque environment configuration:

- *Official Bosque Docs*: https://github.com/microsoft/BosqueLanguage/tree/master/docs
- *Installing Bosque via Docker*: https://github.com/microsoft/BosqueLanguage/blob/master/docs/extras/docker.md
- *ExeGen -- The Bosque Language AoT executable generator*: https://github.com/microsoft/BosqueLanguage/tree/master/impl/src/runtimes/exegen
- *Node Version Manager Docs*: https://github.com/nvm-sh/nvm
- *Getting Started: Building and Running Clang*: https://clang.llvm.org/get_started.html
- *VSCode Extension Marketplace*: https://code.visualstudio.com/docs/editor/extension-gallery

3

Bosque Key Features

At this point, you already know the theory behind Bosque, and you have practical knowledge about running Bosque programs. Now, it is time to dive deeper into the language itself and learn more about its features.

In this chapter, we will present a brief introduction to the most important features of the Bosque language. Keep in mind that Bosque offers far more interesting aspects, all of which will be presented later in this book. In this chapter, we will focus on the most interesting and innovative ones. Detailed descriptions for the rest of the language syntax, operations, and semantics can be found in the upcoming chapters.

In this chapter, we are going to cover the following topics:

- Identifying immutable values
- Introducing typed strings
- Discovering bulk algebraic data operations
- Learning iterative processing in Bosque
- Identifying recursive functions in Bosque
- Validating program behavior using the built-in mechanism

By the end of this chapter, you will be able to recognize the most interesting features and design decisions in Bosque, which will allow you to build reliable software without worrying about side effects.

Technical requirements

Before you jump into the contents of this chapter, it is recommended that you have the following:

- Knowledge about the Bosque project – especially in terms of why it was invented
- The Bosque language installed on your local machine
- How to compile and run Bosque programs

Identifying immutable values

Building software is complex, especially in our rapidly changing world, which has been yearning for bigger and bigger demands. These days, IT systems are handling enormous amounts of tasks and are designed to be scalable and reliable. It is impossible to make the process of developing such systems and the resulting code simple. By seeing how the world changes and how software evolves to make our lives easier, I have come to the conclusion that we are doomed to experience complexity. However, it is not a hopeless situation. There are ways to make the situation a bit better, and I will show you how Bosque tries to overcome this.

Back in *Chapter 1, Exploring Bosque*, you learned about accidental complexity and its main sources. Let's quickly recall what that is.

An accidental complexity, when it comes to building software, is a kind of trap we fall into when we're designing and implementing certain features. At the time the feature is implemented, we can't see any suspicious factors that we may regret in the future. We only start to see them later, once our code has grown, and when it is much more difficult to introduce major changes.

One such source of accidental complexity is mutable state.

Let's consider the following code snippet. It's a JavaScript function that simply adds 1 day to the date, which is given as a parameter:

```
function getTomorrow(date) {
  const d = date;
  d.setDate(date.getDate() + 1);

  return d;
}
```

```
const today = new Date();
const tmrw = getTomorrow(today);

console.log(tmrw);
console.log(today);
```

Assuming today is October 16, 2020, what will be the output of this code?

If you are familiar with JavaScript, you probably know the answer, but if you are not, let's make things clear.

Many people would automatically say that the correct answer is the following output (depending on your locale):

```
Fri Oct 16 2020 19:04:26 GMT+0100 (Central European Standard
Time)
Sat Oct 17 2020 19:04:26 GMT+0100 (Central European Standard
Time)
```

However, this answer is *incorrect*. The correct answer is that *both* console.log() calls will output Sat Oct 17 2020 19:04:26 GMT+0100 (Central European Standard Time).

This happens because, in JavaScript, objects are passed by reference (in fact, you are not passing the direct reference but its copy, which means that if you tried to overwrite the referenced argument, it wouldn't affect the original object). This means that you can modify the contents of the passed object by modifying the argument of the getTomorrow function. In the previous snippet, the getTomorrow(today) call is causing the original today object to be modified by adding 1 day to the current date value. It may not seem obvious because of the following line:

```
const d = date;
```

However, this line does nothing more than just copy the reference to another variable. It is still referring to the original object and we can still modify it using this new reference.

As you can see, this type of language behavior may be confusing. It becomes even more complicated if we were to call the getTomorrow function once again with the today or tmrw variables as an argument – this would cause *all* the dates to increase by one more day, which would result in having all the dates set to Sun Oct 18 2020 19:04:26 GMT+0100 (Central European Standard Time).

The previous example – although very simple – illustrates a whole variety of problems. We can easily imagine a similar function but instead of changing the `Date` object, it would add an entry to some Map. The original Map would be affected by the change through parameter reference, regardless of whether we realize this.

And there are many more examples of this problem in real-world apps, especially in web apps. These days, web applications are becoming more and more complex. It is hard to imagine a web app without JavaScript involved. The more complex the apps become, the more problematic it becomes to maintain their logic. The common solution is to introduce a global shared state, which represents the current state of the whole app. The problem is that, at some point, it is very hard to maintain such a global mutable state. It is caused by the fact that many parts of our application change it, and that it's nearly impossible to follow all the paths that modify it. These problems have accelerated the development of various solutions such as NGRX in Angular, Redux in React, and the RxJS library. They help us manage global state through observables and streams. But even with such libraries, it is still possible (if you are stubborn or not careful enough) to mess things up by modifying the global state by reference.

Another issue in web development is referential transparency, which may sometimes be problematic to achieve in JavaScript without the use of libraries such as ImmutableJS. It is better maintained in languages such as TypeScript, but it can still be tricked by using the `any` type. We, as developers, must think about such side effects all the time, but it's still not enough – we will all fall into this trap eventually. Our lives would be much easier if we didn't have to constantly think about this and could simply focus on the implemented features, wouldn't they? Here's where Bosque shines.

In Bosque, all values are immutable. It doesn't matter if it's a primitive value or some complex type – you are not allowed to modify it once you have assigned it to some constant. Also, you are not allowed to change the values of function parameters unless you explicitly say that the given parameter is meant to be updated. All of this is forbidden by the design and is treated as a compile-time error. This concept is very similar to functional programming, where all the values are also immutable and you cannot change them – they can only be changed if you assign them to a new constant.

Many developers may see this as an impediment because instead of changing some value in-place, we are forced to create a new value. Well, they are right to some extent. However, if we consider mutability as a side effect, then making all the values immutable starts to make sense since we do not need to worry about what happens after some function call. Nonetheless, Bosque introduces the concept of updatable variables, which allow you to reassign them. Surprisingly, under the hood, such a variable is still immutable.

Let's see how these concepts are implemented in Bosque.

The let keyword

First, let's consider the following example:

```
namespace NSMain;


entity User {
    field name: String;
    field id: Int;
}
entity ApplicationContext {
    field emailServiceEnabled: Bool;
    field user: User;
}


function sendEmail(ctx: ApplicationContext): String {
    if (ctx.emailServiceEnabled) {
        return String::concat("Email sent to ", ctx.user.name,
"!");
    } else {
        return "Email service disabled";
    }
}


entrypoint function main(): String {
    let user = User@{ name = "John Doe", id = 1 };
    let context = ApplicationContext@{
        emailServiceEnabled = false, user = user
    };


    let newContext = context.update(emailServiceEnabled =
true);
    return sendEmail(newContext);
}
```

This is a very simple application that simulates an email sending service. We have the `ApplicationContext` entity, which holds two fields: `emailServiceEnabled` and `user`. The first one is just a flag telling us whether our imaginary email service is enabled, while the second one is a user entity representing some user that we want to send an email to. The `sendEmail` function takes the `ctx` parameter, which is of the `ApplicationContext` type, and returns a different `String` based on the value of the `emailServiceEnabled` flag. In the `main` function, we are creating an example user and a context with the default value of `emailServiceEnabled` set to `false`. Then, we are enabling the email service and eventually returning the value of the `sendEmail` call.

Let's focus on the `main` function – especially when it comes to updating the `context` entity. Entities will be discussed individually in *Chapter 12, Namespaces, Concepts, and Entities*. For now, think of an entity as a class from a classic OOP.

As we mentioned previously, in Bosque, all values are immutable. This means that we cannot simply change the value of our context fields as we would normally do in other languages, such as JavaScript. If we tried to do this here, we would get a parsing error because this is considered invalid at the syntax level. To change the value of the `emailServiceEnabled` flag, we must create another constant using the `let` keyword and assign it with a new context value. This is very similar to the concept of functional programming. A detailed description of the `update` method will be provided in the *Bulk algebraic data operations* section. As for now, all you need to know is that this method updates the field value and returns a new, updated entity. We also cannot reassign the `context` constant because it has been declared using a `let` keyword, which means it is immutable.

As I mentioned previously, having to declare a new constant each time some value changes can be frustrating. This is why Bosque has introduced something called updatable variables. Let's take a closer look at them.

The var keyword

Let's get back to the previous example. We had to declare a new constant called `newContext` to switch the value of the `emailServiceEnabled` flag. The concept of immutable values definitely has its advantages because it eliminates a whole bunch of side effects caused by mutability. On the other hand, it is a little bit frustrating for developers as they have to declare tons of variables every time they change some value. What if we could get rid of side effects while also reassigning variables? In Bosque, we can do this using the `var` keyword.

Let's replace the following line in the previous example:

```
let context = ApplicationContext@{
    emailServiceEnabled = false, user = user
};
```

We'll replace it with this one:

```
var context = ApplicationContext@{
    emailServiceEnabled = false, user = user
};
```

The only thing that's changed is the highlighted `var` keyword. Thanks to this little modification, we can reassign this variable with a new value. This means that we can now also replace these two lines:

```
let newContext = context.update(emailServiceEnabled = true);
return sendEmail(newContext);
```

We'll replace these with the following:

```
context = context.update(emailServiceEnabled = true);
return sendEmail(context);
```

So, as you can see, we are now reassigning the `context` variable. The idea of an immutable `context` entity still stands – we cannot simply change the `emailServiceEnabled` flag once we've declared the `context` variable. However, now, we can (sort of) abandon its old value and replace it with the new one. Now, the code is much simpler and nicer, isn't it?

In fact, under the hood, the `context` variable is still constant. If we could see the **intermediate representation** (**IR**) code after compiling this version of this example, we would notice that, in place of the `context` variable, there are two constants that have been initialized with the proper value. Nonetheless, for us developers, the `var` keyword makes writing in Bosque more satisfying.

With that, you now know how to reassign a variable. But the code we have written so far still can be cleaned up. We can extract the `update` method to another function in order to separate the logic. Let's see how that can be done in Bosque.

The ref keyword

We are still considering the previous example. The next modification we are going to make is extracting the update method to some helper function. This helps separate logic and makes the code more understandable. So, let's add this function:

```
function enableEmailService(ref context: ApplicationContext):
ApplicationContext {
    context = context.update(emailServiceEnabled = true);
    return context;
}
```

This function simply wraps the update method. The advantage of such extractions is that you can freely change the way you enable the email service, without having to update multiple places in the code where this mechanism is used.

Now, let's apply this change to the main function. The new version will look like this:

```
entrypoint function main(): String {
    let user = User@{ name = "John Doe", id = 1 };
    var context = ApplicationContext@{ emailServiceEnabled =
false, user = user };
    context = enableEmailService(ref context);
    return sendEmail(context);
}
```

The only difference is the highlighted line of code.

Look closer at those two snippets. They use the ref keyword both in the function declaration and the call. This keyword allows us to update the function parameters by reference. This means that after calling the enableEmailService function, the context variable is going to be changed. Go ahead and compile this example. You should see "Email sent to John Doe!" on the screen. Now, comment out the line that calls the enableEmailService function and compile it again. The output will show "Email service disabled".

So, as you can see, Bosque allows us to achieve the same "side effect" that we can get in other languages. However, in Bosque, you must explicitly state that a given parameter is going to be updated by reference using the ref keyword.

In summary, in Bosque, all values are immutable. However, there are ways to change this behavior. In this section, you learned why mutability may be painful and how Bosque faces this problem. You also how to use the `let`, `var`, and `ref` keywords. The next section describes an exciting feature called typed strings. Let's jump straight into it.

Introducing typed strings

In today's applications, there are many data structures that we need to handle, such as students in school, books in a library, or orders in a shop – if we want to keep the code object-oriented, we need to create a `Student`, `Book`, or `Order` class, respectively. This is because such structures are complex schemas that contain many characteristics that need to be checked. On the other hand, there are lots of less complex data types that are still schematic, and some checks are required to confirm their validity. Some examples include phone number, ZIP code, email address, credit card number, or even simple types such as mass or distance. All these data types can be described with a finite number of rules that define their structure. The problem is that we usually do not create a class for things such as a mass unit and even if we do, we feel like it's overkill because the implementation hides the true intent of a programmer, which is to simply know what type of data we are dealing with. A solution we usually go for is strings.

If we want to store a phone number or a distance unit, we simply store it as a string. This is convenient, but at the same time, it brings terrible consequences. If we operate on strings, then how sure can we be that a given string is actually a phone number? What stops us from – accidentally – passing a string representing a mass unit to a function that expects a ZIP code string? The answer is that we can't be sure at all unless we perform a manual check; nothing stops us unless we perform a manual check. It would be much easier for us if there was a way to tell the compiler to treat some strings as if they were representing some data type – **typed strings**. This is where Bosque shines.

Bosque provides us with two ways to define typed strings: `SafeString<T>` and `StringOf<T>`. Thanks to this, we can address a variety of scenarios where specifying the string type may be very useful. We will cover them separately in the next two sections.

SafeString

Let's continue with our previous example. We have created a `User` entity with an `id` field. Imagine that, in our system, a user ID must have a specific format. In our example, let's say that the ID consists of one uppercase letter, a dash, three lowercase letters, a dash, and a number. There is no such data type that could represent this format. Normally, we would throw this into a string and operate on it. However, thanks to typed strings, in Bosque, you can make a string an actual data type. Let's see how that works.

First, we need to formalize our ID schema. We can easily describe the format using a regular expression:

```
/^[A-Z]-[a-z]{3}-(\d)+$/
```

So, as you can see, we expect an uppercase letter followed by a dash, then three lowercase letters followed by another dash, and in the end, we have at least one digit.

Now, let's define a new type called `UserId` that will represent our regular expression:

```
typedef UserId = /^[A-Z]-[a-z]{3}-(\d)+$/;
```

The next step is to update the type of the `id` field in our `User` entity. This is where we use `SafeString`, parameterized by the `UserId` type:

```
field id: SafeString<UserId>;
```

The last thing we must do is change the line where we create our user:

```
let user = User@{ name = "John Doe", id = UserId'A-bcd-123' };
```

Notice how we use our `UserId` type. The `Type'...'` syntax creates a typed string literal that checks the string format with a given regex. Thanks to that, we can immediately say what a given string represents just by having a quick look at the code. We don't have to go through the code to know that – it is written right before the string itself.

This looks nice, but sometimes, we need to perform more complex parsing to determine if a given string is valid or not. That's why Bosque offers the `StringOf<T>` type.

StringOf

`StringOf<T>` is also a parameterized type. However, here, the `T` type must inherit from the `Parsable` special type. The `Parsable` special type is a concept provided by Bosque's core. It includes one abstract static method called `tryParse` that has the following signature:

```
abstract static tryParse(str: String): Result<Any, String>;
```

It takes a string to be parsed and returns a `Result` object. To understand this, let's continue our example and replace the previous `SafeString` modification with the `StringOf` one. To justify this, let's say that from now, the user ID can accept a special value of "admin" and that in such scenario, we don't want to run our regex on that – we just accept this.

> **Important note**
>
> At the time of writing, the `.accepts()` method is not implemented yet.
> Therefore, the code we will present in the following example will not compile
> in the current version of Bosque. To run it, you will have to remove the regex
> check and play with this example without it.

To do this, we have to create a special entity that provides `Parsable` and overrides the
`tryParse` method:

```
entity ComplexId provides Parsable {
    override static tryParse(value: String): Result<ComplexId,
String> {
        if (value == "admin" || /^[A-Z]-[a-z]{3}-(\d)+$/.
accepts(value)) {
            return ok(ComplexId@{});
        } else {
            return err("Invalid id");
        }
    }
}
```

This is basically a simple `if` statement that returns a valid result if the condition is met
and an invalid result otherwise. Of course, we could replace it with a regex using the |
(OR) operator, but that would make the regex more complex. On the other hand, this
allows us to easily extend the parsing logic.

The `err` and `ok` helper functions are built-in functions that return subtypes of the
`Result<T, E=None>` type: `Ok<T, E>` and `Err<T, E>` respectively.

Now, let's change the `id` field type from `SafeString<UserId>` to
`StringOf<ComplexId>`:

```
field id: StringOf<ComplexId>;
```

The last thing we must do is apply the change to the line where we created our `User` object:

```
let user = User@{ name = "John Doe", id = ComplexId'admin' };
```

It's very similar to the previous version. The only difference is the highlighted part.

Now, go ahead and try providing different values for the `id` field – valid and invalid ones. After compilation, you will see a `"Failed string validation"` error if the provided value is invalid.

In conclusion, I think it's safe to say that typed strings are a truly powerful feature. They add important metadata to an ordinary string, which makes the compiler check if the string's contents is correct. We can be certain that the values we operate on have an expected format, and this is guaranteed by the language. What a cool thing!

Now, it is time to cover another Bosque feature that we already partially used in our earlier example – the `.update()` method and its true nature.

Discovering bulk algebraic data operations

Back in the *Immutable values* section, we used the `.update()` method to update the `ApplicationContext` entity field value. You may be wondering why you can't simply update the field value using a dot, like this:

```
context.enableEmailService = true;
```

Recall that all values in Bosque are immutable and that this kind of syntax implies that we are modifying the `context` value, which is forbidden by design.

This is why we need another way of doing this. But that's not all we have to say about this method, nor is this the only one that is considered a bulk algebraic data operation. Such operations include the following:

- Bulk read
- Bulk update
- Projection
- Merge

We will describe them one at a time, but first, let's add new requirements to our email sending app. This will help us to understand the next few sections.

Imagine that we have three additional integer fields in the `ApplicationContext` entity called `successCount`, `errorCount`, and `leftToSend`. The first two store the number of successfully sent and failed emails, respectively, while the last one tells us how many emails are left to be sent in the current queue. After each sending queue is completed, we want to display a message showing how many emails have been sent in total and what the number of successful and failed emails was.

Let's see how this new requirement can be satisfied with bulk data operations.

Bulk read

First, let's focus on displaying a message once all the emails have been sent.

To do this, we need to access the `successCount` and `errorCount` fields. Having them will help us calculate the total emails sent and then display all the required information. The first thing that should pop into our minds is that we must assign each of the fields to a variable, one at a time, and then proceed with creating the output message. But we can do better.

Bosque allows us to read multiple values from an entity at once. Let's see what this looks like:

```
let {
    successCount = sc,
    errorCount = ec
} = context.{ successCount, errorCount };
```

Here, we have created two variables called `sc` and `ec`, which store the respective values that have been extracted from the context entity. It is similar to object destructuring in JavaScript. This way, we have read two fields at once, without having to do it one at a time. This change can be applied to the `sendEmail` function, as shown in the *Bulk update* section later. For now, it's important to just remember the syntax so you aren't confused once you see it.

This can even be applied to records and tuples, which will be described later in this book. For the sake of this section, I will show what it looks like, but I won't dive into the details.

So, for records, it looks very much the same as it does for the preceding entities:

```
let record = {
    success = true,
    message = "Success!",
    status = 200
};
let { success = suc, message = msg } = record.{ success,
message };
```

This example creates two variables, suc and msg, which store the respective record fields. Notice that the .{...} operator is required for that to work. Without it, you would get an error indicating that there are more fields in the record than there are in the assignment.

We don't have to create separate variables, though. We can just read the required fields from the record and assign them to a singular variable. This is because the bulk read operator, .{...}, returns a record so that the result will get one record with the selected fields:

```
let selected = record.{ success, message };
```

Another bulk read operator applies to tuples. It's pretty similar to the previous one:

```
let tuple = [ 2, 4, 6, 8, 10 ];
let [ third, fifth ] = tuple.[2, 4];
```

In the .[...] operator, we provide a list of indexes and we get a new tuple consisting of the values at these indexes as the result. As for its assignment, we can – similar to the record – extract elements in various ways.

- The following is the first way:

```
let [ first, second ] = tuple.[0, 1];
```

- The following is the second way:

```
[ let first, let second ] = tuple.[0, 1];
```

- The following is the third way:

```
var first: Int;
[ first, let second ] = tuple.[0, 1];
```

All these scenarios will produce the same result. Well, except the last one, where the first variable is defined as var instead of let. This is because let cannot be updated, so we need to use var in such cases. Nonetheless, the last example presents the possibilities of this syntax.

Bulk read can be very handy in various scenarios, as can bulk update. Let's have a closer look at it.

Bulk update

As we mentioned previously, the .update() method is used to update the values of entity fields. You may be wondering why it is called "bulk" if we only use it to update one field of our context entity. In fact, you can update multiple fields at once. And by "at once," I really mean that it is an atomic operation and that it will either succeed or fail the whole update operation. It can be very useful when we must update multiple fields of the same entity. We don't have to update each field one by one.

Let's go back to our new requirements for the email sending app. Now, we must support the successCount, errorCount, and leftToSend fields. For each sendEmail() call, we need to update two fields: increment successCount or errorCount and decrement leftToSend. This is a perfect fit for bulk update. Let's see what it looks like in practice.

First, we need to separate the logic. We have two things we need to do: send an email and then update the context. So, let's rename our sendEmail function to doSend and make it return a Bool indicating a success or error. Also, let's create a new sendEmail function that will call doSend and then update our context. This is what the modified code looks like:

```
entity ApplicationContext {
    field emailServiceEnabled: Bool;
    field successCount: Int = 0;
    field errorCount: Int = 0;
    field leftToSend: Int = 10;
    field user: User;
}


function sendEmail(ref context: ApplicationContext):
ApplicationContext {
    let sent = doSend(context);
    let {
        successCount = suc, errorCount = error, leftToSend =
left
    } = context.{ successCount, errorCount, leftToSend };

    if (sent) {
        context = context.update(
            successCount = suc + 1, leftToSend = left - 1
```

```
        );
        _debug(String::concat("Email sent to ", context.user.
name, "!"));
    } else {
        context = context.update(
            errorCount = error + 1, leftToSend = left - 1
        );
        _debug("Error sending email");
    }
    return context;
}


function doSend(ctx: ApplicationContext): Bool {
    if (ctx.emailServiceEnabled) {
        // real sending logic goes here
        return true;
    }
    return false;
}
```

The doSend function doesn't do much, really. This is because our app does not really send any emails. Normally, we would add some logic that would send an actual message, but for this example, this logic does not matter.

sendEmail has changed a lot. It returns ApplicationContext and accepts a context ref parameter, which is updated later. We can see bulk read and bulk update in action here. It is very useful for such operations. Imagine that the .update() method isn't atomic and that our program stopped working between incrementing successCount and decrementing leftToSend – this is pretty problematic.

Of course, don't forget to change the main function after making these changes. I'll leave this for you as an exercise.

> **Tip**
> You need to change the return type and pass context with the ref keyword to the sendEmail function.

Now, let's look at the next bulk data operation.

Projection

Projection is very similar to bulk read, which we covered earlier. The difference is that it operates on types rather than raw records or tuples. To understand this, imagine that we have a concept called `Context`, which `ApplicationContext` inherits from, and that we have one more field – `taskQueue`.

> **Important note**
>
> At the time of writing, the `.project<T>()` method is not implemented yet. Therefore, the previous code won't compile until this feature is implemented.

Projection can be used to **project** one value to another. I'll explain this with a short code snippet:

```
concept Context {
    field taskQueue: List<String>;
}
entity ApplicationContext provides Context {
    field emailServiceEnabled: Bool;
    field successCount: Int = 0;
    field errorCount: Int = 0;
    field leftToSend: Int = 10;
    field user: User;
}
entrypoint function main(): ApplicationContext {
    var context = ApplicationContext@{ emailServiceEnabled =
false, user = user, taskQueue = List<String>@{"exampleTask"} };
    return context;
}
```

Here, we created `context` and changed the `taskQueue` field from the `Context` concept. Now, imagine that we want to look at the `context` variable in terms of the `Context` concept. So, this means that only `Context` fields matter here. How can we do this? By using projection:

```
var projected = context.project<Context>();
```

The `projected` variable now only has fields from the `Context` concept at has the same values that it had in the `context` variable.

Finally, it is time for the last bulk data operation – `merge`.

Merge

This bulk algebraic data operation is very similar to the bulk update operation. The difference is that in the `.update()` method, you have to specify the exact fields to be updated and you can't really call that programmatically. This is why we have the `.merge()` method. It accepts a record or a tuple as a parameter and merges this with the value it has been called on.

> **Important note**
>
> At the time of writing, the `.merge()` operation is not fully implemented, and merging entities may result in unidentified errors. Currently, only record and tuple merging works.

Let's see an example:

```
let updateRec = { emailServiceEnabled = true, leftToSend = 20
};
context = context.merge(updateRec);
```

Here, we are creating a record with some fields that we would like to update; then, we are just passing this to the `.merge()` method.

It works the same way with records and tuples. For example, to merge two tuples, we can do something like this:

```
var taskQueue = ["taskOne", "taskTwo"];
var extendedQueue = taskQueue.merge(["taskThree"]);
```

This will result in creating a new tuple with an additional task.

And that is all there is to say about bulk algebraic data operations. It is a powerful feature that allows us to efficiently produce easy-to-understand code. Now that you've learned it, you are already more efficient. The next thing we will cover is iterative processing.

Learning iterative processing in Bosque

In this section, we will briefly walk through the process of iteration in Bosque. We will not dive deep into the details here as we will cover it in full in *Chapter 10, Iterative Processing and Recursion*. Here, we will only introduce the concept of available methods and iterators with a simple example.

The first thing to note is that in Bosque, there are no structured loops. Yes, you read correctly – not a single loop. Instead, we have a variety of high-level functions and methods that help us do some iterative job. This means that if we want to iterate over a list of numbers and do something with them, we can use one of many methods defined in the List entity. We don't have to write an imperative loop and worry about edge cases ourselves. We must pick one of the methods available for us and let the computer figure out the best way to perform a task. This is a pretty convenient way to do iterative processing. We only describe our intent; then, we let the machine do the rest.

As we mentioned previously, the concept of iteration and its related collections will be described in detail later in this book. If you wish to jump right into this, you can go directly to *Chapter 9, Collections*, and *Chapter 10, Iterative Processing and Recursion*.

Continuing with our example app, imagine that instead of the user field in ApplicationContext, we have a list of users to send emails to – users. The definition of ApplicationContext would look like this:

```
entity ApplicationContext {
    field emailServiceEnabled: Bool;
    field successCount: Int = 0;
    field errorCount: Int = 0;
    field leftToSend: Int = 10;
    field users: List<User>;
}
```

Thanks to the wide range of available List methods, we can perform a lot of useful things without the need to write a loop statement. For example, if we want to select only administrators from the list, we can use the .filter() method:

```
let filtered = context.users.filter(fn(u) => u.id ==
ComplexId'admin');
```

Alternatively, if we wanted to filter out the administrators, we can use a built-in method called filterNot:

```
let filtered = context.users.filterNot(fn(u) => u.id ==
ComplexId'admin');
```

Another useful method is `defaultFind`, which will return an element from the list or the default value:

```
let filtered = context.users.defaultFind(john, fn(u) => u.id ==
ComplexId'administrator');
```

Here, it will return `john` if it does not find the specified user.

There are a lot more things to cover here. As we've mentioned a few times previously, we will learn about them later in this book. This is just a brief introduction. Now, let's focus on recursion.

Identifying recursive functions in Bosque

As for recursion, things aren't too different in Bosque. The only new thing is the `recursive` keyword, which informs us that a function is meant to be called recursively. This keyword is required both at the function definition and at the call. This may seem a little too problematic and frustrating, but there is a good reason to do this.

Since, in Bosque, there are no loop constructs, there is the risk that some complex iteration structures may be replaced with similarly complex recursion structures. Such solutions obscure the true intent of a programmer and are hard to reason about. This is why Bosque introduces the `recursive` keyword.

Let's see an example:

```
recursive function fibonacciNumber(n: Int): Int {
    return if (n == 0) 0
           elif (n < 3) 1
           else fibonacciNumber[recursive](n - 1) +
fibonacciNumber[recursive](n - 2);
}
entrypoint function main(): Int {
    return fibonacciNumber[recursive](10);
}
```

This is a classical function that returns the *nth* number of the Fibonacci sequence in a recursive way. In case you haven't heard of it, the Fibonacci sequence is a sequence where each number is the sum of the two preceding ones, starting from 0 and 1. As you can see, the `recursive` keyword is used both at the definition and at the time of calling the function. It makes it very clear that the function is meant to be called recursively, and just by looking at the call line, we can tell right away that the function is recursive. Despite the fact that it's exhausting to write this every time, it makes you think about what you are doing and makes you check if your reasoning is correct.

And this is all about recursion for now. More details will be provided in *Chapter 10, Iterative Processing and Recursion*.

Now, it is time to learn about how to perform sanity checks and assertions at the time of writing a program.

Validating program behavior using the built-in mechanism

Let's go back to our example app. Since we've made many changes, let's synchronize the code and make sure that we are on the same page. The following is the current version of `ApplicationContext`:

```
entity ApplicationContext {
    field emailServiceEnabled: Bool;
    field successCount: Int = 0;
    field errorCount: Int = 0;
    field leftToSend: Int = 10;
    field user: User;
}
```

The following code shows the `sendEmail` and `doSend` functions that we currently have:

```
function sendEmail(ref context: ApplicationContext):
ApplicationContext {
    let sent = doSend(context);
    let {
        successCount = suc, errorCount = error, leftToSend =
left
    } = context.{ successCount, errorCount, leftToSend };
    if (sent) {
```

```
        context = context.update(
            successCount = suc + 1, leftToSend = left - 1
        );
        _debug(String::concat("Email sent to ", context.user.
name, "!"));
    } else {
        context = context.update(
            errorCount = error + 1, leftToSend = left - 1
        );
        _debug("Error sending email");
    }
    return context;
}
function doSend(ctx: ApplicationContext): Bool {
    if (ctx.emailServiceEnabled) {
        // real sending logic goes here
        return true;
    }
    return false;
}
```

The rest of the code has not been changed, so I will not include it here. If you have any problems with the code, compare your code with the code that's been published in this book's GitHub repository: https://github.com/PacktPublishing/Learn-Bosque-Programming/blob/main/Chapter03/main2.bsq.

In the ApplicationContext entity, we have the leftToSend field, which holds the number of emails that are left to send. Naturally, we don't want this number to ever be lower than 0. We can perform a manual check at the time of updating the context fields, but we can also use the invariant keyword and delegate the task to check the valid value of that field. Let's see what this looks like:

```
entity ApplicationContext {
    field leftToSend: Int = 10;

    invariant $leftToSend >= 0;
}
```

Here, we have told Bosque to make sure that whenever the value gets updated, it must not be lower than 0; otherwise, an error will be thrown. At this point, it's worth recalling that updating means creating a new object with updated values because of immutability. This means that invariants are checked before an object's construction. Notice the dollar sign. You need to use this to refer to the specific field.

Another useful thing is the use of pre and postconditions. You can add them to a method and be sure that whenever the method is called, they will be checked. The following is an example of such checks:

```
function sendEmail(context: ApplicationContext):
ApplicationContext
    requires context.user != none;
    ensures $return.leftToSend == context.leftToSend - 1;
{
    let sent = doSend(context);
    let {
        successCount = suc, errorCount = error, leftToSend =
left
    } = context.{ successCount, errorCount, leftToSend };

    if (sent) {
        _debug(String::concat("Email sent to ", context.user.
name, "!"));
        return context.update(
            successCount = suc + 1, leftToSend = left - 1
        );

    } else {
        _debug("Error sending email");
        return context.update(
            errorCount = error + 1, leftToSend = left - 1
        );
    }
}
```

We have modified the `sendEmail` function here a bit. It still performs the same logic, but it no longer accept ref parameter and instead of assigning a new value to the context parameter, we are simply returning a new result. Now take a look at the two lines just before the opening curly bracket. Here, we are ensuring that the user field is defined before running the function – this is the precondition and it is expressed using the requires keyword. The second check – postcondition – ensures that the `leftToSend` field has been decreased by one in comparison with the initial parameter value return value is either true or false and it is expressed using the ensures keyword. It's a convenient way to easily add another layer of reliability in Bosque.

Notice the `$return` keyword I used here. It is a special variable that refers to the return value of the function. Since `doSend` returns a `Bool` we compare `$return` to `true` and `false`. However, if the function returned `Int`, we could do something like this: `$return > 0` to ensure that the `return` value is greater than zero. Similarly, you can use it with other return types.

The last thing we will learn about is how to perform sanity checks using the `check` keyword and how to perform assertions using the `assert` keyword. Here is a simple example of their usage:

```
function doSend(ctx: ApplicationContext): Bool {
    check ctx.leftToSend > 1;
    assert ctx.user.name != "";
    if (ctx.emailServiceEnabled) {
        // real sending logic goes here
        return true;
    }
    return false;
}
```

This sanity check is only enabled on optimized builds. You can enable them using the `--level` flag, as described in *Chapter 2, Configuring Bosque Environment*. Assertions, on the other hand, are only enabled in test or debug mode. This can be also changed using the `--level` flag.

All these checks are there for one more reason – the Symtest tool. We will describe this in more detail in *Chapter 13, Testing in Bosque*.

Let's sum up your current knowledge.

Summary

In this chapter, you have learned about a lot of useful Bosque features. Now, you have knowledge about how certain theoretical assumptions have been implemented in the Bosque language and how to use them.

First, you learned that all the values in Bosque are immutable, and you know the reasoning behind that. You also learned that, in some scenarios, updating variables is possible. Here, you learned about three important keywords: `let`, `var`, and `ref`.

The next thing you become acquainted with was typed strings. Now, you know what they are and how to use them. You learned what the main problems of raw strings are and how powerful typed strings may be in real-world applications.

After that, we covered bulk algebraic data operations. You learned about four such operations that are available in Bosque and how to use them. Unfortunately, not all these features have been implemented yet, so you couldn't see them in practice. However, the language is developing quickly, so stay tuned.

Eventually, we took a closer look at iteration, recursion, errors, and checks. Because of this, you know that, in Bosque, there are no loops and that there is a good reason for this. You also learned how Bosque discourages us from using too much recursion thanks to the `recursive` keyword. Finally, we learned how to validate a function's input and output using built-in mechanisms.

At this point, you know enough things to level up your knowledge and jump into more advanced topics. In the next chapter, we will cover some of the most essential features of Bosque in more detail and build a real-world app using the language. Let's not waste any time!

Questions

1. What keyword can you use to declare an updatable variable?
2. How can you update a function parameter by reference?
3. What are the two ways of declaring typed strings? What are the differences between them?
4. What are the four main bulk algebraic data operations we talked about?
5. Are there any loop statements in Bosque?
6. What is the `recursive` keyword for?

Further reading

The following links are to a paper about safe strings, where the reasoning behind them is described in detail, and the official Bosque docs:

- *Representing Strings as Structured Data* `https://arxiv.org/pdf/1904.11254.pdf`

- *Official Bosque Documentation*: `https://github.com/microsoft/BosqueLanguage/blob/master/docs/language/overview.md`

Section 2:
The Bosque
Language Overview

In this part, we describe in detail all of the key features that Bosque provides. After reading this section, you will know what the language looks like and what its main features are.

This section comprises the following chapters:

- *Chapter 4, Entrypoint Function*
- *Chapter 5, Types and Operators*
- *Chapter 6, Statements and Syntax*
- *Chapter 7, Project: Bosque in the Cloud*

4
Entrypoint Function

As we well know, the result of the compilation process is a set of machine code instructions stored in a binary file containing an executable version of our program prepared for running on a computer according to its architecture.

But the programs being written nowadays generally have more than one function, several instructions, or main loops, so how does the processor recognize the first instruction it should execute? Will it execute the first instruction it finds?

To solve these questions, we will discuss the entrypoint functions, which allow programmers to define which is the first instruction to be run regardless of the position in which it has been placed in the code. We will learn how to create our own entrypoint functions in Bosque.

The following topics will be covered throughout this chapter.

- Why do we need an entrypoint function?
- Writing our first entrypoint function
- Passing arguments and returning values

At the end of the chapter, you will understand the importance of entrypoint functions. You will also have learned to create entrypoint functions and enrich our programs through the input parameters and the returning values.

Technical requirements

The following are the requirements for this chapter:

- A successful installation of the Bosque (the complete process for performing this was explained in *Chapter 2, Configuring the Bosque Environment*)

- A text editor of your choice

Why do we need an entrypoint function?

To understand the importance of entrypoint functions in a programming language, it is essential to start with understanding their history and realize how their role has been transcendental for the development of programming languages as we know them today.

It is said that Ada Lovelace wrote one of the first programs written using a programming language, which was an algorithm for calculating the Bernoulli numbers and was written for execution by Charles Babbage's Analytical Engine.

The Analytical Engine represented one of the first instances in the development of machines that were programmable through instructions entered into the machine using input devices, laying the foundation for sequential and single-purpose programs to be developed over the next decade. These first programs had computational and scientific objectives, so their sequential nature did not mean real limitations.

The incursion of computing into business implied the need to have multiple-purpose programs that could serve different execution flows according to the user's needs, so new multipurpose programming languages emerged; FORTRAN was one of the most popular.

FORTRAN 77 implemented the structured programming paradigm, which marked the starting point for executing a program with the PROGRAM statement, a basic form to define an entrypoint in the program code.

The program's execution used to be sequential, running line by line from top to bottom, and altered only through the IF, GOTO, or CONTINUE instructions, allowing each program to be modeled as a flow chart:

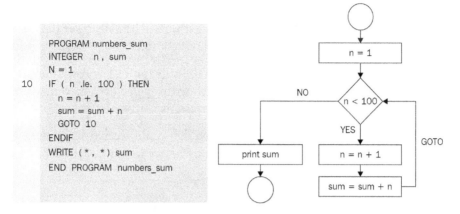

Figure 4.1 – A program written in FORTRAN 77 and its flowchart

But soon, programs became more complex, and could contain multiple files, functions, and subroutines. So it was essential to establish a standard to identify the starting point of a program. The entrypoint function was then established as a high-level abstraction that would allow the compiler to identify the first instruction, thus defining it in the final binary.

Thanks to the entrypoint function, today we can arrange our functions and decouple our programs according to what we consider more intuitive for easy maintenance or legibility without worrying about altering the expected execution flow.

Now that we understand why input functions exist, we will learn how to write our first entrypoint functions in Bosque.

Writing our first entrypoint function

Bosque, like most programming languages, allows us to explicitly establish the start of execution of a program through an entrypoint function. In this section, we will learn how to write one.

In Bosque, the entrypoint function is defined by default as a function named main(), which must be placed within the NSMain namespace, as follows:

```
namespace NSMain;
entrypoint function main(): String {
    return "Hello World, from an Entry Point ";
}
```

When compiling this code, a binary is generated where the first instruction to be executed will be a call to the `main` function, and after running it we will be able to see the message `"Hello world, from an Entry Point"` in our console.

It is possible to define some other function through the **entrypoint** keyword or even define more than one. This is useful for symbolic testing through a data-driven strategy or when we want to program with different compiled versions.

For example, if we would like to create an application that could receive parameters from a web server or via direct execution on the command line, we would have to define two different `entrypoint` functions, as follows:

```
namespace NSYourApplication;
entrypoint function api_request(): String {
    // Do something
}
entrypoint function cli_call(): String {
    // Do something
}
```

When we have more than one `entrypoint` function, it is necessary to define which of these functions should be used for each version during the compilation process.

As we remember from *Chapter 2, Configuring the Bosque Environment*, we have to use ExeGen to compile our Bosque scripts. Additionally, this tool also allows us to define which function will be used as input function through the `-e` or `–entrypoint` parameter, as follows:

```
exegen -o binary_output_file your_script.bsq –entrypoint
"function_name"
```

So to generate a binary to run our program from a web server, we would set the `api_request` function as an entrypoint function, which we do by writing the following in the command line:

```
> exegen -o web_version.exe your_script.bsq –entrypoint "
NSYourApplication::api_request"
```

On the other hand, to generate the command-line version of our program we will use the `cli_call` function as an entrypoint function. We do this by writing the following in the command line:

```
> exegen -o cli_version.exe your_script.bsq -entrypoint
"NSYourApplication::cli_call"
```

This flexibility allows us to have reusable code, writing programs that can respond to different interfaces through dedicated entrypoint functions.

At this point, we are able to write entrypoint functions for our Bosque programs, but we could notice that our programs could be very limited without the ability to pass input data. For this reason, in the next heading, we will learn how to send arguments and define the response types, allowing our programs to be more dynamic.

Passing arguments and returning values

When we design programs, it is customary to think about allowing users to define input variables and choose what to receive in response; that is why Bosque allows including parameters and specifying a return type in the definition of a custom entrypoint.

As we can see in the following script, we have a function that receives two integer parameters which will be multiplied and divided, returning a float value:

```
entrypoint function triangleArea(base: Int, height: Int):
Float64 {
    return ( base * height ) / 2;
}
```

The structure of a custom entry point can be summarized in the following graphic:

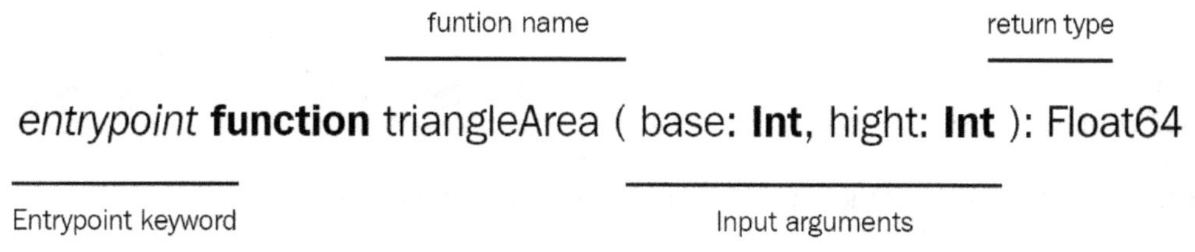

entrypoint **function** triangleArea (base: **Int**, hight: **Int**): Float64

Figure 4.2 – Custom entrypoint structure

Let's see an example. We will write a program that calculates the number in the *n*th position in the Fibonacci series using a recursive function.

First, we have to write a simple Fibonacci generator function:

```
recursive function fibonacciNumber(n: Int): Int {
return if (n == 0) 0
   elif (n == 1) 1
   else fibonacciNumber(n - 1) + fibonacciNumber(n -
2);
```

Then, we prepare our custom `entrypoint` function for receiving n as an input parameter and we set an `Int` type for the returning value:

```
entrypoint function calc_n_pos_fibonacci(n: Int) Int {
       return fibonacciNumber(n);
}
```

Finally, our script is as follows:

```
namespace NSFibonacci
recursive function fibonacciNumber(n: Int): Int {
       return if (n == 0) 0
            elif (n < 3) 1
            else fibonacciNumber(n-1) + fibonacciNumber(n-2);
}
entrypoint function calc_n_pos_fibonacci(n: Int) Int {
       return fibonacciNumber(n);
}
```

To define `calc_n_pos_fibonacci()` as our default entrypoint function in the final binary, we will use the `--entrypoint` param for the compilation process, as we can see in the next command:

```
> exegen -o fibonacci.exe fibonacci.bsq –entrypoint
"NSFibonacci::calc_n_pos_fibonacci"
```

Let's try our binary with some input parameters in the command line:

```
> fibonacci.exe 5
5
> fibonacci.exe 11
```

```
89
> fibonacci.exe 25
75825
```

When run the program, the `calc_n_pos_fibonacci` function is executed immediately, receiving as a parameter an integer number according to the specification of the input function returning the *n*th Fibonacci number as a result.

Summary

The entrypoint functions arise to allow developers to establish the main flow of execution of a program through a high-level function, which, when compiled, will become a set of instructions with a specific main instruction that allows the computer to follow the expected workflow.

In Bosque, the `entrypoint` function is more flexible than in other languages. It allows establishing input parameters and output data types, which is useful for developing serverless functions.

When writing a custom input function or having more than one, it is necessary to specify what the input function should be for the final binary through the `--entrypoint` parameter of the ExeGen compiler.

Finally, we have learned more about `entrypoint` functions. Now you are able to write your own `entrypoint` functions for your Bosque programs. In the next chapter, we will explore the Bosque types and operators in order to expand our knowledge of the language.

Questions

The answer to the following questions can be found in the *Assessments* section at the end of the book:

1. What is an entrypoint function?
2. Why is important to have entrypoints?
3. How can we build a custom entrypoint function in Bosque?
4. How we can pass arguments to a custom entrypoint function in Bosque?

Further reading

- *History of Programming Languages, Volume III*, Barbara Ryder and Brent Hailpern

- *Regularized Programming with the Bosque Language*, Mark Marron

- A sketch of the Analytical Engine, by L. F. Menabrea: `http://www.fourmilab.ch/babbage/sketch.html`

5
Types and Operators

Bosque supports a multiple type system that allows developers to have sufficient flexibility to develop their programs through nominal structured or combined types. To take advantage of the language, it is essential to become familiar with the different supported types and operators that Bosque provides.

In this chapter, we will explore each of the type systems, review the core types, and discover some special types and the main operators that Bosque offers us. For this chapter, we will cover the following topics:

- Bosque type system
- Nominal type system
- Structural type system
- Typed strings
- Operators

By the end of this chapter, you will be able to understand the Bosque type systems, as well as identify and use each operator available to process information from different types.

Technical requirements

The following are the requirements for this chapter:

- It is necessary to have Bosque installed successfully. The complete process to perform this has been explained in *Chapter 2, Configuring a Bosque Environment*.

- A text editor of your choice.

Bosque type system

Bosque provides more than one single type system. It gives us more flexibility and provides us with more options for building our programs. In this section, we will learn more about each type system so that we can understand how each type adds value to the software construction process.

Type systems in a programming language first appeared for the purpose of allowing the programmer to choose how data would be stored in memory.

One of its first implementations can be found in FORTRAN, which allowed us to define whether a variable would store an integer or floating-point data using some specific characters at the beginning of the variable identifiers' names.

Later, type systems were also used to prevent errors in execution time through type checking, which was implemented for the first time in ALGOL 60.

Nowadays, type systems also provide abstraction mechanisms that provide simplified interfaces to interact with data structures, thereby allowing the programmer to have a broader range of tools when solving problems.

The Bosque type system provides three different perspectives so that the programmer can have greater flexibility when building their applications, which are as follows:

- **Nominal type system**: The most familiar type system for programmers with experience in object-oriented languages.

- **Structural type system**: A type system focused on data structures.

- **Combinational type system**: A type system oriented to Boolean algebra operations between types.

Let's look at these type systems in the following subsections in a little more detail.

Nominal type system

The nominal type system provides a familiar interface for programmers who come from object-oriented languages, thanks to the implementation of concepts and entities, which could be interpreted, saving the differences, with abstract classes and classes.

We can create concepts to define abstract types, which allow us to implement inheritance, constants, or static functions. Just like abstract classes, concepts are never instantiated and are declarative or descriptive.

We can define a concept using the `concept` keyword as follows:

```
concept Foo {
    // Something
}
```

A **concept** in Bosque can define and implement static functions, member fields, constants, and methods. Let's see a comparison between JavaScript and Bosque implementations. We see the following snippet in which a simple class with a constructor is declared:

```
// JavaScript
class Foo {
    constructor(x) {
        this.x = x;
    }
}
```

On the other hand, we can see the following snippet written in Bosque, which has a similar implementation using the language's own characteristics, such as concepts and fields:

```
//Bosque
concept Foo {
    field x: Int;
}
```

Furthermore, we could use the `entity` declaration to create types that can instantiate concepts. These inherit the methods, fields, and constants from the concept.

To create an entity, we will use the `entity` keyword as follows:

```
entity Bar provides Foo {
    //
}
```

Let's see an example involving more extensive code. In the following snippet, we have a basic example of inheritance in JavaScript:

```
// JavaScript
class Foo {
    constructor(x) {
        this.x = x;
    }
}
class Bar extends Foo {
    constructor(x) {
        super(x)
    }
}

var baz = new Bar(1)
```

As we can see in the following snippet, the nominal type system allows us to implement a very similar solution using Bosque through concepts and entities:

```
// Bosque
concept Foo {
    field x: Int;
}

entity Bar provides Foo { }

let baz = Bar@{x=1}
```

Do not worry if you don't understand the previous code. We will learn more about these topics later. The important thing is to recognize that Bosque provides us with similar tools, such as languages with object-oriented programming support. As we have seen, this type system allows us to adopt known practices and patterns in object-oriented programming languages. Next, we will see another Bosque type system that will shape our most basic data structures.

Structural type system

The structural type system provides two main types, tuples and records, which are the most basic data structures. They are commonly used to define the arguments received by a function. Let's look at these types more closely in the following subsections.

Tuples

A **tuple** is a list of items providing a type that can be marked as optional. Each tuple is a subtype of the nominal type `Tuple`..

Let's look at some examples of tuple declarations:

```
[ Int ]              // Tuple of an Integer value
[ Int, Bool ]        // Tuple of an Integer and Boolean value
[ Int, ?:Bool ]      // Tuple of an Integer and optional Boolean
value
```

But we could also use a literal constructor syntax, as follows:

```
[]                   // Empty Tuple
[1, 2]               // Tuple of Integer values
[1, "a"]             // Tuple of an Integer and String value
[1, foo()]           // Tuple of an Integer value and the result of
foo()
```

Records

We could understand a **Record** as a map of named elements. Some of these could be marked as optional.

Let's now look at some examples of Record declarations:

```
// Record with an Integer value with an identifier called x
{ x: Int }
// Record with two required values y and z, both Integer
{ y: Int, z: Int }
// Record with an Integer and an optional Boolean value
{ x: Int, b?: Bool}
```

However, as with tuples, we can also use a literal constructor syntax, as follows:

```
// Empty record
{ }
// A record with an Integer value identified by x
{ x = 1 }
// A record with an integer and Boolean values
{ x = 1, y = true }
```

Core types

Bosque provides some basic types established in the definition of the language itself, commonly called **primitive types**. Let's see what they are.

Int

The **Int** type is used to represent positive and negative whole numbers whose values can be in the range from -9007199254740991 to 9007199254740991.

Let's see an example of a declaration and assignment of a Int type identifier:

```
var n: Int;
n = 53;
```

Here is a tiny subset of useful methods available on `Int` type:

Method	Type	Description
`toFloat64(): Float64`	Member	Convert an integer to a floating-point number.
`max (v1: int, v2: int): Int`	Static	Returns the max value between two numbers.
`min (v1: int, v2: int): Int`	Static	Returns the min value between two numbers.
`mod (a: Int, b: Int): Int`	Static	Returns the modulo operation result for two numbers.

Figure 5.1 – Int type available methods

Bool

A **Bool** type can only store a Boolean value (true or false) as a bit representation – 1, 0.

Let's now see an example of the declaration and assignment of a `Bool` type identifier:

```
var flag: Bool;
flag = true;
```

According to the `Bool` implementation, we have the following useful methods:

Method	Type	Description
`stringify(b: Bool): String`	Static	Return a string representation for a Boolean value.
`parse (str: String): Bool`	Static	Return a Boolean value from a string representation.

Figure 5.2 – Bool type available methods

String

A **String** type represents a string of characters commonly used to store text.

Let's now see an example of the declaration and assignment of a String type identifier:

```
var greeting: String;
greeting = "Hello world";
```

According to the `String` implementation, we have the following useful methods:

Method	Type	Description
`length (): Int`	Member	Returns the number of characters in the string
`charAt(idx: Int): String`	Member	Returns the character located in the position indicated by the `idx` parameter within a string
`concat(...args: List<String>): String`	Member	Allows the concatenation of two strings, returning a new string with the result
`substring (start?: Int, end?: Int): String`	Member	Allows the extraction of a segment of the string delimited by the start and end parameters.
`includes (str: String): Bool`	Member	Evaluates if one text string is inside another
`startsWith(str: String): Bool`	Member	Evaluates if a string starts with a specific set of characters
`endsWith(str: String): Bool`	Member	Evaluates if a string ends with a specific set of characters
`indexOf(str: String):Int`	Member	Returns the position of a substring within a string
`lastIndexOf(str: String): Int`	Member	Returns the last position of a substring within a string
`split(sep: String): List<String>`	Member	Divides a string into several segments by returning a list of strings

Method	Type	Description
`trim (): String`	Member	Removes spaces at the beginning and end of a string
`trimStart(): String`	Member	Removes spaces at the beginning of a string
`trimEnd(): String`	Member	Removes spaces at the end of a string
`compare (a: String, b: String): Bool`	Static	Compares two strings

Float64

A **Float64** represents a number in floating-point notation, used to store numbers with a decimal point so as not to lose precision in the case of mathematical operations.

Let's now see an example of the declaration and assignment of a `Float64` type identifier:

```
var f: Float64;
f = 0.54f
```

According to the `Float64` implementation, we have the following useful methods:

Method	Type	Description
`parse (str: String): Float64`	Static	Returns a floating-point value from a string
`toInt(): Int`	Member	Converts a `Float64` value to an integer
`abs (): Float64`	Member	Returns the absolute value
`ceiling (): Float64`	Member	Returns the result of rounding the value to the nearest higher integer
`floor (): Float64`	Member	Returns the result of rounding the value to the nearest lower integer
`root (x: Float64, y: Float64): Float64`	Static	Returns the result of executing the root operation between two operands
`log (v: Float64): Float64`	Static	Returns the result of the natural logarithm for the number passed as a parameter

Method	Type	Description
`sin (): Float64`	Member	Gets the sine of a number
`cos (): Float64`	Member	Gets the cosine of a number
`tan (): Float64`	Member	Gets the tangent of a number
`min (v1: Float64, v2: Float64): Float64`	Static	Returns the lowest value between two numbers
`max (v1: Float64, v2: Float64): Float64`	Static	Returns the highest value between two numbers

The `Float64` Bosque type allows us to use a single type to represent existing types in other languages, such as Float, Decimal, or Double, providing the maximum possible precision with this type.

Typed strings

In addition to the primitive `String` type, Bosque provides two additional types to broaden the possibilities through extra features such as metadata or supporting validation through regular expressions – `SafeString<T>` and `StringOf<T>`. Let's learn more about these in the following subsections.

SafeString<T>

The `SafeString <T>` type is defined by a parameter representing a validation pattern for its content through a regular expression. This feature can be useful for simplifying string formatting or for performing content validation.

Let's consider an example program to convert USD to EUR that are provided as strings with the currency symbol.

> **Important note**
> As of this writing, the methods of the `String` and `Regex` entities presented in the next example are not fully implemented yet. Therefore the code will not compile properly. Keep this in mind while analyzing it.

Have a look at the following practical example:

```
typedef CurrencyFormat = /(\d)+(USD|EUR)/; // Currency valid
format
function convertToUSD (input: SafeString<CurrencyFormat>):
Float64 {
    let strInput = input.string();
    let regexMatch = /(\d)+/.match(strInput);
    let dval = Float64::parse(strInput.substring(regexMatch.
index, regexMatch.index + regexMatch.length));
    if(strInput.endsWith("USD")) {
        return dval;
    }
    else {
        return convertEURToUSD(dval);
    }
}

function convertEURToUSD (euros: Float64): Float64 {
    // return euros * 1.18f;
}
```

In the previous code, we can identify a function called convertToUSD that aims to return an amount in dollars and carry out the conversion if the amount entered is expressed in euros.

In this function, we can see a parameter called input. This is typed as SafeString <T>, which means that if we call the function with an amount expressed with another currency identifier, for example, 100 MXN, this will result in a type error.

Let's see how it would be used with the help of the following example:

```
var amount = CurrencyFormat'100EUR';
return convertToUSD(amount); // 118.0
```

In the previous code, we see how a string with a valid format can be processed by complying with the format expected by SafeString, where finally this process returns a Float64 value that represents the conversion of the numerical part of the string.

StringOf<T>

On the other hand, we also have a more flexible option, the `StringOf<T>` type, which can be defined through a parameter that can be of any type, with the only condition that it implements the `Parsable` concept.

This extra flexibility also means that we must manually specify the parsing process by overwriting the `T::tryParse` method.

Let's look at a practical example:

```
entity PhoneNumber provides Parsable {
    field number: String;


    hidden static parseNumber(str: String): Result<String,
String> {
        if (str.length() <= 9) {
            return ok(str);
        } else {
            return err("Invalid Phone Number");
        }
    }


    override static tryParse(str: String): Result<PhoneNumber,
String> {
        let result = PhoneNumber::parseNumber(str);


        if(result.isErr()) {
            return Result<Any, String>::err(err(result.
failure());
        }
        else {
            let phone = PhoneNumber@{number=result.result()};
            return Result ok(phone);
        }
    }
}


function sendSMSNotification(phone: StringOf<PhoneNumber>:
String {
```

```
    // Send the notification
return String::concat("Send to ", phone.string());
}
```

In this example, we observe a function that aims to obtain a valid phone number from a string to send an SMS notification.

For this purpose, an entity that implements the Parsable concept is generated. The tryParse method is overwritten to implement a more complex method of validating phone numbers in an imperative way instead of just a simple descriptive method through a validation based on regular expressions, opening a range of possibilities as regards custom parsing implementations. The types exposed in this chapter, in addition to improving clarity, enable identification of the text validation parameters' restrictions in a function, thereby enhancing the testability of our applications. Next, we will explain the operators that Bosque provides to carry out between the diverse types available.

Operators

Operators are an intrinsic part of the definition of a programming language. They establish the way in which one or more operands are resolved by an operation expressed through a predefined symbol in the language.

To have a clearer idea of how an operator works, let's remember how we use arithmetic operators in real life:

```
4 + 5
```

As we know, if we find the + symbol located between two numbers, this indicates that when executing the operation, both operands 4 and 5 will be solved by an addition operation, returning 9.

We call this operation a **binary arithmetic operation** since it involves two operators and is defined as employing an arithmetic calculation. Still in a language, we have a set of several diverse types of operators.

In the next subsections, we will explore each available operator in Bosque.

Unary operators

Bosque supports three types of unary operations that are defined by a symbol at the beginning of an expression. The following table shows some of these expressions and its uses:

Symbol	Description
!	This returns a Bool value. It is the result of the negation of the expression. If the expression is None, it returns `true`.
+	This is an indicator of a positive value used just to be explicit.
-	This is an indicator of the arithmetic negative value of the expression.

Let's look at some examples of these:

```
!true       // Returns false
!false      // Returns true
!none       // Returns true
!"hello"    // Type error
!5          // Type error
+9          // Return 9
-5          // Return -5
```

In summary, as in most known languages, a unary operator is represented by a symbol at the beginning of an expression and receives a single parameter located on the right. The common operations are the negation and the explicit indicator for a number's negativity or positivity.

Binary operators

Bosque provides a set of arithmetic operators that can be used when employing the desired operation symbol between two operands or by calling the static methods of Math and passing the operands as arguments.

The following table lists some of these operators:

Symbol	Description
+	Addition
-	Subtraction
*	Multiplication
/	Division

Let's see some examples of these operations in the following code:

```
6 + 8       // 15
9 - 5       // 4
3 * 9       // 27
6 / 2       // 3
```

As we said before, these expressions can also be performed using `Math` methods, as we can see here:

```
Math::sum(6, 8)      // 15
Math::sub(9, 5)      // 4
Math::mult(3, 9)     // 27
Math::div(6, 2)      // 3
```

As we can observe, arithmetic binary operations in Bosque are performed in the same way as in other languages.

Logic operators

Bosque provides the basic logical operators `&&` (**AND**) and `||` (**OR**), which are valid only for Bool type operands. Additionally, the `==>` operator is included, which is only `false` if the first operator is `true` and the second one is `false`.

Let's see some examples:

```
OR
true || false        // true
false || false       // false
AND
true && true         // true
false && true        // false
false && false       // false
Material conditional (→)
true ==> false       // false
true ==> true        // true
false ==> true       // true
false ==> false      // true
```

Order comparison operators

Bosque has operators designed to carry out order operations between two values, that is, to identify whether one is greater or less than another. In the following table, the operands and its use cases are listed.

Symbol	Description
<	Smaller than
>	Greater than
<=	Less than or equal to
>=	Greater than or equal to

Let's see some examples:

```
1 < 5           // true
2 > 0           // true
13 <= 8         // false
9 >= 3          // true
6 > "3"         // error
```

We have intentionally omitted the equality operator, which you will see in the next heading.

Equality comparison operators

To evaluate equality between two operands in Bosque, you can use the antagonistic symbols == (equality) and != (inequality), although it is also possible to use the static `KeyType::equal(a: KeyType, b: KeyType)` method.

An expression containing the == operator will always be evaluated from left to right.

Let's see some examples:

```
5 == 5          // true
"7" == 7        // error
"9" != ""       // false
false == none   // false
```

On the other hand, Bosque does not support reference equality, but it is possible to define an identification key to allow equality operations between more complex types. This identifier can be composite, allowing more than one field within its definition.

Let's see how they work:

```
identifier UniqueID = Int;
entity Resource {
    field id: UniqueID;
    // ...
}

let x = Resource@{1};
let y = Resource@{2};

x == x      // true
y == x      // false
```

In the previous code, we can see a numeric identifier declaration that will become part of the Resource entity. In this way, we can compare different instances through an equality operation.

Now, let's see how a compound identifier works:

```
composite identifier CompoundKey = { id: Int, version: String
};
entity Resource {
    field idkey: CompoundKey;
    // ...
}

let x = Resource@{ idkey: {id: 10, version: "beta"} };
let y = Resource@{ idkey: {id: 10, version: "alpha"} };

x == x      // true
y == x      // false
```

In the previous code, we can see that the identifier is composed of two fields, id and version, which will be evaluated during the equality comparison process.

Select operators

The selection operator evaluates a Boolean condition and returns the value to the left of the : symbol if the condition is `true`, and the value to the right if it is `false`. The use of this operator facilitates improved code readability through a ternary operation. The `none` value is considered false.

Let's see some examples:

```
true ?  "yes" : "no"      // yes
false ? "yes" : "no"      // no
none ?  "yes" : "no"      // no
"" ? "yes" : "no"         // error
```

We have now learned to identify the different type systems and operators that Bosque provides.

Summary

Bosque adopts many of the types and operators that we already know from our experience in other languages, simplifying their adoption. However, it is important to consider the deterministic nature of language, so it is important to understand how Bosque implements them and how they should be used to obtain the expected results while respecting the language's paradigm.

In this chapter, we have learned that the nominal type system is advantageous during the learning process since it allows the reasoning of the well-known object-oriented programming to be imitated.

Still, it is important to try to take full advantage of the structures that the language offers, such as collections and sets, and that not every implementation based on object-oriented programming is necessarily idiomatic or will efficiently take advantage of the paradigm that implements the language.

On the other hand, we also saw that in addition to the basic arithmetic, logic, or comparison operators, Bosque provides some operators that allow us to improve our code's readability as selection operators or none-coalescing operations.

And finally, we learned how Bosque solves the equality evaluation problem by implementing identifier fields and eliminating the need to implement referential equality.

Now we are ready to use these in our programs and continue to familiarize ourselves with the language. In the next chapter, we will explore the syntax of this language with a view to building more complex sentences.

Questions

1. What is a type?

2. How many type systems does Bosque support?

3. Does Bosque implement reference equality?

Further reading

- Jang, H., Dong, L., Xingyuan, Z., and Xiren, X. (2001). *Type system in programming languages*. Journal of Computer Science and Technology, 286–292

- Pierce, B. C. (2002). *Types and Programming Languages*. The MIT Press.

- Cardelli, L. (1996). *Type systems*. ACM Computing Surveys, 263-264.

6
Bosque Statements

A programming language is made up of a series of syntactic rules defined by a specific syntax. This syntax contains units called statements, representing a particular action, controlling the execution flow, or performing a specific action.

Recognizing and understanding the use of statements when writing programs allows us to identify the intention of the written code, so in this chapter, we will review the following topics:

- Writing comments
- Understanding variables
- Using constants
- Using conditionals
- Understanding switch
- Understanding return and yield
- Understanding blocks
- Writing validations

By the end of this chapter, we will have learned to identify and use the main Bosque statements, and we will be ready to understand almost any code written in Bosque.

Technical requirements

In order to get the most from this chapter, it is recommended that you have a successful installation of Bosque (the complete process of installation was explained in *Chapter 2, Configuring the Bosque Environment*) and have the text editor of your choice.

So, let's begin!

Writing comments

Although the writing of comments does not fulfill a specific function during our programs' execution, they are essential for good documentation of the written code and explicitly exposing a particular code segment's intention.

Bosque provides two types of comments that we can use interchangeably:

- Line comments, declared by the characters // at the beginning of a line
- Comment blocks, which will be framed between the characters /* at the beginning of the block and */ at the end

In the following code, we can see how to write each type of comment:

```
// This is an inline comment
```

```
/* This is
a multiline
comment */
```

As we can infer, comments will not be included in the final build, so we should write as many as we consider necessary to allow a better understanding of the code.

Next, we will see how Bosque implements variables, which are a widely used concept in most algorithms.

Understanding variables

Bosque allows imperative programming despite having a functional inclination. Hence, the assignment of identifiers for memory spaces still maintains a relevant role in writing code.

Keeping a deterministic intention, Bosque doesn't support aliasing, as we saw in the *Chapter 1, Exploring Bosque*, preventing hidden behaviors within the variable's assignation.

The following syntax tree defines the declaration of variables in Bosque:

```
VarDecl :=

    var Identifier(: Type)? = Exp;

    var! Identifier(: Type)?( = Exp?);

    ( var | var! ) Structure = Exp;
```

Figure 6.1 – Syntax tree for variable declaration

As we can see in the syntax tree, we have three ways to declare a variable through the `var` keyword. Let's see two ways to write variable declarations:

- **Initialized variables**: A variable can be initialized with a value in its declaration. If the type is not defined, the type will be inferred according to the assigned value:

```
var x: Int = 3;
var y = "abc"
```

- **Uninitialized variables**: It is also possible to declare a variable whose value is initialized later. We can omit the type, which will be inferred in its first assignment:

```
var x: Int;
x = 3;
```

In addition to initialized and uninitialized variables, Bosque supports the declaration and simultaneous assignment of multiple values on the same line, as shown here:

```
[var x, var y] = [3, 5];
var {i=x, j=y} = {i=3, j=5};
```

Now that we understand how to use variables, we will see how to define immutable variables.

Using constants

Bosque allows us to define immutable or constant variables that will maintain a single value throughout the execution life cycle. For this purpose, unlike mutable variables, Bosque provides the reserved word `let`; it is recommended to use these variables when variables don't have to be updated during our programs' execution.

A constant must always be initialized, but the type can be omitted since the type could be inferred from the assigned value.

The following code block shows some constant declarations:

```
let x: Int = 3;
let y = 5;
let x, y = 3, 5;
let {i=x, j=y} = {f=3, g=5};
```

If we try to change the value of a constant through a second assignment, we will get an error message.

It is also possible to have variables and constants within the same declaration, which allows us to simplify our code. This can done in the following way:

```
[var x, let y] = [3, 5];
```

In this piece of code, the variable x is assigned with a value of 3 and the type Int is inferred. On the other hand the constant y is initialized with 5 and its type will also be inferred.

Now that we know how to declare constants, we will see how Bosque implements the execution flow control statements through conditionals in order to build more complex processing flows.

Using conditionals

Conditionals are control structures that allow us to separate the main execution flow into one or more secondary flows of execution from a Boolean evaluation.

Bosque provides if, elif, and else reserved words for writing a conditional block. Additionally, due to Bosque being a curly-bracket language, we have to use curly brackets instead of a reserved word for closing blocks.

The following figure shows different ways to define a conditional:

```
if ( boolean evaluation ) { ... }

if ( boolean evaluation ) { ... }
else { ... }

if ( boolean evaluation ) { ... }
elif ( boolean evaluation ) { ... }
else { ... }
```

Figure 6.2 – Conditional structures

The only restriction in the construction of conditional blocks is that if we use an `elif` block, it is mandatory to have one `else` block.

Let's see an example:

```
if ( x > 10 ) {
        return "error, greater than 10";
elif ( x < 0 ) {
        return "error,  the number must not be negative";
} else {
        return "it's ok, thanks";
}
```

In this code, we can observe a simple validation made through a conditional, which validates whether a number is not negative and less than ten. However, we could also express it using a logical operator to group conditions as follows:

```
if ( x > 10 || x < 0 ) {
        return "Invalid number";
else {
        return "it's ok, thanks";
}
```

On the other hand, as we saw in *Chapter 5, Types and Operators*, we have a selection operator that allows us to write conditionals as ternary operations, so the preceding code can also be expressed as follows:

```
return ( x > 10 || x < 0 ) ? "Invalid number" : "It's ok,
thanks";
```

But conditionals are not the only way to control the execution flow. Let's take a look at the `switch` statement next.

Understanding switch

Another way of constructing conditionals is through the `switch` statement, which simplifies writing code in scenarios where several evaluations must be carried out on the same variable.

But additionally, Bosque has implemented a series of extra functions to enhance this statement using pattern matching, constraints, and type-based dispatch.

First, let's look at the most basic example:

```
switch(x) {
    case 1 => { return "option one"; }
    case 2 => { return "option two"; }
    case _ => { return "any other option"; }
}
```

As we see in the code, the switch block allows us to execute different instructions according to the value of the variable x. The wildcard _ will enable us to establish a flow for the values that do not correspond to any defined cases.

As we mentioned earlier, Bosque also allows us to use switch blocks to evaluate types, as shown in the following example:

```
switch(x) {
    type Bool => { return "is boolean"; }
    type Int => { return "is integer"; }
    type String => {return "is string"; }
    case _ => { return "unknown"; }
}
```

As we can see in the code, we use the type keyword instead of case to specify that the evaluation will be performed on the type of x and not on its value.

Another useful feature of switch statements is the conditioned case through the when clause, which allows us to add a condition to the evaluation that is carried out in the case clause. Let's take a look at the following example:

```
function abs(x: Int?): Int {
    switch(x) {
            type Int when x >= 0 => { return x; }
            type Int when x < 0 => { return -x; }
    }
}
```

In this code, we have a function that returns the absolute value of a number. These instructions evaluate the integer type and assess the positivity through the extra conditionals; then, the negative values change sign through the – operator.

Another exciting feature that Bosque supports is a structured assignment in the `switch` statement. It allows you to perform checks on tuples and records. Let's see how we could apply an example tuple in the `switch` statement:

```
var x = [1, 5];
switch(x) {
    case [1, let y: Int] => { return y; }
    case [2, let z: Int] => { return z; }
    case _ => { return none; }
}
```

Here, we are creating a x tuple and passing it to `switch`. In this case, the first check will match because the first value of our tuple is 1. In that case, a new variable, y, is going to be created, assigned the second value of the tuple and returned. So the result of this `switch` will be 5. If we changed the x tuple to [2, 6], then the second check would match and the z variable would be created, assigned, and returned, and the result would be 6.

We can also do the same with records. Let's see a similar example but with x being a record:

```
var x = {height=1, width=5};
var w: Int;
switch(x) {
    case {height=1, width=w} => { return w; }
    case {height=2, width=w} => { return w; }
    case _ => { return none; }
}
```

As you can see, we define x as a record with two fields: `height` and `width`. Then we are passing it to the `switch` statement and, depending on the `height` value, we are assigning the `width` value to the variable w, which was declared earlier. In each `case` the w variable is returned. In this particular example, the `height` field equals 1 so the result will be 5.

Next, we will see one of the most common statements in the writing of code, and we will explore the particulars of the `yield` clause.

Understanding return and yield

The `return` statement may sound familiar, and indeed the function it fulfills in Bosque scripts is the same function as in most languages. Within a block of code, it ends the invocation returning the expression's value as a result.

Let's understand this with the help of some examples:

```
namespace NSMain;
entrypoint function main(): String {
    return "hello world";
}
```

If we analyze the classic `hello world`, we will see that the input function is composed of a single `return` statement, so when we execute our script, the expression is evaluated, the execution is ended, and the text `"hello world"` is returned as a result.

So, if we try to add a second `return` statement below the first one, the execution of this second line will not be carried out because the first one ends the block's execution. The following code shows the line that won't be executed:

```
namespace NSMain;
entrypoint function main(): String {
    return "hello world";
    return "bye"; // This line will never be executed
}
```

It is possible to have more than one `return` statement in the same function. However, to do this, it will be necessary to have more than one execution flow. For example, we can use conditionals as follows:

```
function isPositive (x: Int): Bool {
    if (x > 0) {
        return true;
    } else {
        return false;
    }
}
```

The blocks are present in many of the statements that we have seen in this chapter, so let's dive deeper and learn more about blocks.

Understanding blocks

The Bosque block statements are nothing more than sequences of statements; they usually define a scope for the variables declared within the block and represent a contained execution context. Typically, they are delimited by curly brackets.

Let's see the next code:

```
var x = 7;
{
    var y = 5;
    y = x + 3;
}
```

As we see in the previous code, we see a variable x declared outside the block's context, which is accessible from the block, but the variable y is available only for the instructions contained by the block.

The blocks are present in several of the statements presented in this chapter. Let's see some examples to identify them better:

```
if ( true ) {
    // this is a block
} else {
    // this is another block
}
```

We have two blocks in a common if declaration. We also have a block in a function declaration:

```
function try(): String {
    // this is a block
}
```

But we can also have blocks like statement expressions, as follows:

```
let a = {| let x = 5; yield x; |}
```

When a block is used as an expression, yield should be used instead of return.

Every written code must have the ability to be tested, so the validation states are especially relevant. For this reason, we will explore this statement in detail next.

Writing validations

Bosque support statements validation through the reserved `assert` and `check` keywords, which are very useful for writing tests; the main difference between them is that the first is available only in debug time, and the second is included in the final build.

A false evaluation is interpreted as an error at debug time. This is provided as a report containing the error line number, an error code, and the call-stack, which are very useful for making corrections. On the other hand, once a build is generated, the errors become generic and indistinguishable.

Let's see an example:

```
function test_nth_prime_number(x: Int): Bool {
    assert nth_prime_number(50) = 229;
    assert nth_prime_number(100) = 541;
    assert nth_prime_number(1000) = 7919;
    return true;
}
```

In the previous code, we can see how to use the `assert` function to do an equality validation in order to test the reliability of the `nth_prime_number` function.

Summary

Bosque provides a reduced number of statements but enough to have the flexibility to write useful programs without losing its deterministic intent to allow writing more reliable code and without unexpected behavior.

In this chapter, we have reviewed the statements available in Bosque that, for the most part, would be familiar to a programmer who has previous experience in other programming languages since Bosque also supports the use of variables, constants, and control structures, among others.

On the other hand, Bosque has certain peculiarities, such as the intentional non-implementation of loops, an extension of the well-known `switch` clause to support different scenarios, and validation of statements to build our programs' tests.

It is essential to always keep in mind the intentionality of the language and the paradigm it implements to take advantage of it to write more reliable, readable, and maintainable code as expected from a program written in Bosque.

In this chapter, we have learned how to use the main characteristic statements of Bosque. Now we are ready to understand almost any piece of code; in the next chapter, we will apply everything we have learned in a practical project to strengthen our skills acquired in the Bosque language.

Questions

1. Which kind of variables does Bosque support?

2. Why does Bosque provide the `yield` keyword in addition to the `classic` return?

3. What is a block?

4. What does the _ symbol represent in a `switch` statement?

Further reading

Marron, M. (2019). *Regularized Programming with the Bosque Language*, Microsoft Research

7
Project: Bosque in the Cloud

Up to this point, we have learned a series of useful concepts that will allow us to build our first applications to solve real world problems.

The emergence of serverless technology has led us to think about building atomic solutions of limited responsibility, which have converted previously complex applications into a set of small specialized services, reducing resource consumption and simplifying maintenance and scalability.

Bosque emerges as an ideal candidate for the construction of small services due to its deterministic nature. We can ensure that our applications will always fulfill their purpose efficiently and be sufficiently legible to facilitate their maintenance.

In this chapter we will build an atomic web service that allows us to estimate the indoor position based on the physical principle that the signal intensity and the distance between transmitter and receiver are usually directly proportional.

To do this we are going to cover the following topics:

- Defining requirements

- Implementing the solution

- Running our program in the cloud

At the end of this chapter, we will have learned to build an application destined to be used on a web server. We are also going to reinforce our knowledge acquired in previous chapters, including creating custom entry points to receive the input arguments for our application, using our understanding of types of data to process the information received, and applying the different type systems that Bosque offers. All this will allow us to reinforce our learning and prepare to use Bosque in real-world projects.

Technical requirements

In order to carry out this project, you will need to meet the following basic requirements:

- A successful installation of the Bosque (the complete process to perform this was explained in *Chapter 2, Configuring Bosque Environment*).

- A text editor of your choice.

- Basic NodeJS knowledge.

Defining requirements

To develop this project, we will start with establishing our objectives. Throughout this chapter, we will write an API that will allow us to calculate a person's indoor position in a floorplan through the Wi-Fi signal intensity measurements concerning three known access points' positions.

Let's look at some theoretical concepts to understand how we are going to implement our program.

As we know, any device that can connect to a Wi-Fi network can identify which is the best signal to use through the **Received Signal Indicator (RSSI)** signal strength indicator. As we can see in the following table, a higher value for RSSI implies a better signal:

RSSI	Receive sensitivity threshold	Signal strength (%)	Signal Quality (%)
30	-30 dBm	100%	100%
25	-41 dBm	90%	100%
20	-52 dBm	80%	90%
21	-52 dBm	80%	80%
15	-63 dBm	60%	50%
10	-65 dBm	40%	35%
5	-89 dBm	10%	5%
0	-110 dBm	0%	0%

Figure 7.1 – RSSI equivalences

However, in addition to allowing us to estimate the signal quality that we have, we will find that there is a direct relationship between the decrease in signal intensity and the increase in distance measured from the signal emitter. To understand this better, let's see the following figure:

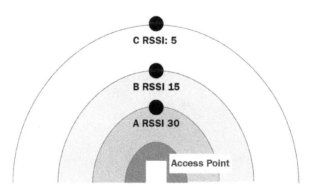

Figure 7.2 – Graphical representation of signal intensity

Next, we have to identify the best way to estimate the distance in meters from the emitter for a specific RSSI value. To simplify this calculation, most manufacturers provide us a *Measured Power* factor, which is a calibrated measure that indicates to us what the expected RSSI is at a distance of 1 meter, and thanks to that, we can deduce the following formula:

$$Distance = 10^{\frac{(Measured\ Power - RSSI)}{(10 \times N)}}$$

In this formula, N is the environmental factor constant (in a range of 2-4), which represents the resistance of the environment for the propagation of the signal. From now on, we will assume that this value is 2, which implies a low resistance or normal conditions.

Now we know how to calculate the distance between the emitter of the signal and our receiving device. Let's see how to use this information to estimate our position within an area.

If we have three different access points, we can estimate the distance from these through the RSSI detected by the receiving device using the formula that we explained.

With this information, we could draw circles containing all the points located at those distances, and in this way, we will find our position right at the intersection of these areas, as we can see in the following figure:

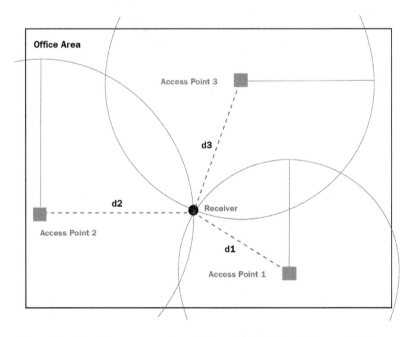

Figure 7.3 – Graphic representation of the position estimate through distances

And finally, we could obtain the exact position from a simple geometric calculation exercise that we will see in detail during the implementation of the algorithm in the *Implementing the solution* section:

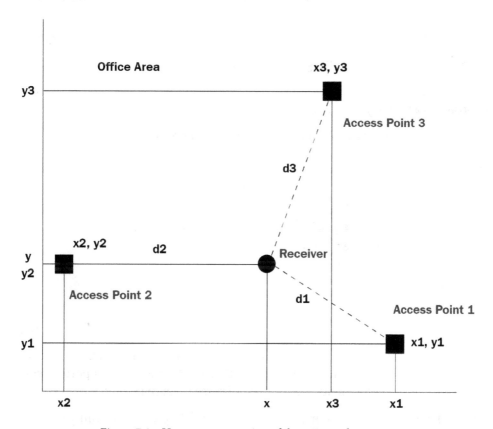

Figure 7.4 – Vector representation of the estimated position

Now that we understand the theory behind the problem, we can summarize the tasks in a series of consecutive steps as follows:

1. Get the RSSI values detected by the receiver concerning three known access points.

2. Calculate the distance in meters using each of the measured RSSIs.

3. Calculate our x, y coordinates using the 2D trilateration method.

4. Build an API to expose our program as a web service.

In the next section, we will implement our solution using Bosque.

Implementing the solution

Now that we are clear about the position estimation approach, we will see how to use Bosque to implement it as a cloud service, using the task list built in the previous section.

Getting the RSSI values detected by the receiver for the three known access points

First, we will write a Bosque program that receives the receiver's values and the access points' positions as *x* and *y* coordinates.

To do this, we should write a custom `entrypoint` function as follows:

```
namespace NSMain;


entrypoint function runner(
    rssi1: String, rssi2: String, rssi3: String,
    x1: String, x2: String, x3: String,
    y1: String, y2: String, y3: String
): Float64 {
// Do something
}
```

We may have noticed that we are using string types for our input parameters despite them representing numbers. This is because in Bosque, `Float64` type is not supported yet in the entrypoint function arguments and we need to parse them manually.

To provide a better structure for our code, we are going to implement an entity to represent each emitter to have a structured representation of our information as follows:

```
entity Emitter {
    field rssi: Float64;
    field x: Float64;
    field y: Float64;


    factory static create(rssi: String, x: String, y: String):
      {rssi: Float64, x: Float64, y: Float64} {
        return {
            rssi=Float64::parse(rssi),
```

```
            x=Float64::parse(x),
            y=Float64::parse(y)};
    }
}
```

As we can see in the previous code, we have built an `Emitter` entity representing each system's access point. We also observe the constructor's implementation that will allow us to convert the string type parameters into `Float64` values to perform the mathematical calculations necessary.

Additionally, we will create an entity called `IndoorPositionEstimation` whose purpose is to represent your program's instance, as follows:

```
entity IndoorPositionEstimator {
    field emitters: List<Emitter>;
}
```

Now that we have the entities created, we will add the instructions to carry the arguments' values to the `IndoorPositionEstimator` instance as follows:

```
entrypoint function runner(
    rssi1: String, rssi2: String, rssi3: String,
    x1: String, x2: String, x3: String,
    y1: String, y2: String, y3: String
): Float64 {

    let estimator = IndoorPositionEstimator@{
        emitters=List<Emitter>@{
            Emitter@create(rssi1, x1, y1),
            Emitter@create(rssi2, x2, y2),
            Emitter@create(rssi3, x3, y3)
        }
    };
// ...
```

Now that the arguments have been stored in a known structure, we will go to the next step in our checkpoints list.

Calculating the distance in meters using each of the measured RSSI values

Now that we know that each access point's respective values have been stored as fields, we can deduce that the method to calculate the distance using the intensity of RSSI should be implemented as an `Emitter` entity method.

If we remember this method, it must represent the following formula:

$$Distance = 10^{\frac{(Measured\ Power - RSSI)}{(10 \times N)}}$$

Its implementation in Bosque can be seen as follows:

```
entity Emitter  {
    field measured_power: Float64 = -69.0f; // Provided by the
    manufacturer
    field rssi: Float64;


    // . . .


    method calcDistance(): Float64 {
        let n = 2.0f; // Environmental factor constant
        let ratio = (this.measured_power - this.rssi) / (10.0f *
          n);
        return Float64::pow(10.0f, ratio);
    }
}
```

As we can see, we have added a field to the `Emitter` entity to store the value of the `measured_power` constant, which the manufacturer gives. To simplify our code, we have manually set this value to -69.

Additionally, we observe the `calcDistance` method, which contains the necessary instructions to implement the distance formula.

To better understand how this formula works, let's now look at an example.

If we try to calculate the distance from an access point to our receiver, we will take the value that it registers as the RSSI value. For this example, let's say it is -60.

So, assuming that the values of n and `measured_power` are 2 and -69, respectively, when replacing our formula's variables, we would have the following:

$$Distance = 10^{\frac{(-69-60)}{(10\times2)}}$$

$Distance = 0.35\ meters$

So when we call the `measured_power ()` method with the same arguments, we should get the same result.

Now that we have implemented the distance calculation method, we can calculate our position's coordinates using the trilateration method, as we will see in the next step.

Calculating our x, y coordinates using the 2D trilateration method

Now that we have the estimated distances from each access point to our position, we can draw circles that contain all the possible locations where we might find ourselves considering the estimated distance, as we see in the following figure:

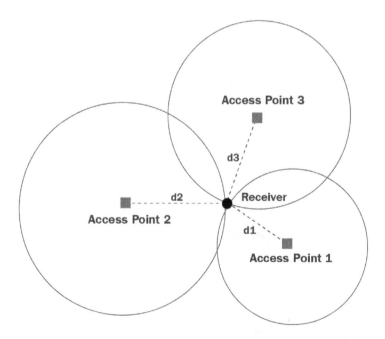

Figure 7.5 – Trilateration method graphical representation

In the preceding figure, we can see that one single point is intersected by the three estimated distances simultaneously. This process of estimating position from distances is called 2D trilateration.

> **Important note**
>
> Please note that the trilateration method that we are going to use is not perfect. It strongly relies on the RSSI measure, which may not be precise. Therefore, the resulting coordinates may not be 100% accurate. In general, the trilateration method taps out at an accuracy of about 1-2m. In order to improve that, we would have to use some other way harder methods, such as triangulation. You can read more about this in the documents linked in the *Further reading* section.

In order to implement the 2D trilateral algorithm using Bosque, we must review some mathematical concepts that will allow us to deduce a mathematical model that is easier to translate into code.

As we know, the circles can be expressed as mathematical equations. So we can represent each circle containing all the points located in the measured distance through the following formula:

$$(x - x_i)^2 + (y - y_i)^2 = d_i{}^2$$

In the preceding formula, *xi* and *yi* represent each access point's known coordinates, and *di* is the distance calculated in the previous step.

So we can describe the three circles as follows:

$$(x - x_1)^2 + (y - y_1)^2 = d_1{}^2$$

$$(x - x_2)^2 + (y - y_2)^2 = d_2{}^2$$

$$(x - x_3)^2 + (y - y_3)^2 = d_3{}^2$$

If we expand the equations, we get the following:

$$x^2 + 2x_1x + x_1{}^2 + y^2 - 2y_1y + y_1{}^2 = d_1{}^2$$

$$x^2 + 2x_2x + x_2{}^2 + y^2 - 2y_2y + y_2{}^2 = d_2{}^2$$

$$x^2 + 2x_3x + x_3{}^2 + y^2 - 2y_3y + y_3{}^2 = d_3{}^2$$

Additionally, as we know, our position is determined by the point x, y where the three equations are fulfilled simultaneously. So we can subtract the second equation from the first and the third from the second in order to simplify our formulas.

This results in the following summarized equations:

$$(-2x_1 + -2x_2)x + (-2y_1 + -2y_2)y = d_1^2 - d_2^2 + x_1^2 - x_2^2 - y_1^2 + y_2^2$$

$$(-2x_2 + -2x_3)x + (-2y_2 + -2y_3)y = d_2^2 - d_3^2 + x_2^2 - x_3^2 - y_2^2 + y_3^2$$

Now, in order to solve for x and y, we can do the following variable substitutions:

$$A = (-2x_1 + -2x_2)$$

$$B = (-2y_1 + -2y_2)$$

$$C = d_1^2 - d_2^2 - x_1^2 + x_2^2 - y_1^2 + y_2^2$$

$$D = (-2x_2 + -2x_3)$$

$$E = (-2y_2 + -2y_3)$$

$$F = d_2^2 - d_3^2 - x_2^2 + x_3^2 - y_2^2 + y_3^2$$

So the solution to the system of equations for x and y can be represented as follows:

$$x = \frac{CE - FB}{EA - BD}$$

$$y = \frac{CD - AF}{BD - AE}$$

As you will have noticed, we receive all the values required to calculate x and y as parameters and represent the coordinates of each access point and the estimated distance using the measured RSSI.

At this point, we can deduce that when translating our system of equations into code, we are implementing the method that will allow us to calculate our position.

Next, we will see the code of the previously explained algorithm as the method within the `IndoorPositionEstimator` entity:

```
entity IndoorPositionEstimator {
    field emitters: List<Emitter>;

    method calcPosition(): {x: Float64, y: Float64} {
```

```
    let d1 = this.emitters.get(0).calcDistance();
    let d2 = this.emitters.get(1).calcDistance();
    let d3 = this.emitters.get(2).calcDistance();

    let a = (-2.0f * this.emitters.get(0).x)
      + (-2.0f * this.emitters.get(1).x);
    let b = (-2.0f * this.emitters.get(0).y)
      + (-2.0f * this.emitters.get(1).y);

    let c = (Float64::pow(d1, -2.0f) - Float64::pow(d2, -2.0f))
-
          (Float64::pow(this.emitters.get(0).x, -2.0f)
            + Float64::pow(this.emitters.get(1).x, -2.0f)) -
          (Float64::pow(this.emitters.get(0).y, -2.0f)
            + Float64::pow(this.emitters.get(1).y, -2.0f));

    let d = (-2.0f * this.emitters.get(1).x)
      + (-2.0f * this.emitters.get(2).x);
    let e = (-2.0f * this.emitters.get(1).y)
      + (-2.0f * this.emitters.get(2).y);


    let f = (Float64::pow(d2, -2.0f) - Float64::pow(d3, -2.0f))
-
          (Float64::pow(this.emitters.get(1).x, -2.0f)
            + Float64::pow(this.emitters.get(2).x, -2.0f)) -
          (Float64::pow(this.emitters.get(1).y, -2.0f)
            + Float64::pow(this.emitters.get(2).y, -2.0f));

    let x = (c * e) - (f * b) / (e * a) - (b * d);
    let y = (c * d) - (a * f) / (b * d) - (a * e);
    return {x=x, y=y};
  }
}
```

Once our position calculation method is implemented, we will make the corresponding call in our `entrypoint`, as follows:

```
entrypoint function runner(
    rssi1: String, rssi2: String, rssi3: String,
    x1: String, x2: String, x3: String,
    y1: String, y2: String, y3: String
    ): {x: Float64, y: Float64} {

  let estimator = IndoorPositionEstimator@{
    emitters=List<Emitter>@{
      Emitter@create(rssi1, x1, y1),
      Emitter@create(rssi2, x2, y2),
      Emitter@create(rssi3, x3, y3)
    }
  };
  return estimator.calcPosition();
}
```

Now that we have completed our code in Bosque, we are ready to expose our program as a web service, which we will see next in the next and last step.

Building an API to expose our program as a web service

As we saw in *Chapter 1*, *Exploring Bosque*, Bosque eliminates some of the sources of undetermined behavior, such as I/O sources. So the responsibility for handling external requests shifts to the Bosque runtime host.

This implies that it will be necessary to create an intermediate layer that allows receiving and processing the HTTP requests and converts them into a Bosque binary call. There are many different ways to do this. Here we list some strategies:

- Write an N-API to create a Bosque binary wrapper that could be used as a NodeJS add-on.
- Run our Bosque binary through the FastCGI protocol.
- Write a simple webserver to wrap our Bosque binary as a child process call.

To simplify our code, we have decided to use the third strategy by building a server written in NodeJS using Express.

Next, we see the code of a minimalist web server that doesn't have any endpoints defined yet:

```
var express = require('express');
var app = express();

var server = app.listen(8081, function () {
  console.log("Running")
})
```

This small server will serve as an interface between the user and our binary, so now we have to define what our API signature will be.

We will build an endpoint under the /calc_position route that will receive the parameters through a JSON payload that contains the information about the position of the endpoints and the RSSI detected from each of them.

Our JSON payload will look like the following snippet:

```
{
    "emitters": [
        {
            "rssi": -60,
            "x": 10,
            "y": 20
        },
        {
            "rssi": -86,
            "x": 30,
            "y": 40
        },
        {
            "rssi": -10,
            "x": 27,
            "y": 12
        }
    ]
}
```

Next, we add the `calc_position` endpoint to our Express server. From this endpoint, we will call our binary through the `child_process` package, as follows:

```
var express = require('express');
var exec = require('child_process').exec;
var bodyParser = require('body-parser');

var app = express();
app.use(bodyParser.json());

app.post('/calc_position', function (req, res) {
  let params = req.body;
  let args_string    = `${params["emitters"][0]["rssi"]} `;
  args_string       += `${params["emitters"][1]["rssi"]} `;
  args_string       += `${params["emitters"][2]["rssi"]} `;
  args_string       += `${params["emitters"][0]["x"]} `;
  args_string       += `${params["emitters"][0]["y"]} `;
  args_string       += `${params["emitters"][1]["x"]} `;
  args_string       += `${params["emitters"][1]["y"]} `;
  args_string       += `${params["emitters"][2]["x"]} `;
  args_string       += `${params["emitters"][2]["y"]} `;

  let command = `/src/bosquebin ${args_string}`;
  exec(command, function (err, stdout, stderr) {
    if (err) return res.sendStatus(500);
    if (stderr) return res.status(400).send(stderr);
    res.send(stdout);
  });
})

//...
```

In the previous code, we can see the new endpoint's implementation where the JSON payload is received, and the list of parameters to be sent to our binary is built.

Finally, the response that the execution of our binary returns is stored in the variable result and is returned as a response to the current HTTP request.

Next, we will see a practical example of the use of the code that we have written.

Running our program in the cloud

The best way to test our written code is by comparing the expected values with the result of the execution of our program. For this, let's imagine a scenario where the *x* and *y* positions of the receiver are known, as we can see in the following figure:

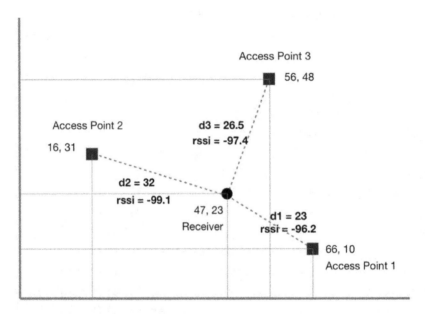

Figure 7.6 – Real case graphical representation

In the previous figure, we can see a real scenario with all the known data. This will allow us to validate our program output after entering the requested parameters.

Next, we will carry out the step-by-step execution of our application and will check the results according to the following list:

1. Compile the Bosque program.

2. Run the Express server.

3. Make an HTTP request to our exposed API.

By the end of these steps, we will have verified the correct operation of our program, and you will also be able to validate your own implementation.

Compiling the Bosque program

As you may have noticed in the previous section, we have created a custom `entrypoint` that will receive all the parameters that our program requires to function. For this reason, it will be necessary to use the `--entrypoint` argument at the time of compilation, and to do this we run the following command:

```
exegen script.bsq -o bosquebin --entrypoint "NSMain::runner"
```

The execution of the previous command creates a binary file called `bosquebin`, which we place in the same folder that we are going to place our web server script that we will run in the next step.

Running the Express server

Now that we have located the binary in the same location as our server (we have placed it under the `/src/bosquebin` path). Then we launch our server using the following command:

```
node server.js
```

The execution of this command starts a web server that will listen for requests on port `8081`.

Next, we will see how to make the HTTP request to calculate our receiver's estimated position.

Making an HTTP request to our exposed API

Once the Express server has been initialized, we can make a `POST` request, passing our test payload to port `8081` using `curl` as follows:

```
curl --location --request POST '0.0.0.0:8081/calc_position' \
--header 'Content-Type: application/json' \
--data-raw '{
    "emitters": [
        {
            "rssi": -96.2,
            "x": 66,
            "y": 10
        },
        {
```

```
            "rssi": -99.1,
            "x": 13,
            "y": 31
        },
        {
            "rssi": -97.4,
            "x": 56,
            "y": 48
        }
    ]
}'
```

After executing the previous command, we should obtain a result similar to the following:

```
47.000, 23.000
```

If you get a similar result, it means that you have correctly implemented the project outlined in this chapter.

Summary

In this chapter, we have applied the concepts learned in the previous chapters such as entrypoints, nominal type system, core types, operators, and statements to be able to build a web service that allows us to calculate a device's position within an area using the signal strength captured from three access points, which could be Wi-Fi routers.

This represents one of our first applications in a real-world scenario of the knowledge we've acquired so far. We also have learned how to present our Bosque programs as consumable web services and ready to be deployed to our cloud servers. You can use this acquired experience as a reference for the elaboration of your own personal projects.

In the next chapter, we will review a set of Bosque expressions, starting from the most frequent expressions in other languages, such as arguments or scoped access, until we reach the most specific Bosque expressions, such as type projection and PCode constructors.

Further reading

- Veli Ilci, R. M. (2015). *Trilateration Technique for WiFi-Based Indoor Localization.* The 11th International Conference on Wireless and Mobile Communications

- Aubakirov, S. (2018). *RSSI Based Bluetooth Low Energy Indoor Positioning.* IEEE 12th International Conference on Application of Information and Communication Technologies

- Cantón Paterna, V., Calveras Augé, A., Paradells Aspas, J., & Pérez Bullones, M. A. (2017). *A Bluetooth Low Energy Indoor Positioning System with Channel Diversity, Weighted Trilateration and Kalman Filtering. Sensors (Basel, Switzerland), 17*(12), 2927. https://doi.org/10.3390/s17122927

- Navidi, W., Murphy, W.S., & Hereman, W. (1998). *Statistical methods in surveying by trilateration.* Computational Statistics & Data Analysis, 27, 209-227

- Triangulation on Wikipedia (`https://en.wikipedia.org/wiki/Triangulation_(surveying)`)

Section 3: Practicing Bosque

In this part, we describe the core language features. After reading this section, you will know what the language looks like and how it can be used in practice to solve a variety of problems.

This section comprises the following chapters:

8
Expressions in Bosque

So far, you have built a solid Bosque foundation. At this point, you have a theoretical background and are able to identify key Bosque concepts. On top of that, you have also gained practical knowledge that allows you to write programs using this language. It is now time to dive deeper into the language specification and learn more about the available features.

In this chapter, we will cover a set of Bosque expressions starting from the most obvious ones such as *arguments* and *scoped access* and ending with Bosque-specific ones such as *typed projection* and *PCode constructors*.

Here is a list of topics that we are going to go through:

- Understanding parameter handling in Bosque
- Learning about scoped access and invocations
- Chaining in Bosque
- Introducing PCode types and constructors
- Identifying access operators

By the end of this chapter, you will have sufficient knowledge about expressions in Bosque to use them in practice. You will see how some well-known concepts are implemented in Bosque, as well as discovering a few unique features available in Bosque and how they are useful.

Technical requirements

In order to get the most out of this chapter, the following are recommended:

- Have installed the Bosque language on your local machine.
- Know how to compile Bosque programs.
- Know the syntax and key constructs that are required to write valid Bosque programs.
- Get acquainted with the examples shared on GitHub here: https://github. com/PacktPublishing/Learn-Bosque-Programming/tree/main/ Chapter08.

Understanding parameters handling in Bosque

Parameters in Bosque are not a big surprise for any programmer who has used some of the popular programming languages. The majority (or even all) of the examples in the chapter will look very familiar if you have used languages such as JavaScript, TypeScript, or even Java and others. This is why we will go through this topic pretty quickly.

The first thing to note is that all parameters **must have a declared type**. If you don't provide the type of a parameter, a compile-time error will be thrown. We can't expect auto type detecting to work here.

A simple example of providing and accessing a parameter in a function looks like the following:

```
function addOne(num: Int): Int {
    return num + 1;
}
```

As discussed in *Chapter 5, Types and Operators*, we define a parameter by providing its name followed by a colon and its type. We can access a parameter using its name. In the previous example, we have defined a parameter called num of the Int type and we are accessing it using its name.

You can also declare an **optional parameter** for situations where a parameter is not required and can be skipped. An optional parameter is declared by using a question mark followed by a colon, instead of just a colon. An example looks like this:

```
function greeting(name?: String): String {
    var n = if (name != none) name else "friend";
    return String::concat("Hello, ", n);
}
```

Here, we have defined an optional parameter called `name`. You don't need to provide it when calling the `greeting` function. Of course, you can mix optional and required parameters when defining a function. However, you are not allowed to define optional parameters before the required ones. It will raise an error when you try to compile this. The reason is quite clear (as in other languages). If we have a function whose optional parameters precede the required ones, and we call it with only one parameter, then the computer has no way to determine which parameter we provided a value to – the first or the second one.

> **Important note**
>
> In the previous example, we have used the `none` keyword. For now, it's enough to know that it is similar to the `null` value known from other programming languages. To learn more about `none`, please refer to the *Chaining in Bosque* section later in this chapter.

As you can see, this is all pretty obvious and straightforward. So, let's not waste more time on this and instead discuss further features.

Recognizing named parameters

Bosque supports named parameters – a very handy feature known from languages such as Python (to be precise, in Python, they are called keyword arguments), for instance. Bosque allows you to provide a value directly to a named parameter without remembering the order of the parameters. Moreover, you are able to skip some of the optional parameters if you wish to provide values only for some of them.

Let's see some examples to understand this better.

The function in the following code block is an expanded version of the previous one. It prints a greeting based on the provided parameters:

```
function greeting(firstName: String, lastName?: String,
nickname?: String): String {
    let ln = if (lastName != none) String::concat(" ",
lastName) else "";
    let nn = if (nickname != none) String::concat(" AKA ",
nickname) else "";

    return String::concat("Hello, ", firstName, ln, nn);
}
```

The difference is that it has more parameters – one required, firstName, and the other two optional, that is, lastName and nickname.

If we want to provide only the first argument, we can obviously do so like this:

```
greeting("John");
```

This will return the "Hello, John" text. Now, let's say we want to greet someone by their first name and a nickname but without providing their last name. We can do this using named parameters:

```
greeting("John", nickname="Strongman");
```

The result will be "Hello, John AKA Strongman". We have skipped the second argument and provided a value to the nickname parameter directly.

Named parameters allow us to forget about the parameter order or even mix named parameters with a positional one. In the following example, we are providing all three arguments but we have changed the order of the first two and provided the last one in the normal way:

```
greeting(lastName="Smith", firstName="John", "Strongman");
```

This will return the "Hello, John Smith AKA Strongman" text.

Named parameters are very handy and are a convenient way to provide function parameters. Now let's see two more features related to parameters. The first one is rest and spread operators.

Using rest and spread operators

Bosque supports another handy and pretty well-known feature – the ability to use rest and spread operators. These can be used when we expect an undetermined amount of arguments to be passed to our function or when we are willing to pass a list of arguments wrapped in a tuple.

Let's say that we have a list of people in a file. Each line consists of a token, the first name, the last name, and the nickname of a single person. We want to send personalized web push notifications to each user using the data from the file – that's why we need a token. Our function for sending the notification will look like this:

```
function sendPush(token: String, firstName: String, lastName?:
String, nickname?: String): Bool {
    let ln = if (lastName != none) String::concat(" ",
lastName) else "";
    let nn = if (nickname != none) String::concat(" AKA ",
nickname) else "";
    let title = String::concat("How are you, ", firstName, ln,
nn, "?");
    let body = "Today is November 16th and it's going to
be rainy and windy. Better stay home with a cup of hot
chocolate!";
    return doSend(token, title, body);
}
function doSend(token: String, title: String, body: String):
Bool {
    _debug(String::concat(token, " | ", title, " | ", body));
    return true;
}
```

So, as you can see, we are defining a sendPush function with four parameters, where the last two are optional similar to in the previous function called greeting. We are simply building a personalized message title and (for now) a hardcoded message body. The values are being passed to the doSend function, which is pretty trivial and doesn't do much.

Now, getting back to our people list, let's assume that after parsing the file, we have a list of tuples of lengths from 2 to 4 each. The token and the first name are always there, but the last name and nickname may be omitted. Normally, in order to call our sendPush function for each person, we would have to extract each value using index notation and check the existence of the third and fourth indexes, and then call the sendPush function with the extracted values. Fortunately, thanks to the spread operator, we don't need to do that. We can simply *spread* each tuple into the sendPush arguments list and the values will be automatically assigned to the parameters. Let's see what that would look like:

```
let entry = ["faketoken", "John", "Smith", "Strongman"];
let result = sendPush(...entry);
```

Since nickname is not a required parameter, we can omit that one. This is what it would look like:

```
let entry = ["faketoken", "John", "Smith"];
let result = sendPush(...entry);
```

We can also omit all of the optional arguments and provide only the required ones, like this:

```
let entry = ["faketoken", "John"];
let result = sendPush(...entry);
```

So, as you can see, the spread operator can be pretty powerful.

Now, let's modify our requirements a little bit. From now, both last name and nickname are required and aside from the current data, we also store users' favorite activities, which we want to include in our personalized message body just to remind them what they can do in their free time. The problem is that we don't really know how many activities a user likes. We just know that it's going to be a list of activities – empty or arbitrarily long. With the rest operator, we can define a rest parameter called activities, which will allow us to pass any number of arguments – four as a minimum, but without the maximum bound – to our sendPush function.

> **Important note**
> You can't have optional and rest parameters in one function. Bosque will not allow you to do that and a compile-time error will be thrown. The reason is similar to why we cannot have required parameters after optional ones – it would be impossible for a computer to guess what parameter a programmer is referring to at the function call.

Let's see an example of how the rest operator can be implemented to meet our
new requirements:

```
function sendPush(token: String, firstName: String, lastName:
String, nickname: String, ...activities: List<String>): Bool {

    let ln = String::concat(" ", lastName);
    let nn = String::concat(" AKA ", nickname);

    let title = String::concat("How are you, ", firstName, ln,
nn, "?");
    let userActivities = String::concat(...activities);
    let body = String::concat("Today is November 16th and
it's going to be rainy and windy. How about doing one of your
favorite activities: ", userActivities, "?");

    return doSend(token, title, body);
}
```

So, as you can see, we have added one more parameter, called `activities`, which is
automatically converted to `List`. Thanks to the rest operator, we don't need to know how
many arguments are going to be passed to our function – everything after `nickname`
will be added to the `activities` list. Look at the following example to see how it can
be invoked:

```
let res = sendPush("faketoken", "Johnny", "Silverhand",
"Samurai", "singing", "dancing");
```

The last two arguments are converted to the `activities` list. The previous code will
produce the following output:

```
"faketoken | How are you, Johnny Silverhand AKA Samurai?
| Today is November 16th and it's going to be rainy and
windy. How about doing one of your favorite activities:
singingdancing?"
```

> **Important note**
>
> As you have probably noticed, we have used the `String::concat()`
> method, which produces a bit of a hard-to-read result. Normally, we would use
> `String::join()` like this:
>
> `String::join(", ", activities);`
>
> However, as of the time of writing, the `String::join()` method is not
> implemented yet and if you try to compile it, an error will be thrown.

This shows how useful the rest operator can really be. If we don't know how many arguments are going to be passed to our function but we want to treat them similarly regardless of the amount, we can use the rest operator and make use of an automatic conversion to `List`.

Key-value argument notation

There is also one more notation called key-value argument notation. It is used for creating maps and will be described in more detail in *Chapter 9, Collections*. At this point, it's enough to just show what it looks like:

```
let studentsPresence = Map<String, Bool>@{ "John Smith" =>
true, "Alice Doe" => false };
```

So, as you can see, we are passing a list of users using the `key => value` notation, where `key` is an expression of the map key type and `value` is the value expression.

This sums up the handling of parameters in the Bosque language. As you have probably realized, this topic is quite clear and the features are similar to other programming languages. Now, it is time to take a quick look at the next topic, which you may also find pretty familiar – scopes in Bosque.

Learning about scoped access and invocations

Similar to the previous topic, this one will also not be of any surprise to anyone who has experience with other object-oriented programming languages. Most of the features presented here will probably look very familiar but there is one feature that is unique to Bosque – conjunction type scoped access and invocations.

We will quickly go through this topic while taking a closer look at the unique feature. Firstly, we will see how variable scoped access works, and then we will have a look at scoped invocations.

Understanding variable scoped access

Let's start with the most common thing, which is a local variable or parameter. As mentioned in the *Understanding parameters handling in Bosque* section, we access them using their name. So, if we have a function with a usersCount parameter, we can access it like this:

```
let approxRevenue = usersCount * 10;
```

Simple as that. The same is done with local variables – the ones we define inside a function or a method.

We can also define global variables in the current namespace. Although it is not recommended to abuse this feature (not only in Bosque but also in general), there are scenarios where it is required, for example, with some kind of config variables that multiple functions refer to. An example of this global variable is presented in the next example:

```
namespace NSMain;
global apiURL: String = "http://myapi.com/v1";
```

If we want to access this variable, we can do so like this:

```
let url = NSMain::apiURL;
```

So, as you can see, first we provide the namespace name, then a double colon, and then the global variable name.

The next common thing is the need to access some kind of a static field of some type. For example, instead of defining the config values as global variables, we may want to have an Environment entity to wrap more values. We would do that like this:

```
entity Environment {
    const apiUrl: String = "http://myapi.com/v1";
    const dbHost: String = "host.database.com";
    const dbUser: String = "db_user";
    const dbPass: String = "db+P4ssw0rd";
}
```

Now, to access those values, you need to write something like this:

```
let url = Environment::apiUrl;
```

If we want to parametrize the `Environment` entity to make it generic, then we need to provide the type in a chevron:

```
let url = Environment<String>::apiUrl;
```

Things work exactly the same for concepts. You can try this out by changing the entity keyword to `concept`. The result will be exactly the same.

The last and most interesting feature is conjunction type scoped access. This is unique to Bosque and can be useful in some scenarios. First, let's define what a conjunction is.

A conjunction, written as `TypeA & TypeB`, can be defined as follows: if `TypeC` is of type `TypeA & TypeB`, then `TypeC` provides both `TypeA` and `TypeB`. So basically, it means that `TypeC` has all members from those types. This is pretty similar to the intersection types in TypeScript. The difference is that in Bosque, a conjunction is limited only to concept types.

This feature is extremely useful when we need to access some field without knowing in which concept or entity it has been defined. Normally, we would have to manually check the type and use the proper one. In Bosque, we can make use of conjunction scoped variable access.

Suppose we are building a module that communicates with an external API. We have the `Environment` concept (defined as in the previous example with the difference that now it is a *concept* not an *entity*) and a new `ModuleProperties` concept. This way, we are separating the global config from the module-specific configuration. The `ModuleProperties` concept looks like the following:

```
concept ModuleProperties {
    const apiClientId: String = "abcdef-gh123-45ij";
    const apiClientSecret: String = "xc9087-23igh_
sdfHJ1213ij/.";
    const resources: Tuple = ["email", "profile"];
}
```

For simplicity, we can define a new type called `Config`, which is a conjunction of `Environment` and `ModuleProperties`:

```
typedef Config = Environment & ModuleProperties;
```

Thanks to this feature, now we don't have to remember in which concept a `resources` field is. We can simply access it like this:

```
let res = Config::resources;
```

Bosque will take care of the type resolution for us. This is a very convenient way of accessing such variables.

Put simply, the conjunction type creates a new type that combines all of the types joined with &. In fact, this: `typedef Config = Environment & ModuleProperties;` is effectively the same as the following: `concept Config provides Environment, ModuleProperties {};`.

So you can use `Config` to get properties that exists in both types: `Environment` and `ModuleProperties`. Conjunction is limited only to concept types so you can't instantiate `Config` here.

> **Important note**
>
> As of the time of writing, this feature is still not fully implemented. In some scenarios, it will not work properly. Be careful when trying to access a variable like this: `TypeA&TypeB::variable;` or inheriting like this: `entity TypeA provides TypeB&TypeC {};` – such usages will currently cause unexpected errors. There are existing issues opened on the official GitHub repo but the problems have not been addressed yet.

Learning about scoped invocations

As for scoped invocations, there's also not much difference from other popular object-oriented languages. However, it's a useful thing in Bosque because it allows you to call functions without assigning the result to any variable. When writing programs in Bosque, you have a functional mindset where every function returns a value and in order to invoke one, you are forced to assign the result to some variable. Although this has many advantages, there are scenarios where we want to invoke a function and simply don't care about the result. Thanks to scoped invocations, we are able to achieve that.

Imagine you want to write a function that logs messages to the console. Of course, we have the `_debug()` function but we want to additionally format the messages by adding the log level and a label. We don't want to concatenate strings every time. Instead, we want to have a function that wraps the concatenation logic and prints formatted text based on some parameters. This kind of function can be written as follows:

```
namespace NSMain;

function log(msg: String, label?: String, level?: String): None
{
    let lvl = String::concat(
```

```
        "[",

        (if (level != none) level else "info"),

        "]"

    );

    let lbl = String::concat("[", (if (label != none) label
else ""), "]");     let lbl = String::concat(

        "[",

        (if (label != none) label else ""),

        "]"

    );
    _debug(String::concat(lvl, lbl, " ", msg));
    return none;
}
```

We are doing some basic formatting here. As you can see, the function returns the none value. In fact, we don't really care about it. We just want to display a log message, that's all. Thanks to namespace scoped invocations, we can write something like this:

```
NSMain::log("This is a log message", "main");
```

This way, we don't need to assign the result to any variable. This invocation will cause the "[info] [main] This is a log message" text to appear on the screen.

Similarly to what was mentioned in the *Understanding variable scoped access* section, if our function was parametrized, we would be able to call it like this:

```
NSMain::log<InfoLevel>("This is a log message", "main");
```

The next thing is pretty trivial, which is type scoped invocation. In fact, we've been using it all the time in this book, even in the `log` function. The `String::concat()` invocation is an example of type scoped invocation. In this case, `String` is a type and `concat` is a static method that can be called using the double colon operator, similarly to namespace scoped functions.

Analogically to what was mentioned previously, if our type was parametrized – for example, `List` – we would be able to call it like this:

```
List<String>::concat("quick ", "brown ", "fox ");
```

We can mix generic types and if our parametrized `log` function were wrapped in some generic wrapper called `LogService<T>`, we would call it like this:

```
LogService<LabelMain>::log<InfoLevel>("This is a log message");
```

One last feature is – analogically to what was presented in the *Understanding variable scoped access* section – conjunction static type invocation. The definition of conjunction is the same here and the behavior is the same with the difference that now we are invoking static functions instead of accessing static fields.

To better understand this, let's take our logger example a bit further. Imagine that in our application we are using two kinds of loggers: `StandardLogger`, which simply sends the message to the standard output, and `QueueLogger`, which sends our log messages to some kind of messaging system for further processing. The definitions would look like this:

```
concept StandardLogger {
    static log(msg: String, label?: String, level?: String):
None {
    let lvl = String::concat(

        "[",

            (if (level != none) level else "info"),

        "]"

    );

    let lbl = String::concat(
```

```
        "[",

        (if (label != none) label else ""),

        "]"

    );

    _debug(String::concat(lvl, lbl, " ", msg));
    return none;
    }
}

concept QueueLogger {
    static queueLog(msg: String, label?: String, level?:
String): None {
let lvl = String::concat(

        "[",

        (if (level != none) level else "info"),

        "]"

    );

    let lbl = String::concat(

        "[",

        (if (label != none) label else ""),

        "]"

    );
```

```
        _debug(String::concat("Sent to log queue: ", lvl, lbl,
" ", msg));
        return none;
    }
}
```

So, as you can see, the first concept provides a static `log` function and the second one provides a `queueLog` function. In this example, they are quite similar, but in a real app, they would differ a lot.

Again, to make things simpler, we can define a `Logger` type, which will be a conjunction of those two concepts:

```
typedef Logger = StandardLogger & QueueLogger;
```

And from now, we can use the `Logger` type to access any of the two methods without worrying about the type:

```
Logger::queueLog("Test log");
```

This is a pretty powerful feature that takes type resolution to the next level.

Important note

As mentioned in the *Understanding variable scoped access* section, currently, this feature is still lacking some functionality, so be careful when using it as unexpected errors may appear. There are existing issues opened in the official GitHub repo that have not been addressed yet.

Chaining in Bosque

Alright, now it is time to introduce a fresh concept! In Bosque, there is a special `none` value that is basically – as the name suggests – a value representing no value. It is pretty similar to the `null` value from other languages, or – in some cases – to `undefined` if you are familiar with JavaScript.

Every programmer who has faced the challenge of handling such *no-value values* knows how hard is it, especially when we need to perform chaining where one of the middle components may be none (or null). I'm pretty sure you already know what chaining is but in case you don't, it is worth reminding that chaining is the process of accessing values or calling methods that are nested deep inside each other. An example of such a nested structure can be seen in the following example:

```
let merchCategories = {
    accessories = {
        kitchen = {
            cups = ["Cup for work with code", "Cup with a
unicorn", "Red cup"],
            cutlery = ["knife", "fork", "spoon"]
        },
        room = {
            clocks = ["Big oak clock", "Red clock", "Clock for
a programmer"]
        }
    }
};
```

In order to access the merchCategories | accessories | kitchen | cups value, we can do the following:

```
let selected = merchCategories.accessories.kitchen.cups;
```

The selected variable will hold the following value:

```
["Cup for work with code", "Cup with a unicorn", "Red cup"]
```

Pretty straightforward, isn't it? Now imagine that we can't be sure whether a certain category exists, or whether a subcategory exists. If it does, we want to select the next sub-element, but if it doesn't, we want to return a none value. Normally, we would use if statements to check for none at each nesting level. Although this does work, it totally obscures the true intent of a programmer, which is simply to go deeper unless the sub-element exists – that's all. Here's where we can use the None-chaining operator operator:

```
let selected = merchCategories.electronics?.mobile?.android;
```

This syntax is pretty familiar from other languages such as JavaScript (optional chaining available in ES2020). This way, the value of the `selected` variable will be the value of the nested `android` field or `none` if any of the preceding fields do not exist. In this particular example, `selected` would be `none`. This is a very easy and convenient way of accessing fields that are possibly `none`.

Alright, things have been pretty easy so far, and the presented features might have been familiar. Now it's time to see some more Bosque-specific aspects. Let's start with PCode functions.

Introducing PCode types and constructors

The name may be a bit confusing. The long name is **parameter code blocks** but we will be using the short one – **PCode** functions. So, a PCode function is a special type and value in Bosque that is similar to lambda functions in other popular languages. The difference is that PCode functions cannot be stored in any variables or entity fields – they must be used as literals in the place of invocation.

It is worth separating this section into two topics, that is, PCode types and PCode constructors.

The former refers to the way we define a PCode function and its signature, while the latter refers to how we actually use PCode functions, that is, how to create a PCode function of a specified type. The syntax is a little bit different when defining PCode and using it.

In order to better understand what we are talking about, let's see an example right away and discuss it later. Let's get back to our previous example, where we created a function to send web push notifications. It wasn't perfect as it had pretty much hardcoded the message body. It is time to fix this and make this function a bit more universal.

The following is the new version of the `sendPush` function:

```
function sendPush(
    token: String,
    firstName: String, lastName: String, nickname: String,
    buildMsg: fn(date: String) -> String
): Bool {
    let ln = String::concat(" ", lastName);
    let nn = String::concat(" AKA ", nickname);

    let title = String::concat("How are you, ", firstName, ln,
nn, "?");
    let body = buildMsg("November 16th");

    return doSend(token, title, body);
}
```

Notice the highlighted parts of the code. We have added the `buildMsg` parameter of the PCode type and we are using it to build the message body. The function looks much better because we do not hardcode the whole message. As for the date, normally, it would be taken from the server, but for the sake of this example, it is simply hardcoded.

Now, let's see how to use this new version of the `sendPush` function:

```
let userActivities = String::concat("running", "cooking");
let result = sendPush(
    "faketoken", "John", "Smith", "Strongman",
    fn(date: String): String => {
        let body = String::concat(
            "Today is ", date, " and it's going to be rainy
and windy. How about doing one of your favorite activities: ",
userActivities, "?"
        );
        return body;
    }
);
```

Again, take a closer look at the highlighted code. Here, we are creating a PCode function that builds a message body and returns it. The value is then used back in the sendPush function as shown in the first example.

Alright, now we will take a step back and discuss the two mentioned aspects of this example.

Recognizing PCode types

Let's focus on the buildMsg parameter in the first example. This is how we define a parameter code block type. We must use the fn keyword followed by parentheses, where we can specify the arguments that our PCode function will accept. The rules for arguments are the same as described in the *Understanding parameters handling in Bosque* section, including optional and named parameters and rest parameters.

One additional thing is the special _ parameter. This a special parameter that means that we don't care how the parameter will be named. It's important to remember because parameters' names are also part of the PCode signature – this is due to named parameters support. If we don't care about the given parameter name provided in the PCode constructor, we can use the special _ parameter.

At the end, we must put a thin arrow (->) followed by a type name. This tells what kind of value the PCode function will return.

Once we define a PCode type parameter, we can access it using its name the same way we access any other parameter. The difference is that this time, we can treat this parameter as a function and call it with arguments specified in the definition. An example is shown in the first example shown previously, where we assigned the body variable with the result of the buildMsg function.

You have learned how to define a PCode type. Now it's time to learn how to create an actual PCode function. Let's not waste time and jump straight into it.

Discovering PCode constructors

Creating a PCode function is very much similar to defining it. There are a few key differences that are required. The first difference is that we don't provide the name of the function. We start right with the fn keyword followed by parentheses, inside which we provide a list of parameters. Since parameter names are part of the PCode signature, we must provide exactly the same names as in the PCode type definition – except the _ parameters, which can have any name.

In general, Bosque is able to infer some obvious types, so it's not necessary to provide them in various situations. In the case of PCode functions, we can skip parameter types and the function return type. We can obviously choose to provide them anyway – as we did in the previous example. But in most cases, it is quite redundant, and choosing not to provide types makes the code a little bit cleaner.

> **Important note**
>
> If you choose to provide argument types, you must also provide the return type – and vice versa. You can't provide only one argument type or only a return type. All types must be provided or none of them.

After the parentheses (and optionally a return type), we must put a fat arrow (=>) followed by a body expression. Here we have two options. The first one is to add braces and the body of the PCode function inside them, as we have done. However, in many scenarios, such function bodies are very simple, consisting of a single line of code. In such cases, you can skip the braces and put the single line of the body right after the fat arrow. You must keep in mind that in these cases, the body expression must still return the expected value type. An example of a PCode constructor is presented in the second example shown previously. Just to remind you, it looks like this:

```
let userActivities = String::concat("running", "cooking");
let result = sendPush(
    "faketoken", "John", "Smith", "Strongman",
    fn(date: String): String => {
        let body = String::concat(
            "Today is ", date, " and it's going to be rainy
and windy. How about doing one of your favorite activities: ",
userActivities, "?"
        );
        return body;
    }
);
```

It's worth recalling that PCode functions cannot be stored in any variable or field. They must be placed as literals as we did here.

You have learned how to create and use PCode functions. You have a very powerful tool in your hands now. Let's discover the last type of expressions available in Bosque – access operators.

Identifying access operators

In this section, we will discuss three types of access operators – tuple typed, record typed, and nominal typed. These operators are a very convenient way of retrieving data from various data structures. We will go through them one by one. Let's get started.

The tuple typed access operator

This feature is pretty similar to what was described in *Chapter 3*, *Bosque Key Features*, in the *Bulk algebraic data operations* section. We will review this in more detail based on our web push notification-sending app example.

So, imagine that in our source file where we get our user data from the user properties are provided in a different order than you expect them to appear in the sendPush function. After parsing and splitting a single line, you get this kind of tuple:

```
let user = ["faketoken", "Warsaw", 24, "Doe", "John", "Bird"];
```

So first, we have a token, then a city, age, last name, and first name, and lastly, a nickname. Our function expects only four values out of these six, provided in a specific order. We can make use of the . [] operator and extract values from certain indexes in a specified order:

```
let args = user.[0,4,3,5];
```

This way, we have extracted only the required fields. Notice that we are also changing the order of the values. The args variable now holds a new tuple value that looks like this:

```
["faketoken", "John", "Doe", "Bird"]
```

We can go even further and make use of the bulk read operation and as a result, we will have something like this:

```
let user = ["faketoken", "Warsaw", 24, "Doe", "John", "Bird"];
let [token, fname, lname, nick] = user.[0,4,3,5];
let sent = sendPush(
    token, fname, lname, nick,
    fn(date) => String::concat("Today is ", date, ". Have a
great day!")
);
```

So, as you can see, we used the tuple typed access operator to extract the exact data that we wanted.

We can also access an element at a specific index using this syntax:

```
let firstName = user.4;
```

In fact, the tuple typed access operator is chainable, which means that we can connect it using a dot. In order to grab only the first name and last name from the previously extracted data, we can do so in one line like this:

```
let [firstName, lastName] = user.[0,4,3,5].[1,2];
```

So first, we create a new tuple of size four, and then we immediately take elements at the given indexes from the newly created tuple. As the result, the firstName variable will hold the John value, and lastName will hold Doe.

We can also reshape a tuple into a value pack. Value packs were described in *Chapter 6, Bosque Statements*. An example can be seen here:

```
(|let firstName, let lastName|) = user.(|4, 3|);
```

The .(|...|) operator creates a value pack and from that value pack, we are taking the first and second one and assigning it to the firstName and lastName variables, respectively.

The tuple typed access operator is a very useful tool that allows us to reshape any tuple according to our needs. Let's now see the next access operator.

The record typed access operator

Similar to the tuple typed access operator, this one was also covered briefly in *Chapter 3, Bosque Key Features*. We will expand our knowledge a little bit here.

Analogically to the previous problem of user data in our source file, now imagine that after parsing, you have created a record for each user. Each user entry has been transformed into something like this:

```
let user = {
    token = "faketoken",
    lastName = "Smith",
    firstName = "Alice",
    nickname = "Slippy",
```

```
        age = 34,
        city = "Washington"
};
```

It is a totally different data structure from what we need to pass to our `sendPush` function. Fortunately, we can make use of the `.{}` operator to reshape our record and extract only the needed data. We can do so like this:

```
let user = { token="faketoken", lastName="Smith",
firstName="Alice", nickname="Slippy", age=34, city="Washington"
};
let { token=tok, firstName=fname, lastName=lname, nickname=nick
} = user.{token, firstName, lastName, nickname};
  let sent = sendPush(
    tok,
    fname,
    lname,
    nick,
    fn(date) => String::concat("Today is ", date, ". Have a
great day!")
);
```

This way, we have extracted only the desired values from the entire large record containing more properties.

Similar to the tuple typed access operator, this one is also chainable. This means that we can connect them using dots:

```
let { token = tok } = user.{token, firstName, lastName,
nickname}.{token};
```

Last but not least, we can also reshape our record into a value pack. You can achieve that like this:

```
let valuePack = user.(|firstName, lastName|);
```

Just like the previous one, this operator is also very powerful as it allows you to transform your records into any structure you need.

Now it's time to jump into the last access operator type.

The nominal typed access operator

This one is very similar to the previous operator. The difference here is that we operate on nominal types and not raw records.

Imagine that instead of creating a record for each user, you decide to create a `WebPushUser` entity and wrap each user entry into the mentioned data type. Here's an example definition of such an entity:

```
entity WebPushUser {
    field token: String;
    field firstName: String;
    field lastName: String;
    field nickname: String;
    field age: Int;
    field city: String;
}
```

This is an example of a user object wrapped in this new entity:

```
let user = WebPushUser@{
    token = "faketoken",
    firstName = "Alice",
    lastName = "Smith",
    nickname = "Slippy",
    age = 34,
    city = "Washington"
};
```

From now on, you can manipulate your data in exactly the same way as in the case of records. So, our example usage of the nominal typed access operator will be almost the same as before:

```
let user = WebPushUser@{
    token = "faketoken",
    firstName = "Alice",
    lastName = "Smith",
    nickname = "Slippy",
    age = 34,
    city = "Washington"
};
```

```
let {
    token = tok,
    firstName = fname,
    lastName = lname,
    nickname = nick
} = user.{ token, firstName, lastName, nickname };
let sent = sendPush(
    tok, fname, lname, nick,
    fn(date) => String::concat("Today is ", date, ". Have a
great day!")
);
```

It works pretty much the same. The only difference is the handling of value packs, which works the same as in the case of tuples:

```
(| let fname, let lname |) = user.(|firstName, lastName|);
```

Alright, now you have yet another powerful tool in your hands that will make your life as a programmer easier. Let's sum up the knowledge you gained from this chapter.

Summary

You learned a lot of useful things in this chapter, but mostly, you now have a much better understanding of the code you write and know about a few useful constructs that make things easier.

Firstly, you learned about a few well-known topics, such as parameters handling, scoped access, and chaining, and how those concepts are implemented in Bosque. You can see that they do not differ much from other popular programming languages.

The next things we covered were PCode types and constructors. You learned what they are and how to use them. They are very useful for injecting specialized behavior into other functions. You are able to point out the difference between the PCode type and a PCode constructor.

Eventually, we took a closer look at access operators, which we talked about in previous chapters. You learned about them in more detail and are able to use them in a real-world app. These operators allow you to reshape tuples, records, and nominals according to your needs, which may save you some time as you now don't need to do that manually.

In the next chapter, we will review the core library of collections in Bosque. Bosque has a few popular collections implemented as core types, along with a ton of useful methods that make them really powerful. Let's jump right into it.

Questions

1. Does Bosque support named parameters?
2. What are the rules for placing optional parameters in the parameters list?
3. What are rest and spread operators?
4. How can you call a function without assigning its value to a variable?
5. When is the none chaining operator useful?
6. What is the keyword used to define a PCode function?
7. Is providing types in a PCode constructor required?
8. What are two ways of accessing a tuple element at a specified index?

9
Collections

I think we can say without hesitation that vast majority of programs makes use of some kind of a container for data – a collection. Almost every real world app, at some point will need to store a collection of data in order to perform some operations. For example a CRM system needs to retrieve a collection of contacts from a database and probably sort them; or a calendar app that shows all events planned for a given day – that's also a collection of elements that needs to be retrieved and displayed. In fact, it is hard to imagine a program that does not need any collection – well, maybe except a "Hello, world" or alike.

In this chapter, we will learn about Bosque core collections. We will cover concepts such as List, Map, and Set and their useful methods. We will also mention collections that are not fully implemented yet (at the time of writing).

In this chapter, we are going to cover the following topics:

- Learning about List and ListOf
- Getting familiar with Map and DynamicMap
- Understanding Set and DynamicSet
- Discovering Stack and Queue

After reading this chapter, you will be able to name the collection types that are available in Bosque, as well as use them in practice. You will learn what particular data structures are and what methods Bosque offers with them.

Technical requirements

To better understand the concepts described in this chapter, as well as to be able to actually try them out, it is strongly recommended that you have knowledge about the following topics:

- The syntax and key constructs that are required to write valid Bosque programs

- Expressions such as PCode functions or key-value notation

You can also get acquainted with the examples in this chapter on GitHub, here: `https://github.com/PacktPublishing/Learn-Bosque-Programming/tree/main/Chapter09`.

Learning about List and ListOf

Let's focus on `List` first. Lists are very popular data structures in the programming world. They are containers that store an ordered sequence of elements, such as arrays in many programming languages. It is parameterized by a type, `T`, which determines what kind of elements are going to be stored in the list. In Bosque, it is implemented as an entity (entities will be described in detail later in this book; they are similar to classes in OOP), which allows us to create an instance of a `List`. The `List` entity provides the `Expandoable` concept, which means that we can use the spread operator on them (as seen in *Chapter 8, Expressions in Bosque*).

The most important thing to remember here is that **in Bosque, all lists are immutable**. This means that once we create an instance of a `List`, we cannot add more elements to it, nor can we update or delete any of them. It may seem weird and inconvenient, but as we explained in *Chapter 3, Bosque Key Features*, mutability causes many unpredictable behaviors in our programs and because of this, in Bosque, everything is immutable; this helps us avoid such problems. So, when we are creating a `List` instance, we must provide all the values that will be stored there right away.

One of the strongest advantages of Bosque `List` entity is the number of methods available for us to use. At the time of writing, there are **84** (eighty-four) methods available in the core `List` implementation. Let's be honest – that's a lot. We will not describe all of them because that would be very time-consuming and not especially necessary. Instead, we will split the description into two parts. Firstly, we will review the most obvious and expected ones. Then, we'll go through the most interesting ones that remain (in my opinion). So, let's not waste any time and see what Bosque `List` has to offer.

Reviewing standard List methods

Despite having a lot of methods that are simply a replacement for loops, Bosque offers a range of "standard" List methods. By "standard," I mean methods that are often implemented in List-like collections in many languages, including, but not limited to, Java, C#, PHP, JavaScript, and C++.

We will review them in groups with similar or connected functionalities.

List::concat() and List::fill()

These are the only two static methods available in the List entity. Their behavior is probably clear just by looking at their names, but for the sake of formalities, let's take a look at them in more detail:

- The `List<T>::concat()` method is used to concatenate more lists into a new one. It accepts an arbitrary list of List elements (thanks to the rest operator) and connects them, producing a new List containing all the elements from all the lists. We can use it like this:

```
let admins = List<String>@{"Alice", "John"};
let mods = List<String>@{"Margaret", "Bob"};
let users = List<String>@{"Percy", "Christine",
"Joffrey"};
let allUsers = List<String>::concat(admins, mods, users);
_debug(allUsers);
```

  So, as you can see, we have three lists of users and we are creating a fourth one by concatenating all of them into one.

- The `List<T>::fill()` method is used to create a List of a given size and fill it with a specified value. It accepts two arguments in the mentioned order. The type of the second argument must match the `T` type provided on the call. It's worth mentioning that this method does not copy just the reference to the provided value – it deeply copies the value so that the list is not populated with references to the single object. It's actually populated with different objects. This is pretty obvious for primitive types, but for complex ones, it may not be so obvious – especially for JavaScript developers, for instance. Again, it's all about immutability, as described earlier in this book.

  Let's look at a simple example of how we can use this method in Bosque:

```
entity User {
        field name: String;
```

```
    }
    var u = User@{ name="John" };
    let list = List<User>::fill(3, u);
    _debug(list);
```

This way, we are creating a list of three identical users that are deeply coupled.

The .size() and .empty() methods

Those two methods are pretty obvious, aren't they? These are standard methods that are implemented in most List-like structures and are responsible for returning a number of elements in the list and returning a Boolean value, depending on whether the list is empty or not, respectively. In fact, the .empty() method returns exactly the same value as this line of code:

```
    let empty = list.size() == 0;
```

And that's exactly how it is implemented internally.

We can use these simple but useful methods for a variety of things. For example, in the *Shopping list* app, you could store list items in the List concept and display the number of added elements using the .size() method. Or you could make use of the .empty() method to decide whether some text informing your user that their list is empty should be shown or not. Another example of usage would be to use the .size() method to indicate how many users are in a mail list so the user of your *Newsletter* app could know how many users will receive their message. Similarly, the .empty() method could be used in a condition that checks if the user should be informed that the list is empty.

The .front(), .back(), and .get() methods

The next three methods are also well-known. The first two are not implemented in every programming language. However, C++ programmers will find them familiar:

- Let's start from the end. The .get() method is used to retrieve the *n*th element of the List, where *n* is the index value. For example, if we want to get the second element of our users list, we would do so like this:

```
    let user = list.get(1);
```

It's important to remember that Lists in Bosque are zero-indexed, which means that the index values start from 0. So, here, if we want to get the second element, we would use index 1.

- The `.back()` method is just shorthand for the following:

```
let back = list.get(list.size() - 1);
```

It just returns the very last element of the list. It is easier and faster to call `.back()` than to write it as shown in the preceding example every time. The list must have at least one element inside it for this to work.

- The `.front()` method returns the first element of the List. Of course, it requires the List size to be more than 0. If this precondition is met, the very first element of the List will be returned. It is more convenient than calling `.get(0)` every time we want to get the first element.

The .contains(), .find(), and .indexOf() methods

All these methods are pretty self-explanatory. Nonetheless, we will walk through them one by one to ensure you know how they work:

- The first one – `.contains()` – as its name suggests, returns a Boolean value depending on whether a given element exists in the List or not. For primitive types such as `String` or `Int`, it works intuitively. However, we may also want to look for a complex type. In such a case, our complex type must implement the special `KeyType` concept and implement the `equal()` and `less()` methods. Unfortunately, in the current version of Bosque, it is not implemented yet, and compilation fails when complex types are used. At the time of writing, it is better to use `.find()` for such cases.

- The `.find()` method accepts a PCode function as an argument and looks for an element in the list by applying the PCode function to each element. It returns the first element that's found or throws an error if no match is found (in release mode, it just aborts the program). If you are not sure if your element actually exists in the list, try the `.tryFind()` or `defaultFind()` methods, which will be described later.

- The `.indexOf()` method is very similar to the previous two. This one accepts up to three arguments: the element we are looking for, the index we wish to start the lookup on, and the index where we wish to stop the lookup. It is also required – as in `.contains()` – that the element implements the `KeyType` concept, which itself is not fully implemented yet, so the `.indexOf()` method can only be used on primitives. For complex types, you can use the `.findIndexOf()` method instead, which is pretty much a mix of `.find()` and `.indexOf()` – it accepts a PCode function and two additional boundary integer parameters that determine the indexes that start and stop the lookup.

The .slice(), .map(), and .sort() methods

It's time to quickly go through the last three well-known method picks from the List concept. Let's start with .slice():

- The .slice() method is responsible for... slicing the list! This means we can only take elements between certain indexes from the list. It accepts two optional arguments that specify the boundary indexes – the part of the list that we want to slice. Remember that the second boundary index is exclusive, meaning that the element on that index will not be included in the resulting list. It can also be used to clone the list. If we won't provide any arguments, it will return a new List of the same size with the same elements. Similar to the .fill() method, it will return deeply copied elements and not just the copied references. To create a list of elements from index 3 (included) to index 7 (excluded), we can do the following:

```
var list = List<Int>@{1,2,3,4,5,6,7,8,9,0};
var sliced = list.slice(3, 7);
```

The sliced list will contain elements 4, 5, 6, and 7 (indexes 3, 4, 5, and 6, starting from 0).

- Another common method is the .map() operation. As the name suggests, it is used to map elements of the list from one value to another. In fact, we can map the elements from one type to another. Let's say that we want to return a List of names from the users list we defined previously. We can easily map the List of User entities to a List of Strings, like this:

```
let userNames = list.map<String>(fn(u) => u.name);
```

As you can see, the .map() method is parameterized. We need to provide the type we are mapping our elements to. In this case, we will change the list elements from the User type to a String type, so we provide the String type as the parameter.

- Last but not least, we will review the .sort() method. It is not hard to guess that this one is responsible for sorting the list. It accepts a single argument, which is a PCode function that's used for comparing two elements. If the PCode returns true, the elements will be swapped; otherwise, they will not. For example, to sort the list of numbers in ascending order, we can do the following:

```
let numbers = List<Int>@{1,5,3,5,89,4,3,6,83,2,5,10};
let sorted = numbers.sort(fn(a, b) => a < b);
```

To sort it in the descending order, just change the condition to a > b.

Of course, these are not all of the standard methods available in the `List` concept. There are many more that we will not review here as you wouldn't learn much from doing so – they are quite well-known and they work pretty much as you would expect them to. Let's just jump into some more interesting ones so that you can actually learn something new.

Discovering Bosque additions to List

Except for a ton of well-known methods, Bosque offers a wide range of more specialized operations that remove the need to have structured loops. We will review a short subset of them that I have found useful, but note that there are many more to explore in the core library. Similar to the previous section, we will review them in groups of connected functionality.

The "try" and "default" prefixes

In a Bosque `List`, there are many methods that have similar names but additional prefixes; that is, *try* or *default*. For example, we have the `.front()` method, but also `.tryFront()` and `.defaultFront()`. We also have the `.find()`, `.tryFind()`, and `.defaultFind()` methods. This can be applied to many more methods, such as `.back()`, `.get()`, `.single()`, and `.indexOf()`, and they always behave similarly. Let's have a look at the three variations of these methods:

- The *raw* method – meaning without any prefix – will throw a runtime error when the operation fails. In `release` mode, the program will be aborted. For example, if we were to call the `.front()` method on an empty list, the operation would fail. Similarly, if we were to call `.find()` on the list and an element isn't found, this means that the operation will fail. This is because it's guaranteed they return a value of a single and precise type. If we call `.get()`, we expect the `T` type, while if we call `.indexOf()`, we expect the number – nothing else. That's why they throw an error.

- If we prefix the method name with the *try* word, the method behaves a bit differently. It will no longer throw a runtime error if the operation fails. In such a case, the special none value will be returned instead. So, while the `.back()` method fails on an empty list, the `.tryBack()` method will return none. The same applies to other, similar methods, such as `.findLast()` and `.tryFindLast()`. It is pretty convenient if we don't care about the resulting type that much. If the None type is acceptable for us, we should go with the *try* methods.

- We can also use the *default* prefix for the same methods. These kinds of methods also guarantee the return T type, but instead of throwing an error on failure, they return the default value of T type (the same as the List elements), provided as an argument. For example, if we want to get the fifth user from our list and, if they're not present, return the first one, we can do the following:

```
let userOrDefault = list.defaultGet(4, list.front());
```

So, if the user at index 4 does not exist, the first one will be returned. This is how the *default* prefix changes the methods.

The "not" suffix

Despite the aforementioned prefixes, Bosque also offers the Not suffix, which basically reverses the behavior of a method. For example, if we want to find elements in a list that do not match the specified criteria, we can use the Not suffix to achieve that. To understand this, let's look at a very simple example. The following line of code creates a list of users named *Bob*:

```
let bobs = list.filter(fn(u) => u.name == "Bob");
```

To reverse the lookup, meaning to get users that are not named Bob, you can use the Not suffix:

```
let bobs = list.filterNot(fn(u) => u.name == "Bob");
```

This suffix applies to many more methods, such as .countIf() or .find().

The .allOf(), .noneOf(), .anyOf() and .count() methods

This set of methods is quite self-explanatory. However, I will describe them briefly to ensure you know what they do.

Before we begin, let's introduce one entity and a list that we will work on to better understand the next few methods' behavior. This is a simple User entity:

```
entity User {
        field name: String;
        field age: Int;
}
```

Here is the list of users that we will work on:

```
var users = List<User>@{
        User@{"Alice", 25}, User@{"Bob", 20},
        User@{"Charlie", 18}, User@{"Dwayne", 34},
        User@{"Ellie", 25}, User@{"Fiona", 24}
};
```

Now, let's jump into the method's descriptions and examples.

The first three are very similar. They all accept a single PCode function as an argument, which is applied to every element of the list. Based on the result, the result of the whole operation may change. The `.allOf()` method returns `true` if all the List elements meet the condition specified by the PCode function. If any of them do not, this method returns `false`. Analogous to the `.allOf()` method, `.noneOf()` will only return `true` if none of the elements meet the criteria. The last one – `.anyOf()` – will return `true` if any of the elements meet the condition. The following are example usages of these three methods:

```
var allof = users.allOf(fn(user) => user.age < 30);
var noneof = users.noneOf(fn(user) => user.age < 30);
var anyof = users.anyOf(fn(user) => user.age < 30);
```

In summary, `allof` will be `false` because of one user who is not under 30. `noneof` will also be `false` because there are 5 users who are under 30. `anyof` will be `true` because some of the users (5, in this case) are under 30.

The `.count()` method accepts a single value argument and returns the number denoting how many times the given element occurs in a list. Again, it is required for the value type to implement the `KeyType` concept to allow Bosque to perform a proper comparison. So, you can't use it for our `User` entity, but you could use it for a list of numbers and, if you wanted, to count the number of occurrences of number 6 in a list:

```
var cnt = list.count(6);
```

You can do this as shown in the preceding code.

The .takeWhile() and .takeUntil() methods

These two similar methods are also pretty self-explanatory, just by looking at their names. They both accept a PCode function as an argument and return a new list consisting of elements that match the criteria specified by the argument.

The difference is that the .takeWhile() method will return elements from the original list, up to the first occurrence of an element that doesn't match. Even if, later in the list, there are elements that satisfy the condition, they will not be included. On the other hand, the .takeUntil() method will include the elements for the new list, as long as they do not satisfy the condition. In other words, the former method includes the value *while* the expression is true, while the latter includes the value *until* the expression is true. As you can see, the difference is quite subtle, but I hope this example will help you understand this:

```
var takewhile = users.takeWhile(fn(user) => user.age < 30);
var takeuntil = users.takeUntil(fn(user) => user.age <= 20);
```

Here, takewhile will consist of three users – Alice, Bob, and Charlie – because in our list, these first three users are under 30 and the next one – Dwayne – is 34 years old, so takeWhile() stops here, without including this last user. takeuntil will consist of only one user – Alice – because, starting from the first index in our users list, Alice is the only one who does not satisfy the <= 20 condition. The next user – Bob – is exactly 20 and as such, satisfies this condition, so he is not included in the resulting list and takeUntil() stops here.

Now, let's have a quick look at a small helper concept available in Bosque called ListOf.

Introducing ListOf

In Bosque, there is another ListOf concept that is pretty small as it only has three static methods. Despite this, those three methods are quite useful, and we are going to describe them briefly. To understand their behavior, let's create another list (except the previous one – users – and the User entity) called activities, which will consist of a list of activities:

```
var activities = List<String>@{
        "Cooking", "Swimming", "Running", "Reading",
"Partying", "Shopping"
};
```

Now, let's see how we can use these three methods:

- The first one is called `ListOf::zip<T, U>()`. As you can see, it is a parameterized method that provides two types as its type parameters. It also accepts two required arguments – two lists of the `List<T>` and `List<U>` type, respectively. This method takes these lists and returns another list that contains pairs of elements from both lists, wrapped in tuples. If we wanted to zip the users and activities lists, we could do this like so:

```
var zip = ListOf::zip<User, String>(users, activities);
```

In the result, `zip` would be a list of tuples that looks like this:

```
{
        [NSMain::User{ "Alice", 25 }, "Cooking"],
        [NSMain::User{ "Bob", 20 }, "Swimming"],
        [NSMain::User{ "Charlie", 18 }, "Running"],
        [NSMain::User{ "Dwayne", 34 }, "Reading"],
        [NSMain::User{ "Ellie", 25 }, "Partying"],
        [NSMain::User{ "Fiona", 24 }, "Shopping"]
}
```

So, as you can see, we have six tuples containing a user and an activity. The values are taken from both lists at the same indexes and put into one tuple for each pair, so the resulting list is of the same length.

- The second method is called `ListOf::unzip<T, U>()`, which is the exact opposite of the previous one. It takes a single list argument and returns a pack value consisting of two lists of the `List<T>` and `List<U>` types, respectively. To handle the result of this method, we will need to use the `(|...|)` operator, like this:

```
(| var userList, var actList |) = ListOf::unzip<User,
String>(zip);
```

So, as you can see, we are providing the previously zipped `zip` list and extracting each of the lists from the pack value.

- The last method is a very useful helper method called `ListOf::range()` that accepts two numbers as arguments and returns a list of numbers from the provided range. For example, if you want to generate a list of powers of 2 up to the 20th, you could do so like this:

```
var powers = ListOf::range(1, 21).map<Int>(fn(n) =>
Float64::pow2(n.toFloat64()).toInt());
```

Notice that we need to provide 21 as the second argument as this boundary is exclusive. Also, we had to convert `Int` into `Float64` to perform the power operation as we don't have a similar helper in the `Int` type.

And that's pretty much it about this concept. Now, let's get familiar with another kind of collection in Bosque – maps.

Getting familiar with Map and DynamicMap

Similar to lists, maps are one of the most popular data structures that are broadly implemented in various programming languages. A map is a collection of key-value pairs with the characteristic that the key must be unique while the values can repeat inside of a map.

In this section, we will describe two data types in Bosque – `Map` and `DynamicMap`. The difference between them is that the former – similar to the `List` concept – creates an **immutable Map instance**, which means that once it has been instantiated with some values, you cannot change it. The latter allows you to modify the map once it's been created. Both `Map` and `DynamicMap` provide the `Expandoable` concept, which means that the spread operator can be used on them.

First thing's first, let's see how a `Map` can be instantiated. The following example shows how to create a `Map` instance in Bosque:

```
let map = Map<String, Int>@{
        "John" => 12,
        "Alice" => 15,
        "Bob" => 14
};
```

So, as you can see, `Map` is parameterized by two data types: one describing the data types of the keys and the second one describing the data types of the values that will be stored in the map. To put elements in a `Map`, we can use the key-value argument notation described in *Chapter 8, Expressions in Bosque*. The important thing to remember is that the key data type must provide the `KeyType` concept. Otherwise, Bosque will not be able to properly compare the keys, and errors will be thrown.

In the next few sections, we will introduce both concepts by reviewing their methods. We will not cover all the methods, just a subset to show the idea behind them. Let's start with Map itself.

Reviewing standard Map methods

Similar to List, we will look at the small subset of the common methods that you can expect from any map-like structure. We will follow the same pattern throughout this chapter – methods grouped by similar functionality.

For the examples presented in this section, we will be using this kind of map:

```
var students = Map<String, Int>@{
        "Alice" => 25,
        "Bob" => 20,
        "Charlie" => 18,
        "Dwayne" => 34,
        "Ellie" => 25,
        "Fiona" => 24,
};
```

Now, let's have a look at the first group.

The .size() and .empty() methods

These two methods are trivial, aren't they? The first one returns a number denoting how many elements there are in a map, while the second one is responsible for returning Boolean true when the map does not have any elements or Boolean false otherwise. Some example usage is presented in the following example:

```
var size = students.size();
var empty = students.empty();
```

Here, size will return 6 as this is the number of keys in our map. The empty variable will be false as our map is certainly not empty. There's nothing more to add here, so let's not waste any time and jump to the next set of methods.

The .keys(), .values(), and .entries() methods

Similar to the previous two, these three methods are also very well-known. The .keys() method returns a List<K> of keys that are present in the map, where K is what's provided during the instantiation of Map. The second method – .values() – returns a List<V> of values stored in the map, where V is the same type that's provided during the instantiation of Map. Some example usages are presented in the following example:

```
var keys = students.keys();
var values = students.values();
```

So, keys will be a list of strings representing students' names and values will be a list of integers representing the age of each student.

The last method, called .entries(), also returns a list. This time, however, the list contains elements of the MapEntry<K, V> type. These are small objects containing two fields, key and value, you can access when dealing with such data types. The following is an example of how to use this method:

```
var entries = students.entries();
```

Here, entries will look like this:

```
{
        MapEntry<String, Int>{ "Alice", 25 },
        MapEntry<String, Int>{ "Bob", 20 },
        MapEntry<String, Int>{ "Charlie", 18 },
        MapEntry<String, Int>{ "Dwayne", 34 },
        MapEntry<String, Int>{ "Ellie", 25 },
        MapEntry<String, Int>{ "Fiona", 24 }
}
```

And that's all there it to say about these three simple methods. Let's look at the last group of standard methods available in Bosque Map.

The .has(), .hasAll(), and .get() methods

You certainly know these methods already. The .has() method accepts a single parameter of the K type, where K is the type of keys in the map. It returns a Boolean value, depending on the key's existence in the map. The .hasAll() method is very similar, except that it accepts comma-separated list of keys that we want to check are present in the map instead of a single key. If all the keys are present, the method returns true, or false otherwise.

The following example shows how you can use these methods:

```
var has = students.has("Bob");
var hasall = students.hasAll("Alice", "Gregory", "Fiona");
```

The has variable will be true because we have such a student in our map. The second one – hasall – will be equal to false because we don't have Gregory defined in the map.

The .get() method is responsible for extracting a value by key. It's important to remember that this method will throw an error if the key does not exist in the map. We can prevent this by adding the *try* or *default* prefixes, just like we did in the *Bosque additions to List* section. The behavior of this method changes in the same way we described it there. In case you need an example, this is how you can use it:

```
var ellieAge = students.get("Ellie");
var maybeJohnAge = students.tryGet("John");
var defaultLucyAge = students.defaultGet("Lucy", 22);
```

So, ellieAge will be equal to 25 because that's what is defined in our map. maybeJohnAge will be none as we don't have such a student. The last one will be 22 because although we don't have Lucy in the students map, we are providing the default value for such a case – 22.

Discovering Bosque additions to Map

As well as the List concept, Bosque offers a bunch of useful Map methods that are more specialized and resolve specific problems. Let's have a look at the most interesting ones (in my opinion), organized into groups.

The .domainSubsetOf() method

This method is quite similar to the .hasAll() method. The difference is that instead of accepting a list of keys, it accepts a Set of keys and returns true if all the Set elements exist in the map as keys. If any of the Set elements are not a key in the map, it will return false. Sets will be described in the *Understanding Set and DynamicSet* section. Its usage is pretty simple. Have a look at the following example:

```
let groupA = Set<String>@{"Alice", "Bob"};
let groupB = Set<String>@{"John", "Martha"};
let users = Map<String, Int>@{
        "John" => 12,
```

```
        "Alice" => 15,
        "Bob" => 14
};
let allPresentA = users.domainSubsetOf(groupA);
let allPresentB = users.domainSubsetOf(groupB);
```

We have a map of users and their points scored in a test. One of the students – Martha – wasn't present that day and is not included in the map. We also have two sets of names – one for each group. The last two lines are testing if all the students from both groups were present by invoking the .domainSubsetOf() method. This may be useful in scenarios were we are forced to use sets to achieve uniqueness in elements and simply can't use the .hasAll() method. Let's have a look at some more methods.

The .toDynamicMap() and .remap() methods

The first method, .toDynamicMap(), converts the map into another kind of structure – DynamicMap – as described in the *Introducing DynamicMap* section. As we mentioned previously, Map creates an immutable map of key-value pairs. However, sometimes, we may want to modify it a bit – such as by adding a new key. In such scenarios, we can use the .toDynamicMap() method to create a new mutable map.

> **Important note**
>
> At the time of writing, the .toDynamicMap() method has not been implemented yet. Therefore, any program that uses it will not compile. Be careful when you're playing with Map.

The .remap() method is used to modify our map and turn it to a different one. Let's say that you want to add 10 points to every student that attended the test. You can do so like this:

```
let awarded = users.remap<Int>(fn(name, points) => points +
10);
```

So, as you can see, we must provide the new value type after the remap keyword. The .remap() method accepts a PCode function as the parameter. This PCode is used to "remap" all the current map entries into the new ones:

```
{
        "John" => 22,
        "Alice" => 25,
        "Bob" => 24
}
```

At the end, a new modified Map instance is returned, which looks like as shown in the preceding code snippet.

The .excludeAll(), .excludeSet(), .projectAll(), and .projectSet() methods

These four methods are responsible for filtering the map's contents. The first two return a new Map instance without the keys provided as arguments. The .excludeAll() method accepts an arbitrary list of arguments of the K type, where K is the type of keys in the map. This means that we can provide them either by separating each of them by a comma or we can use the spread operator on a List. It will return a Map that does not include any of the provided keys. The .excludeSet() method works exactly the same, with the difference that it accepts a single parameter, which is a Set of keys that we want to exclude from our map. To see the difference, here is an example of how to use both methods:

```
var excludeall = students.excludeAll("Alice", "Charlie",
"Ellie");
var names = Set<String>@{"Alice", "Charlie", "Ellie"};
var excludeset = students.excludeSet(names);
```

So, as you can see, the first one accepts a comma-separated list of arguments, while the second one takes a set of values. The result of both operations will be exactly the same – Alice, Charlie, and Ellie will be excluded, and a new map will be returned (modified).

The .projectAll() and .projectSet() methods are complete opposites of their "exclude" twins. While the latter filters out provided keys, the former returns a new map that only includes the keys provided as arguments. They accept the same argument types – .projectAll() accepts an "expandable" list of keys to include (meaning we can either use the spread operator on List or provide an arbitrary number of comma-separated arguments), while .projectSet() accepts a Set of such keys. The following example is similar to the previous one, in that it shows how to use these two methods:

```
var projectall = students.projectAll("Alice", "Charlie",
"Ellie");
var names = Set<String>@{"Alice", "Charlie", "Ellie"};
var projectset = students.projectSet(names);
```

As opposed to the exclude operation, we are now creating a new map that contains only listed keys.

Now, it's time to learn about the DynamicMap helper concept.

Introducing DynamicMap

Let's quickly recall that the Map concept creates an immutable instance that cannot be modified once created. While it does resolve the problem with mutability, it may be problematic. It's not hard to imagine a scenario where we don't know all the keys that will be stored in a map, or where we need to update some values stored under a specific key. One such scenario may go like this: imagine that you have a shopping app and you are implementing the "Review Cart" feature. After picking some products, your user can see the Cart's contents and modify it by updating the quantity or removing some products. One way to implement the Cart is by using a map, where the keys would be the product IDs and the values could be the quantities (in a more advanced scenario, the values would probably be some more complex data types). And here's the problem – you can't do that with Bosque Map because you don't know what product will be chosen by your user, and at the same time, you can't add new products to an already-created map.

This is why there is something called DynamicMap in Bosque. Simply put, we can say that DynamicMap is a mutable version of the Map concept. It has the same methods as its immutable twin but also has additional ones that let us modify the map's contents. These methods are well-known and are self-descriptive, so we will just briefly introduce them here.

> **Important note**
>
> At the time of writing, the DynamicMap concept is not fully implemented yet. None of its methods will work – you can only create an instance of DynamicMap and nothing more. Please be careful when you try out this feature.

The DynamicMap concept – once implemented – will have nine additional methods. The .toMap() method simply converts the current dynamic map into an immutable Map instance. This may be useful when we want to freeze the current state of our map. The .add() and .insert() methods allow us to insert another key-value pair into the map. They both accept the same arguments – a key of the K type and value of the V type, where K and V are the same types that are provided during the dynamic map's instantiation. The .addAll() and .insertAll() methods are similar to the previous two, but with the difference that they accept a comma-separated list of MapEntry<K, V> objects. The MapEntry type was described in the *Reviewing standard Map methods* section. The .update() and .updateAll() methods are responsible for updating the map entries. The difference between them is analogous, as in the previous methods – the first one accepts the key and value arguments, while the second one accepts a comma-separated list of MapEntry<K, V> elements. The last two additional methods – .remove() and .removeAll() – as their names suggest, allow us to delete elements from a map. The first one accepts a single argument, which is the key we want to get rid of. The second one accepts an arbitrary number of keys that we don't want in our map anymore.

All these methods return a new `DynamicMap` object (except `.toMap()`) with a modified state so that the immutability principle in Bosque is not broken.

And that concludes the `Map` and `DynamicMap` concepts in Bosque. Now, it's time to become familiar with another type of collection available in Bosque – Sets.

Understanding Set and DynamicSet

The next collection type we are going to discuss is `Set`. Sets are containers for unique values with constant access time. This means that no matter how many values we have in a set, accessing a value will take the same amount of time, regardless of the value we are looking for. It's worth repeating the fact that all the elements of a set must be unique. Depending on their implementation, adding a duplicated element to a set will either throw an error or simply do nothing. Another characteristic of a set is that there is no such thing as element order. You cannot retrieve, for example, the 5th element from a set – there's simply no such thing because, in sets, there are no any indexes that would determine an order. In fact, there is also no such thing as *retrieving* an element from a set – we can only check if a given element is already in the set or not. And it makes a lot of sense if you think about it. You can think of a Set as if it were a bag – we can put some elements in there and we can check if we have certain elements in there already; we cannot put another identical thing into this bag. With these rules in mind, do we need some `.retrieve()` operation?

Imagine you are writing your thesis and you must create a bibliography where you will list all of the papers and references that your work is based on. In the bibliography every entry must be unique, so you can't have two – for instance – Martin, R. C. (2009). *Clean code: A handbook of agile software craftsmanship* entries (how much sense would it make anyway?). Now, let's say that you are willing to put this very title into your list of references. The first thing you need to do is to check if there is already such an item. So you open some kind of a bibliography manager and type the full citation. If it's already on the list, it won't be added but if it's not, it will be saved. You can also decide to get rid of some entry – it's allowed to do so and once it's done, you can add a new entry with the same value. But do you need to ever retrieve a single item from your list? It would require you to provide the full citation so that the bibliography manager could find such an item – and since you have already provided a full citation, what else would you like to retrieve? You already have the item you were looking for!

At this point, you are probably not surprised that, in Bosque, `Set` is an immutable data structure – similar to the previous ones. If you want to have a mutable set, you need to use the `DynamicSet` concept. Both `Set` and `DynamicSet` provide the `Expandoable` concept, which enables them to be used with the spread operator.

Let's review some of the methods that are available in both concepts. First, we'll review some standard methods that are quite well-known from other programming languages. Then, we'll take a look at some methods that have been added by the creators of Bosque that enhance the implementation of these concepts. After that, we will discuss the `DynamicSet` structure. Everything will follow the same pattern we've been using throughout this chapter.

Reviewing standard Set methods

In general, Sets offer a rather small range of methods that allow developers to operate on them. In Bosque, we can also expect these popular methods to be available to us. Despite being quite self-explanatory, let's have a quick look at them. But before we do that, let's create an example set that we will use for our examples:

```
var customers = Set<String>@{
        "John", "Kate", "Peter", "Wade", "Xavier", "Zack"
};
```

Now, let's continue.

The .size() and .empty() methods

These two are pretty obvious and do not require any deep explanation. The first one returns an `Int` value denoting the number of elements that are currently stored in the set. The second one – `.empty()` – returns a Boolean value of `true` or `false`, depending on whether the set has zero elements or more. Let's quickly learn how to use these methods:

```
var size = customers.size();
var empty = customers.empty();
```

In our case, `size` will equal 6 and `empty` will be false since the set is not empty.

And that's basically all there is to say about these two. Let's discuss the rest of the standard Set methods.

The .has(), .hasAll(), and .entries() methods

Similar to the previous two, these are also pretty easy do understand just by looking at their names. The `.has()` method accepts a single parameter and returns a Boolean value of `true` or `false`, depending on whether the given element is already stored in the set or not. This is how you can use it:

```
var has = customers.has("Peter");
```

`has` will be `true` because we have Peter in our set.

> **Important note**
>
> At the time of writing, `Set` is not fully implemented, and the following two methods will not work. An attempt to use them will result in a similar error:
>
> `Error -- AssertionError [ERR_ASSERTION]: Need to implement -- NSCore::Set::s_entry_list`
>
> Please be careful when playing with `Set`.

`.hasAll()` is somewhat similar, with the difference that it accepts an arbitrary number of parameters, separated with a comma. If all the values are present in the set, it returns `true`; otherwise, `false` is returned. The `.entries()` method does not accept any parameters and simply returns a `List<T>` of values that were stored in the set, where `T` is the type of elements. Here is an example usage of these methods:

```
var hasall = customers.hasAll("John", "Zack", "Kate");
var entries = customers.entries();
```

This will result in `hasall` being `true` and `entries` being a list of customer names. Notice that in `hasAll()`, the order of the elements does not matter – it will be `true` because we have all the names in the set.

And that concludes the standard `Set` methods. Now, let's have a look at some more interesting Bosque additions.

Discovering Bosque additions to Set

In this section, we will review a few useful methods available in the `Set` concept. They are implementations of mathematical operations on sets, which might turn out to be handy.

> **Important note**
>
> As we mentioned earlier, `Set` is not fully implemented yet, so none of these methods will work. If you try to use it and compile a program, Bosque will throw an error, similar to this one (depending on the method used):
>
> `Error -- AssertionError [ERR_ASSERTION]: Need to implement -- NSCore::Set::s_subsetof`
>
> Please be careful when playing with `Set`.

The .toDynamicSet() method

The first method, called `.toDynamicSet()`, converts the set into a previously mentioned `DynamicSet`. It's described in more detail in the *Introducing DynamicSet* section. As we mentioned previously, `DynamicSet` is a mutable version of `Set`, which means that we can add or remove values. To convert a regular `Set` into this editable structure, we can use the `.toDynamicSet()` method, like this:

```
var dynamicSet = customers.toDynamicSet();
```

Let's now see the next set of methods.

The .subsetOf(), .disjoint(), and .equal() methods

For the sake of this whole section, let's introduce a scenario that will help us understand the upcoming `Set` methods. Imagine that you have created a personality test and asked two people to complete it. It has five single-choice questions. Every question has three choices, and every choice has a unique ID, starting with 1 and ending with 15, meaning that the first three choices have IDs 1, 2, and 3, the next three have IDs 4, 5, and 6, and so on. You don't have to answer all the questions. Bob and Alice have filled in your test. Now, you want to look at the results from various points of view. We can use sets for that.

But why not a map? Well, a map would be more convenient in a similar scenario for sure. But in this particular example we don't really care about the keys (questions) – we care only about values (answers) so a set is more optimal as we don't waste memory for things we don't use (keys in this case). We can still easily tell what question a particular answer (value) belongs to without the need to have it stored in a map as a key – it results from the requirements.

Having said that, let's define the results as follows:

```
let bob = Set<Int>@{2,4,9,10,14};
let alice = Set<Int>@{1,9,12};
```

We can tell that Bob answered all the questions and that Alice skipped the second and last one, just by looking at the answer's IDs.

Using `.subsetOf()`, we can check if Alice gave the same answers as Bob. In other words, we can see if Alice's answers are a subset of Bob's answers, like this:

```
let result = alice.subsetOf(bob);
```

We can also check whether they gave totally different answers by using the
`.disjoint()` method, which returns true if the sets are not overlapping – they don't
have common values:

```
let result = alice.disjoint(bob);
```

Alternatively, we can check whether they gave exactly the same answers by using the
`.equal()` method:

```
let result = alice.equal(bob);
```

The previous examples will result in `result` being `false` in all of them.

Let's see what else we can do with the test results by using different methods.

The .union(), .intersect(), difference(), and .symmetricDifference() methods

The first thing we may want to see is all the answers that were given on your test. You
made a personality test for a reason, right? Let's say you want to give Alice and Bob a piece
of advice for every given answer. In such a case, you may want to see what advice you need
to prepare – that's why you want to see all the given answers (there's no reason to prepare
advice for answers that weren't given at all). We can see that by using the `.union()`
method, which returns a new `Set` containing all the unique values from both of them:

```
let result = alice.union(bob);
```

This will result in a set containing these values: 1, 2, 4, 9, 10, 12, and 14.

You can also see if there were any common answers by using the `.intersect()`
method, which returns a new `Set` containing elements that are in both sets:

```
let result = alice.intersect(bob);
```

This time, the result will equal {9} because this is the only common answer.

Another thing worth checking is what aspects of Bob's personality differs from Alice's,
and vice versa. You can do that using the `.difference()` method, which returns a new
`Set` that only contains elements from the current set that are not in the set being passed
as an argument. This means that this operation is not symmetric – Alice "minus" Bob is
not the same as Bob "minus" Alice. You can use this method like this:

```
let aliceWithoutBob = alice.difference(bob);
let bobWithoutAlice = bob.difference(alice);
```

Here, the results will be as follows: `aliceWithoutBob` - {1, 12},
`bobWithoutAlice` - {2, 4, 10, 14}.

To get all the different answers that were given, we can use the
`.symmetricDifference()` method, which returns a new `Set` that
contains only non-common elements from both sets:

```
let result = alice.symmetricDifference(bob);
```

This will return a new set that looks like this: {1, 2, 4, 10, 12, 14}.

This summarizes the most interesting `Set` methods in Bosque. Now, let's learn about the
concept of `DynamicSet`.

Introducing DynamicSet

As we mentioned previously, `DynamicSet` is very similar to a regular `Set`, except
that it's mutable. In fact, `DynamicSet` provides all the same methods as `Set` but also
introduces a few additional ones that are for modifying dynamic sets.

> **Important Note**
>
> At the time of writing, the `DynamicSet` concept is not fully implemented
> yet. None of its methods will work – you can only create an instance of
> `DynamicSet` and nothing more. Please be careful when trying out this
> feature.

The `DynamicSet` concept will have seven additional methods. The first one, called
`.toSet()` simply, converts the current dynamic set into a regular one. This can be
useful when we want to freeze a set and disallow further changes. The next two methods
– `.add()` and `.addAll()` – are responsible for adding new elements to the set. The
first one accepts a single parameter, which is the value to be inserted. The second one
accepts a comma-separated list of values to be added. The next two – `.insert()` and
`.insertAll()` – are aliases to the previous ones and work the same way. The last two
additional methods, called `.remove()` and `.removeAll()`, are responsible for deleting
elements from the set. The first one accepts a single parameter, which is a value to be
removed, while the second one accepts an arbitrary number of values as parameters.

All these methods return a new `DynamicSet` object (except the `.toSet()` one) with
a modified state so that the immutability principle in Bosque is not broken.

And that concludes the `Set` and `DynamicSet` concepts in Bosque. It's time to get
familiar with another type of collections available in Bosque – stacks and queues.

Discovering Stack and Queue

The last two data structures that we are going to cover in this chapter are `Stack` and `Queue`. These are built-in Bosque collections and – unlike the previous ones – do not have *dynamic twins*. At the current stage of Bosque development, these concepts are rather small and do not offer much functionality. However, it's likely that they will be enhanced in the future.

Important note

At the time of writing, the `Stack` and `Queue` concepts have not been implemented yet. Any attempt to use them will result in errors. The concepts itself are declared in Bosque but they lack any internal implementation.

Since these concepts are quite small and not implemented yet, we will only review their basic methods because currently, they do not work at all.

Reviewing Stack methods

In general, stacks are data structures that have one specific characteristic; that is, you can only retrieve elements from them in the reverse order they were added. In programming, we call it a **LIFO** queue – **Last In, First Out** – which means that the last element to be added will be the first one to be taken out of stack. I'm sure it's not a surprise that, in Bosque, `Stack` is an immutable data type.

Bosque `Stack` offers a basic set of methods that are quite well-known. `.size()` and `.empty()` are trivial and we use them to check the number of elements stored in the stack and to check if it's empty. The `.pop()` method is used to take the last element from the stack and remove it from the structure. Since `Stack` is immutable, `.pop()` returns multiple values (two, in this case) – the element and a new modified `Stack` instance. We also have the `.peek()` method, which only returns the last element without removing it, so it only returns one value. In order to push another element on top of the stack, we can use the `.push()` method, which accepts a single parameter value and returns a newly modified `Stack` instance.

Reviewing Queue methods

As opposed to a stack, a queue is characterized by the fact that we remove elements from it in the same order as they were added. In programming, we call it a **FIFO** queue – **First In, First Out** – which means that the first element to be added will be also the first one to be handled. Similar to other data types, `Queue` is also immutable in Bosque.

The `Queue` concept in Bosque also has a basic set of methods available. We can use methods such as `.size()` or `.empty()` to perform standard checks, as described many times in this chapter. The `.dequeue()` method is similar to the `.pop()` method from `Stack`. The difference is that it returns (and removes from the queue) the first element instead of the last one to be added. It returns two values as well – the element and modified `Queue` instance. The `.peek()` method is identical to the one described with `Stack`. The `.enqueue()` method accepts a single parameter value, adds this element to the end of the queue, and returns a new modified `Queue` instance.

That concludes all the collection types in Bosque. Let's sum up the knowledge you gained in this chapter.

Summary

This was a long chapter, wasn't it? You learned a lot about the collection types that are available in Bosque. Now, you know about how Bosque implements some popular collections, as well as Bosque-specific ones.

The first thing you learned about were the `List` and `ListOf` types. You became familiar with the standard methods that are available for you to use, and also discovered new ones that have been added by the creators of Bosque. You also found out that there is the `ListOf` concept, which is a type of helper that has a few static methods.

Then, you jumped into the `Map` and `DynamicMap` concepts. You learned that `Map` is an immutable type and cannot be modified after creation. You also discovered the mutable version of `Map`, called `DynamicMap`. You know how they differ and what methods they offer, but also that the latter is not fully implemented yet.

You also become familiar with `Set` and its mutable twin, called `DynamicSet`, which has also not been implemented yet. Here, you learned about sets in general and how this data type has been implemented in Bosque. Similar to maps, you learned about the differences between `Set` and `DynamicSet` and their methods.

Eventually, we covered the `Stack` and `Queue` types. You faced the sad truth that they are not implemented yet and cannot be used, but regardless of that, you learned what a stack and queue are in general and how these types have been implemented in Bosque.

Now, it's time to dive deeper into iterative processing and recursion in Bosque. Earlier in this book, we mentioned that there are no loops in Bosque. In the next chapter, we'll look closer at this and see if it's true after all.

Questions

1. How does the `ListOf` concept differ from List? What can you use it for?

2. How does `DynamicMap` differ from `Map`? When it can be useful?

3. How does `DynamicSet` differ from `Set`? When it can be useful?

4. What is a stack and how does it differ from a queue? Can you use `Stack` or `Queue` in Bosque?

Further reading

Here is a recommended list of books about data structures:

- Aho, A. V., Hopcroft, J. E., Ullman, J. D. (1983). *Data Structures and Algorithms.* Bell Telephone Laboratories, Incorporated.

- Drozdek, A. (2001). *Data Structures and Algorithms in C++, Second Edition.* Brooks/Cole.

10
Iterative Processing and Recursion

I bet the first time you read that there are no loops in Bosque, you were confused. And you probably were even more confused when you read that there are operations on concepts such as List that look like they are doing some iterative work. It wouldn't come as a surprise to me if you were asking yourself, *What is going on here? Does Bosque support iteration or not?* In this chapter, we will shed some light on this topic as well as recursion. First, we will learn why (and if) there are no loops available and how we can solve various problems related to iteration in Bosque. Next, we will take a closer look at recursion and restrictions that Bosque sets to simplify recursive calls in our programs – we will simply recall and slightly expand the knowledge that you gained in *Chapter 3, Bosque Key Features*. We will also cover the NSIterate namespace and its implemented methods.

Here is a list of topics that we are going to cover in this chapter:

- Learning about structured loops
- Practicing iterative processing without structured loops
- Discovering the NSIterate namespace and its helper functions
- Recursion and the recursive keyword

After reading this chapter, you will have a good understanding of the iteration and recursion concepts in Bosque and will be able to use it in practice. You will learn how you can solve problems that require iteration or recursion using Bosque.

Technical requirements

In order to better understand the code shown in this chapter, you are encouraged to have a knowledge of the following topics:

- Core collections available in Bosque and their methods that do iterative work

- Expressions in Bosque, such as `PCode` functions or scoped invocations

You can also become acquainted with the examples shared on GitHub here: `https://github.com/PacktPublishing/Learn-Bosque-Programming/ tree/main/Chapter10`.

Learning about structured loops

I think we cannot argue that in programming, one of the fundamental concepts is the iteration construct. The ability to perform certain repetitive tasks using a single structure that is both expressive and flexible has been an inherent part of the development process since the rise of the structured programming paradigm. For years, programmers have been using loops to enclose parts of their code into smaller chunks that are responsible for accomplishing one thing. Over the years, programming languages have been improving gradually to the point where we know them today – high-level languages that allow us to tell computers what to do in a fairly easy-to-understand, human-readable way.

You may be wondering why I am telling you this. The answer is that I want you to have some background before you learn what this "no loops" concept in Bosque is all about.

So today, we have a wide range of programming languages that have changed a lot since their beginnings. In most of them, we don't have to bother allocating and releasing memory or thinking about the platform we are targeting. We have compilers, transpilers, garbage collectors, and many more tools that handle the dirty work for us. Also, the iteration process has changed. Back in the old days, the way to perform "iteration" was to use `goto` instructions and it was all about *jumping* from one *label* to another. Today, we have all kinds of loop statements, for example:

- The `while` loop
- The `for` loop
- The `do...while` loop

And we could name even more, such as `foreach`, `repeat...until`, `for...in`, or `for...of` loops. While these constructs do give us – developers – a lot of flexibility, they introduce a new set of problems. The more you are allowed to do, the higher the chance that you will do something wrong. This even applies to day-to-day life, but also to the iteration concept in programming. The most obvious mistake when dealing with loops is stepping out of the bounds of the array (or any other indexed structure). I agree that it's easy to fix, but it does happen and you need to waste time doing a facepalm and fixing the bug.

This is why Bosque has taken another step ahead in improving the programming experience and has removed the source of these kinds of problems – the loop construct itself. Please note that I didn't say "loop **concept**" – I said "loop **construct**." And this is where the confusion may arise. Let me shed some light on this.

The truth is that Bosque did not remove the iteration completely. What the creators did is they removed structures like the ones we mentioned previously: `while`, `for`, `do...while`, and so on. Instead, every iterable data structure (such that we can perform an iteration on it) that is available in Bosque is equipped with a ton of methods that are performing iterative processing internally. The only thing we have to do is to pick the ones that will satisfy our needs and make use of them. This may seem like an impediment because we simply got used to structured loops. But in reality, for the price of some level of flexibility, we are better able to understand the code we write.

At this point, you may be wondering how does this increase the readability of the code and is it really worth losing some flexibility? The real question you should ask is, do we really need that much flexibility? Do we really make use of it? Research has shown that we don't.

In 2018, a group of researchers, including Mark Marron – the creator of Bosque –analyzed millions of lines of code and detected some patterns that 90% of loop structures followed. They call such patterns idioms. Without going into the details too much (the link to the whole paper is provided in the *Further reading* section), they found that there is a space to replace repetitive patterns with language constructs that will do the job for us. It seems that after all, we don't use the flexibility that "raw" loop constructs offer – intentionally or not, we repeat ourselves all the time. Of course, we can't simply ignore the 10% of loop structures that are not covered by the built-in collection methods. This last part can be handled with the `NSIterate` namespace, which provides a more generic iteration method.

What's also very important is that in Bosque, there is no `break` and `continue` statement. Since there are no structured loops, you can't use these two, so it may also feel inconvenient. However, once you learn all of the available methods and helper functions, you will get used to it and won't require these statements that much.

So, it is now time to finally answer the question: does Bosque support iteration? Yes, it does, but we don't have any loop constructs available to use. Instead, what we do have are lots of methods that cover common loop patterns that we can use on any iterable data structure, depending on requirements and the structure that we use. Additionally, as mentioned before, there is an `NSIterate` namespace, with a few namespace-scoped functions that we can make use of when we need to perform iteration. More on these is described in the *Discovering the NSIterate namespace and its helper functions* section.

Alright, following this introduction, you can now learn more about iterative processing without structured loops in practice. Let's not waste time and jump right into it.

Practicing iterative processing without structured loops

As stated in the previous section, as well as in *Chapter 3*, *Bosque Key Features*, in order to perform iteration, we need to utilize ready-to-use methods depending on the task we are solving and the data structure we use. In this section, we will play with the `List` concept and see how we can iterate over it in various ways and solve a few practical problems.

Multiplying vectors

The first problem we are going to solve is the multiplication of vectors. However, before we jump into the code, let's clarify how we multiply vectors in the first place.

Let's begin by explaining what a vector actually is. Since this book is not a mathematics textbook, I won't provide you with a formal definition. For the sake of this example, it's enough to know that a vector is a set of *n* numeric components. In programming, vectors can be represented as arrays of numbers. In Bosque, we can represent a vector using a tuple or a List – we will go with the second approach since there are more methods available to play with it. An example vector written in Bosque looks like the following:

```
let vectorA = List<Int>@{ 3, 7, 2 };
```

Our task is to take two similar vectors of arbitrary, but equal, length and multiply them.

There are several ways of multiplying vectors. One of these is the **dot product** approach. A dot product of two vectors is a sum of products of elements in the same positions. For instance, a dot product of vector a = (1, 2, 3) and vector b = (4, 5, 6) is equal to 32 because this is the result of the following calculation:

$$a \cdot b = 1 \times 4 + 2 \times 5 + 3 \times 6 = 32$$

Hence, our function, which will be doing the calculations, will accept two arguments of the `List` type and will return a single number. Let's define it.

In the next example, you can see the definition of our function. Please note that it lacks the body implementation – don't worry, we will take care of this shortly:

```
function multiplyVectors(
    vector1: List<Float64>,
    vector2: List<Float64>
): Float64 {
}
```

As you can see, we have a function called `multiplyVectors` that accepts two arguments of the `List<Float64>` type and returns a `Float64` value. Now, let's implement it.

As described previously, we need to multiply numbers at the same positions and summarize them. So, we need to actually iterate over the vectors and perform these operations. In JavaScript, we could simply use a single `for` loop like this:

```
function multiplyVectorsJS(vector1, vector2) {
    let result = 0;
    for (let i = 0; i < vector1.length; i++) {
        result += vector1[i] * vector2[i];
    }
    return result;
}
```

In Bosque, we don't have any structured loops, so we need to take a different, more functional approach. We could achieve the same result as follows, for example:

```
function multiplyVectors(
    vector1: List<Float64>,
    vector2: List<Float64>
): Float64 {
    return Float64::sum(
        vector1.mapIndex<Float64>(
            fn(el, i) => Float64::product(
                List<Float64>@{ el, vector2.get(i) }
            )
```

```
        )
    );
}
```

As you can see, we are using the `.mapIndex<U>()` method available in the `List` concept, and we wrap it in `Float64::sum()`. This way, we are iterating over the vectors multiplying the elements and summarizing all of them at the end. Note that in order to get the product of two `Float64` numbers in Bosque, we need to use the `Float64::product()` method, which accepts a `List` of numbers. Let's now see the full example showing how we can use our function to multiply two vectors:

```
namespace NSMain;
function multiplyVectors(
        vector1: List<Float64>,
        vector2: List<Float64>
): Float64 {
  return Float64::sum(
          vector1.mapIndex<Float64>(
                fn(el, i) => Float64::product(
                    List<Float64>@{ el, vector2.get(i) }
                )
            )
    );
}
entrypoint function main(): Float64 {
        let va = List<Float64>@{ 2.0f, 4.0f, 7.0f, 12.0f };
        let vb = List<Float64>@{ 8.0f, 4.0f, 32.0f, 6.0f };
        return multiplyVectors(va, vb);
}
```

Try to compile and run this program with the same and changed vector elements and see what result it returns. After running this example in the untouched form, the result will be as follows:

```
328.000000
```

Please keep in mind that both vectors must have the same length. Our function should make sure that they do, but we did not implement that. This can be achieved using the `requires release` precondition, which has already been mentioned in *Chapter 3, Bosque Key Features*, and which will be discussed in more detail in *Chapter 13, Testing in Bosque*.

Now, let's see another example of iterative processing without using any loop structure.

Grouping list elements by key

Grouping is a very popular problem that we may encounter in any real-world application. Imagine the following scenario: you are building some kind of car market application. In one of the views, you need to show all cars manufactured in a particular year that are available for sale grouped by the make of car.

So, on the backend side of your application, you are grabbing all of the cars from the database and, as a result, you are getting a list of Car entities:

```
let cars = List<Car>@{
    Car@{ "Audi", 2001 }, Car@{ "Ford", 2002 }, Car@{
    "Ford", 2002 },
    Car@{ "Ford", 2004 }, Car@{ "Audi", 2003 }, Car@{
    "BMW", 2020 }
};
```

The Car entity is very simple, and looks like this:

```
entity Car {
    field name: String;
    field year: Int;
}
```

This structure requires some processing on the frontend side in order to be easily displayed according to requirements. Ideally, we would like to send the data formatted as follows:

```
let result = Map<String, List<Int>>@{
    "Audi" => List<Int>@{ 2001, 2003 },
    "Ford" => List<Int>@{ 2002, 2002, 2004 },
    "BMW" => List<Int>@{ 2020 }
};
```

So, as you can see, this is much easier to display in a readable form on the frontend side. We have a map where the keys are car brands, and the values are years of manufacturing. Notice that for `"Ford"`, the `2002` year occurs twice – this is fine, it just means that there are two cars from that year available for sale (plus the third one from another year).

Such problems require some kind of iteration to perform the grouping operation. How can we solve this problem using Bosque? The answer is quite obvious at this point: Let's use some of the built-in methods!

In the `List` concept, there are two methods that are going to be crucial here: `.joinGroup<U>()` and `.transformToMap<K, V>()`.

> **Important note**
>
> As of the time of writing, the `.transformToMap<K, V>()` method is not yet fully implemented and therefore throws unexpected errors.

Having said that, let's understand what these methods do before we use them:

- The `.joinGroup<U>()` method is used to perform two operations at once – joining with grouping. It accepts one type parameter, `U`, which tells Bosque what type of elements the second list has. It also accepts two arguments. The first one is the second list we want to join with the original one. The second one is a `PCode` function that is called for every pair of elements from both lists and returns a Boolean value depending on whether the element from the second list should be added as a group element to the current element from the original list or not. The `.joinGroup<U>()` method returns `List<[T, List<U>]>`, which represents a list of tuples where the first element is a "key" from the first list and, at the second position, there is a list of group elements from the joined list. In our case, this will allow us to group cars by their names.

- The `.transformToMap<K, V>()` function, as the name suggests, is used to transform the current list into a map. The type parameters indicate what the key and value types are going to be. It accepts two `PCode` function arguments. Both of them accept a single argument – the current element of the list – and are called for each of them. The first one is supposed to return a key for the current element, while the second one is used to return a value for the given key. In our case, it will help us to transform the result of the previous method into an actual map.

So, the general idea of how are we going to solve our problem is to separate the car brand names from the manufacturing years, group them using the `.joinGroup<U>()` method, and finally transform the partial result into a complete result using the `.transformToMap<K, V>()` method.

> **Important note**
>
> The program presented in the next example is not going to use the
> `.transformToMap<K, V>()` method because, as of the time of writing,
> it is not fully implemented yet and causes unexpected errors. That's why we
> need to work around this problem slightly. However, there is an alternative
> approach presented later in this section that demonstrates how to use this
> method once it gets fixed.

As mentioned, we need to work around the original problem so that it can be solved
without the unimplemented method. For that, we will require another entity called
CarGroup, which is going to be a special grouping entity:

```
entity CarGroup {
        field name: String;
        field years: List<Int>;
}
```

It consists of a car brand name and a list of manufacturing years. The result we are hoping
to get now should look like this:

```
let result = List<CarGroup>@{
    CarGroup@{ "Audi", List<Int>@{ 2001, 2003 } },
    CarGroup@{ "Ford", List<Int>@{ 2002, 2002, 2004 } },
    CarGroup@{ "BMW", List<Int>@{ 2020 } }
};
```

So, as you can see, we want to have a list of entities consisting of grouped elements – quite
similar to the list of tuples returned from the `.joinGroup<U>()` method.

Now, let's define a function called groupCars that accepts a cars list as an argument.
The return type is going to be the list of CarGroup elements presented earlier. The
function solves the grouping problem by separating the car brand names from the
manufacturing years, groups them, and then finally removes the duplicates and maps
them to the CarGroup entities:

```
function groupCars(cars: List<Car>): List<CarGroup> {
        let names = cars.map<String>(fn(c) => c.name); /* 1. */
        let years = cars.map<Int>(fn(c) => c.year); /* 2. */

        let joined = names.joinGroup<Int>( /* 3. */
                years,
```

```
        fn(name, year) => cars.anyOf(
            fn(c) => c.name == name && c.year == year
        )
    );
    let result = names.unique().map<CarGroup>( /* 4. */
        fn(n) => {
            [let name, let years] = joined.find(fn(t) => n
                == t.0);
            return CarGroup@{ name, years };
        }
    );

    return result;
}
```

Let's break this code down line by line.

Understanding the code

The first two lines, marked in the highlighted comments as **1** and **2**, are responsible for separating the cars list into two – names (car brands) and years (manufacturing years).

Then, these two lists are used with the .joinGroup<Int>() method, marked as **3**. The PCode function returns a Boolean, true, if there is a car with the current name and year – in such an instance, the year is going to be added under the current name "key." The result of this line looks like the following:

```
{ ["Audi", {2001, 2003}], ["Ford", {2002, 2002, 2004}], ["Ford",
{2002, 2002, 2004}], ["Ford", {2002, 2002, 2004}], ["Audi",
{2001, 2003}], ["BMW", {2020}] }
```

So, as you can see, we have a list of tuples containing the car brand name with a list of manufacturing years. Notice that the tuples are duplicated here. This is because, in our input list, there are Car entities with the same name and the PCode function in the line marked as **3** checks whether there is *any* element matching the criteria. This is why we need to use the last method, which will ignore duplicates and create a readable map.

The last line, marked as **4**, takes only unique brand names from the names list and maps them from just a brand name into the CarGroup entity. It is not the best approach because, for each element, the .map<CarGroup>() method is called and, in each of the calls, we are calling .find(), which looks for the element in the whole joined list, which may reduce performance. However, this is a working example of how we can perform iterative processing using the tools offered by Bosque. The result of this operation is the desired result of our program:

```
{
    NSMain::CarGroup{ "Audi", {2001, 2003} },
    NSMain::CarGroup{ "Ford", {2002, 2002, 2004} },
    NSMain::CarGroup{ "BMW", {2020} }
}
```

The full code of our program looks like this:

```
namespace NSMain;
entity Car {
    field name: String;
    field year: Int;
}
entity CarGroup {
    field name: String;
    field years: List<Int>;
}

function groupCars(cars: List<Car>): List<CarGroup> {
    let names = cars.map<String>(fn(c) => c.name); /* 1. */
    let years = cars.map<Int>(fn(c) => c.year); /* 2. */

    let joined = names.joinGroup<Int>( /* 3. */
        years,
        fn(name, year) => cars.anyOf(
            fn(c) => c.name == name && c.year == year
        )
    );
    let result = names.unique().map<CarGroup>( /* 4. */
        fn(n) => {
```

```
                [let name, let years] = joined.find(fn(t) => n
                == t.0);
                return CarGroup@{ name, years };
        }
    );


    return result;
}
entrypoint function main(): Map<String, List<Int>> {
    let cars = List<Car>@{
        Car@{ "Audi", 2001 }, Car@{ "Ford", 2002 },
        Car@{ "Ford", 2002 }, Car@{ "Ford", 2004 },
        Car@{ "Audi", 2003 }, Car@{ "BMW", 2020 }
    };
    return groupCars(cars);
}
```

As mentioned earlier, this code is a workaround that was necessary due to a lack of the full
`List` implementation. The next section introduces a solution to the same problem that
will use the `.transformToMap<K, V>()` method, **but it won't run until the missing
feature gets implemented.** Let's have a look at the code.

Using an alternative solution

Since the `.transformToMap<K, V>()` method is not yet fully implemented,
our program will not compile correctly. But if you are curious about how it could be
implemented if the method worked, this is the right place to look. Here, we won't require
the `CarGroup` entity any longer, as now we will return a map with keys being car brand
names and values being a list of manufacturing years.

In order to transform the previous solution, you need to delete the `CarGroup` entity.

Let's recall the result we are hoping to get now. It should look like this:

```
let result = Map<String, List<Int>>@{
    "Audi" => List<Int>@{ 2001, 2003 },
    "Ford" => List<Int>@{ 2002, 2002, 2004 },
    "BMW" => List<Int>@{ 2020 }
};
```

So, it's a very convenient map of car brand names and their manufacturing years.

Now, we need to change the previous approach to grouping. The algorithm will be quite similar because we still want to separate the brand names from manufacturing years and still want to group them using the `.joinGroup<U>()` method. However, the final step will be completely different and much more effective as we will use the `.transformToMap<K, V>()` method, which won't call more iterations internally as we did in the previous approach. The new version of the `groupCars` function is presented in the next example:

```
function groupCars(cars: List<Car>): Map<String, List<Int>> {
  let names = cars.map<String>(fn(c) => c.name); /* 1 */
  let years = cars.map<Int>(fn(c) => c.year); /* 2 */

  let joined = names.joinGroup<Int>( /* 3 */
    years,
    fn(name, year) => cars.anyOf(
      fn(c) => c.name == name && c.year == year
    )
  );
  let result = joined.transformToMap<String, List<Int>>( /*4*/
    fn(entry) => entry.0,
    fn(entry) => entry.1
  );

  return result;
}
```

The only thing that has changed is the highlighted line marked as **4** and the return type. Now, we are calling the `.transformToMap<String, List<Int>>()` method on the `joined` list, which produces the desired result. The first PCode function passed as an argument extracts the key from the current tuple, which lays on the position 0. The second one takes the second element of a current tuple and returns it as a value for the given key. The result of this operation is the desired result of our program:

```
{"Audi" => {2001, 2003}, "BMW" => {2020}, "Ford" => {2002,
2002, 2004}}
```

Up to this point, you have learned how to deal with problems requiring iteration in Bosque using available methods. Now, it's time to take a closer look at the `NSIterate` namespace, which provides us with a few useful functions that are used to perform iteration in a more universal way.

Discovering the NSIterate namespace and its helper functions

Except for a number of methods available in Bosque core collections, there is one more way in which to do iteration in Bosque. We can make use of the `NSIterate` namespace and its functions. While I'm writing this, there are four functions in this namespace that we will discuss here:

- `while<S>()`
- `until<S>()`
- `steps<S>()`
- `reduce<T>()`

We will now cover these briefly one by one. Let's start with the last one mentioned – the `reduce<T>()` function.

The reduce<T>() function

In functional programming, reducing is an operation that processes a data collection in order to produce a result using some kind of a function that combines the collection elements. So, in other words, reducing means transforming the whole collection of data into one end result. The `reduce<T>()` function in Bosque is used exactly for that. It's parametrized by a type, `T`, and accepts a number of arguments in order to produce a valid result. The type parameter, `T`, tells Bosque what type of result is going to be produced as well as what type of elements are stored in the collection. **This means that in Bosque, using the reduce operation means creating a result of the same type as the type of collection elements.** This is important to keep in mind, as sometimes we may wish to reduce a collection into some different type of value. It's hard to imagine every possible case, but if you'll need to produce a value of another type, you would probably need to use a map operation first to transform your collection to a different type. Then, the reduce operation could be applied to produce a single value.

As for the arguments, the first one is an initial value of type T for the whole operation. This is used both for the first iteration step and is returned if the collection is empty. The second argument is List<T> of elements – this is the collection that we are reducing. The third argument is a PCode function that combines the collection elements. This PCode function is called for each element of the list and, on each call, there are two arguments provided – the accumulated value and the current element. Let's look at an example in order to better grasp the idea of this function.

Imagine that you are developing a fantasy game. In your game, you can play (among others) as a mage. In order to improve the character's statistics, you can use potions. A potion can increase your health points, speed, and magic level by various amounts of points. You wish to improve the UI of your game and introduce a new feature – stacking the potions inside a player's inventory. This means that if the player has multiple potions, they can put them all on the same slot, which will save some space in the inventory. The player can take one potion at a time or all of them at once; in such a case, you want to show a summary of all the potions' effects so that the player can see immediately how much their stats are going to improve after taking all of the potions at once. This is where reduce<T>() can be very useful.

In your game, we can represent a potion as a new type called Potion:

```
typedef Potion = {hp: Float64, speed: Float64, magic: Float64};
```

It has three fields – hp, speed, and magic – of the Float64 type. As mentioned in *Chapter 5, Types and Operators*, the Float64 type is used to represent floating-point numbers in Bosque, as opposed to Int, which represents only integer values.

The stack of potions can be represented as List<Potion> like this:

```
let potions = List<Potion>@{
    { hp = 1.2f, speed = 2.0f, magic = 9.2f },
    { hp = 4.3f, speed = 2.1f, magic = 13.4f },
    { hp = 10.5f, speed = 1.2f, magic = 0.8f }
};
```

So, as you can see, we have three potions with various amounts of points for each statistic. Please note the syntax for floating-point number literals. If you use the Float64 type, you need to add the decimal part of a number followed by the letter f. Even if the number does not have a decimal part, it should be specified as 0, for example, 9.0f.

Now, in order to show a summary of all of the potions, we can create a new
`Potion` object that has all of the stats summed up. We can achieve this by using the
`reduce<Potion>()` function as follows:

```
let summary = NSIterate::reduce<Potion>(
    { hp = 0.0f, speed = 0.0f, magic = 0.0f },
    potions,
    fn(acc, curr) => ({
        hp = acc.hp + curr.hp,
        speed = acc.speed + curr.speed,
        magic = acc.magic + curr.magic
    })
);
```

Here, we are calling the `reduce` function using namespace-scoped invocation. If you
don't remember this topic, please refer to the *Scoped access and invocations* section in
Chapter 8, *Expressions in Bosque*. We are providing `Potion` as a type parameter and then
a list of parameters. The initial value is just an empty potion with every value zeroed.
In the `PCode` function, we are returning a new record (matching the `Potion` type
definition), with each stat being summed with the accumulated value and the current
potion value. By way of a result, we end up with a new potion that looks like this:

```
{hp=16.000000, magic=23.400000, speed=5.300000}
```

Now you can display these values to the player so that they know how much HP, magic,
and speed their character will gain after drinking the entire stack of potions at once.

Let's now have a look at the `steps<S>()` function.

The steps<S>() function

This function is very much similar to a classic structured `for` loop. It's used to iterate an
arbitrary number of times, changing a state each time. Of course, the number of iterations
doesn't have to be hardcoded – you can specify this by providing the size of a list that you
want to iterate over, for example, using the `.size()` method. The mentioned state is just
a value that we want to modify in each iteration. At the end, the modified state is going to
be returned.

Similar to the previous function, the `steps<S>()` function is parameterized by the type S, which indicates the data type of the state. It could be anything – a simple number of the `Int` type or a custom complex data type. The second parameter is the number of steps to perform. This is an integer value denoting how many times the third argument will be called. And the third argument is a `PCode` function that takes the current state as an argument and returns a new, modified state on every iteration. Let's now have a look at a quick example of how we can utilize this function.

Imagine you are writing a chat app. You are queueing the messages to be sent in order to maintain a better performance. The messages queue is stored in an application context. Now, we want to send a message for each of the messages from the queue. The `steps<S>()` function is a perfect bet here.

Let's define our app context:

```
entity Context {
    field currentMessage: Int = 0;
    field messages: List<String> = List<String>@{ "Hey",
    "Hi", "Hello" };
}
```

So, as you can see, we have three messages in our queue, which is `List<String>` for the sake of this example. Now we need to create a function called `sendMessage()`, which will grab the data from the context and simulate sending a message while updating the `currentMessage` value. Here is what this function could look like:

```
function sendMessage(ctx: Context): Context {
    let { currentMessage = curr } = ctx.{ currentMessage };
    let msg = ctx.messages.get(curr);
    _debug(msg); // simulate sending a message
    return ctx.update(currentMessage = curr + 1);
}
```

This function takes the context as an argument and returns a new context that is modified – the `currentMessage` value is incremented on each call.

The final missing part is the iteration itself. Let's utilize the `steps<S>()` function in order to send all of the messages stored in the context:

```
var context = Context@{};
context = NSIterate::steps<Context>(
    context,
    context.messages.size(),
    fn(ctx) => sendMessage(ctx)
);
```

Here, we are creating a `Context` instance and run the `steps` function parameterized with the `Context` type. The initial state is our context, with `currentMessage` set to 0. The second argument is just the size of the messages list – we want to iterate over all of them. The `PCode` function calls our `sendMessage` function with the current context state and returns a new state since the `sendMessage` function updates and returns it. So, as the result, Bosque will iterate three times and call our function for every message that needs to be sent. Here is the full code of this example:

```
namespace NSMain;

entity Context {
    field currentMessage: Int = 0;
    field messages: List<String> = List<String>@{ "Hey",
      "Hi", "Hello" };
}

function sendMessage(ctx: Context): Context {
    let { currentMessage = curr } = ctx.{ currentMessage };
    let msg = ctx.messages.get(curr);
    _debug(msg); // simulate sending a message
    return ctx.update(currentMessage = curr + 1);
}

entrypoint function main(): Int {
    var context = Context@{};
    context = NSIterate::steps<Context>(
        context,
        context.messages.size(),
```

```
            fn(ctx) => sendMessage(ctx)
    );
    return 0;
}
```

After running this program, you should see something like this:

```
"Hey"
"Hi"
"Hello"
0
```

This will mean that it works correctly and that you managed to successfully perform iteration in Bosque. In case you are wondering what the 0 is at the end of the output, this is because our main function must return something and since, in this example, we don't have anything interesting to be returned, it just returns 0.

It's now time to learn about the last two functions available in the NSIterate namespace.

The until<S>() and while<S>() functions

These final two functions are very similar to each other and they are both quite similar to the well-known while loop. At the same time, they are pretty similar to the steps<S>() function, which we just discussed.

> **Important note**
>
> As of the time of writing, the until<S>() and while<S>() functions are not yet implemented. If you try to compile a program that uses them, you will see a similar error:
>
> ```
> Error -- AssertionError [ERR_ASSERTION]: Need to
> implement -- NSIterate::while
> ```
>
> Please be careful when playing with them.

Let's briefly discuss these two functions. The first one – `until<S>()` – logically works pretty much the same as the standard `while` loop. The difference is that it will stop once the condition becomes true, as opposed to the `while` loop, which will break once the condition is false. On the other hand, the `while<S>()` function from the `NSIterate` namespace behaves exactly the same as the standard `while` loop – as long as the condition is true, it will continue operating. As soon as the condition becomes false, the iteration stops.

Both of the functions have the same signature. They are parameterized by the type `S`, which denotes the data type of state that we want to change iteratively. The first argument is the initial state itself. At every iteration, it is going to be changed and replaced by the result of the second argument. The second argument – `step` – is a `PCode` function that will be called at every iteration step with the current state as a parameter. In each step, we need to return a result of type `S` declared as a parameter. The last argument is also a `PCode` function that accepts a single parameter – current state – and returns a Boolean value. This function acts as a condition that is checked prior to each iteration. Depending on the function and the return value, the iteration will continue or stop. They both return the state changed after all iterations. Let's see two analogous examples to see them in action.

Let's implement an algorithm that prints every number of the Collatz conjecture, starting from *n*. In case you don't know what this is, suffice to say that it's a conjecture that generates a sequence of numbers following two rules, starting from any positive integer:

1. If the previous number is even, the next one is one half of the previous term.

2. If the previous number is odd, the next one is three times the previous one plus 1.

The sequence ends when the conjecture reaches 1.

This problem can be easily solved using both the `until<S>()` and `while<S>()` functions. Let's now look at them doing the same thing in order to see the difference. This is how we could use `until<S>()` to achieve it:

```
entrypoint function main(n: Int): Int {
    return NSIterate::until<Int>(
        n,
        fn(c) => {
            _debug(c);
            return if (Int::mod(c, 2) == 0) c / 2 else 3 *
            c + 1;
        },
```

```
        fn(c) => c == 1
    );
}
```

So, as you can see, we are printing the current number in sequence and returning a new one on each step until the c == 1 condition is true. Once that is true, the iteration will stop.

We can do the same thing using the while<S>() function like this:

```
entrypoint function main(n: Int): Int {
    return NSIterate::while<Int>(
        n,
        fn(c) => {
            _debug(c);
            return if (Int::mod(c, 2) == 0) c / 2 else 3 *
                c + 1;
        },
        fn(c) => c != 1
    );
}
```

Here, we are doing exactly the same thing as previously, but the condition has changed. As long as c != 1 is true, the iteration will continue to operate.

And this is all that needs to be said regarding the NSIterate namespace. Without doubt, it is a very convenient thing as it provides ways to perform iteration in a more universal manner. These four functions cover the majority of things that developers would want to do in terms of iterative processing. Basically, if you can't do something with the built-in methods provided that are available in Bosque collections, you should be able to achieve it using one of these four methods. Of course, you can't forget about certain limitations, such as the lack of continue or break statements. Another limitation is the restriction on reducing that allows you to reduce only to the same type of data as the collection elements. This is something that you simply need to get used to and find a way to work around. Nonetheless, most of the time, you won't need to complicate things and I believe that once Bosque is developed further, fewer tricks and workarounds will be required.

Having said that, let's now take a brief look at recursion in Bosque.

Recursion and the recursive keyword

As mentioned in the *Recursion* section in *Chapter 3, Bosque Key Features*, there is not much difference between Bosque and other popular programming languages when it comes to recursive processing. The only thing that is different is the `recursive` keyword. In the aforementioned chapter, we learned that in order to declare and call a recursive function, we need to decorate it with the `recursive` keyword. Without doubt, this practice helps a lot as we can just take a quick look at the code and tell immediately whether a function is recursive just by looking at the way it is called. However, we can declare a recursive function without using this keyword and it will work just fine. Have a look at this example:

```
function power(base: Float64, exp: Int): Float64 {
    return if (exp == 0) 1.0f
        else if (exp < 0) 1.0f / power(base, 0 - exp)
        else Float64::product(
            List<Float64>@{ base, power(base, exp - 1) }
        );
}
```

Here, we are declaring a function that calculates the `base` to the power of `exp`. It is recursive, but we did not use the `recursive` keyword. The full example would look like this:

```
namespace NSMain;

function power(base: Float64, exp: Int): Float64 {
    return if (exp == 0) 1.0f
        else if (exp < 0) 1.0f / power(base, 0 - exp)
        else Float64::product(
            List<Float64>@{ base, power(base, exp - 1) }
        );
}

entrypoint function main(): Int {
    return power(2.0f, 3);
}
```

And the result will be `8.000000`. Or we can call `power(4.0f, -1);`, for example, which will return `0.250000` as the result. The disadvantage is that we lose the ease of determining whether this function is recursive or iterative.

It is important to remember that as long as you don't provide the `recursive` keyword, you don't need to use it. But if you declare a function with it, you must use it at the call, otherwise Bosque will throw an error.

That sums up the concept of iterative processing and recursion in Bosque. Let's now recap what you've learned so far.

Summary

In this chapter, you learned a lot about iterative processing and acquired additional knowledge of recursion. Now you are fully aware of the motivation that stands behind the no-loops concept and what the Bosque approach is to solving problems that require iteration.

First, you covered a bit of theory regarding loops and the research that Bosque creators did before they decided to get rid of structured loops entirely. You learned about loop patterns that developers follow and how they can be replaced by built-in collection methods.

Then, you covered the practical side of iterative processing without using structured loops. You wrote a lot of practical programs that require some kind of iteration using core collection methods. You also saw how you can work around problems that can't yet be solved in Bosque in the easiest manner possible.

Reading further, you discovered the `NSIterate` namespace and its useful functions that help us perform iteration in a more universal way. Now you know that this may be a very convenient replacement for collection built-in methods in certain scenarios.

Last but not least, you acquired some additional information regarding recursion. You realized that you don't actually need to use the `recursive` keyword when declaring recursive functions, but nonetheless it does help in identifying such calls.

Alright, I must admit that if you survived up to this point, it means that you learned a ton of things about Bosque and you are ready to create an actual project. One of the main goals of the Bosque project was to create a language that is easy to reason about, both for humans and machines. So, if Bosque was partially created for AI-based tools, why don't we create an AI project in order to keep Bosque close to ML? Let's not waste any time and jump right into this in the next chapter.

Questions

1. Does Bosque support iterative processing? How?

2. What are loop idioms?

3. What is the `NSIterate` namespace?

4. Do you need to use the `recursive` keyword when declaring a recursive function?

Further reading

Here is a research paper that helped Mark Marron identify the aforementioned loop idioms and replace them with ready-to-use collection methods:

- M. Allamanis, E. T. Barr, C. Bird, P. Devanbu, M. Marron, and C. Sutton, *Mining Semantic Loop Idioms*: `https://web.cs.ucdavis.edu/~devanbu/tse-coils-paper.pdf`.

11
Project: AI Classifier

One of Bosque's main goals was to support easy reasoning for machines. Its IR language is designed in such a way that facilitates in-depth automated code analysis and therefore creates a space for inventing new, next-level development tools or compilers. When we read about this, presumably one of the first thoughts that comes to mind is that Bosque will be used or analyzed by some kind of AI-powered systems. So, if Bosque is designed to be – in some way – close to the AI world, I think it's a good idea to try it in a project that employs machine learning.

In this chapter, we will utilize the features that we have learned so far and build a simple AI project. The idea is to create a basic classifier that predicts an output based on two input values. In this example, we will try to train our model so that it will be able to tell which quadrant of the Cartesian coordinate system a point belongs to just by looking at the X and Y coordinates.

Here is a list of topics that we are going to cover in this chapter:

- Defining project requirements
- Implementing the intelligent model
- Testing the program
- Improving the code
- Enhancing ideas and suggestions

After this chapter, you will know how Bosque can be applied in simple AI solutions.

Technical requirements

The contents of this chapter will be easier to understand if you have knowledge of the following topics:

- Core collections that are available in Bosque and their methods that do iterative work

- Expressions in Bosque

- Iterative processing using built-in methods and the `NSIterate` namespace

You can also get acquainted with the examples shared on GitHub here: `https://github.com/PacktPublishing/Learn-Bosque-Programming/tree/main/Chapter11`.

Defining project requirements

As mentioned earlier, the goal of this chapter is to create an intelligent program that will be able to tell which quadrant of the Cartesian coordinate system a point belongs to, based on its X and Y coordinates. In case you don't know what the Cartesian Coordinates System looks like, take a look at the following diagram:

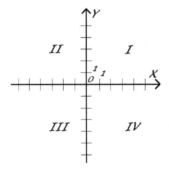

Figure 11.1 – Cartesian Coordinates System along with quadrant numbers

So, as you can see, it consists of two axes – X and Y – that meet at a single point called the origin. We distinguish four quadrants, numbered I to IV in counterclockwise order, starting from the top-right quadrant. On the Cartesian Coordinates System, we can mark points. A point has two coordinates – numbers corresponding to the two axes – that are called the X- and Y-coordinates.

For example, we can define a point, A(2, 4). Its *X*-coordinate is equal to 2, while the *Y*-coordinate is equal to 4. This point is placed in quadrant I. Another point, for instance, B(-2, -5) will belong to quadrant III.

The goal of our project is to create a program that will learn that rule by looking at examples and, as a result, will be able to correctly guess in which quadrant a point is placed based on its coordinates.

At this point, you may be thinking that the problem we are trying to solve is straightforward and that the entire program simply requires one if statement, and that's all, as follows, for example:

```
namespace NSMain;
entrypoint function main(x: Int, y: Int): String {
    return if (x > 0 && y > 0) "Quadrant 1"
          elif (x < 0 && y > 0) "Quadrant 2"
          elif (x < 0 && y < 0) "Quadrant 3"
          else "Quadrant 4";
}
```

Well, you're right. The problem could be solved like this but … this is boring! Let's have some fun and create a program that will actually learn the rule that we just described and will use that knowledge for predictions. Moreover, our program will be universal enough to be used not only in this particular (and rather simple) case, but in many more scenarios. Basically, it will be able to solve almost any task that requires distinguishing between objects based on two features.

Alright, now that we have a goal, it is time to define the actual requirements. Our end result should consist of two programs. The first one should be used to train and test our intelligent model and return trained values (we'll talk about these in the next section). The second one should accept those learned values as parameters plus two coordinates – *X* and *Y* – and return a string that will indicate which quadrant the point with these coordinates belongs to.

The reason we need two programs instead of one is that we don't want to train and test our model every time we want it to predict a quadrant. Instead, we want it to be trained once and then use the trained parameters for predictions. And that can be achieved by splitting the logic into two programs; the second one will take as parameters the values returned from the first one and make use of them. I think this approach makes much more sense than forcing the training over and over again.

Now that we know what we would like to achieve, let's focus on *how* we are going to do that.

Understanding the approach

In order to better understand what we are going to build, we need to learn a little bit about neural networks – how they work and what are they built of. We will not dive deep into the details of how some big neural networks work internally as this is beyond the scope of this book. We will only cover topics that are essential for understanding the approach in our particular case.

Brief introduction to neural networks

For many people, AI seems to be an exciting new technology. However, the truth is that it was invented decades ago (the whole subject of deep learning dates back to the 1940s) and it simply became more popular in the 21st century. The reason is that today, unlike in the past, we have very powerful computers and zillions of gigabytes of data that can be fed into the neural nets in order to train them properly. This is why this concept has become so popular in the last decade or two.

Neural networks are mathematical structures that are designed to perform calculations by using a collection of nodes called neurons. An artificial neuron is an elementary unit of a neural network. Basically, it's a mathematical function that receives input and produces output. The artificial neuron usually has multiple input values (input vectors) that are weighted (weight vectors). The input and weight vectors are multiplied and passed through a non-linear function known as an activation function. Each neuron produces a single output value that can be passed as an input to another neuron – that's how neural networks are built. In order to better understand this, have a look at the following diagram, which shows a single artificial neuron:

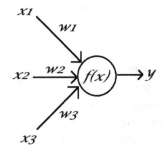

Figure 11.2 – Artificial neuron

If we connect multiple neurons with one another, we will create an artificial neural network. However, I won't dive deep into the details of such complicated structures as we will not be building a big neural network to solve our problem. In fact, we will need two perceptrons.

A perceptron is a special kind of a neuron whose activation function is a step function. One such function is a threshold function. This is a very simple function that returns only two results. If the function argument is greater than zero, it returns 1, otherwise, it returns 0.

This characteristic of a perceptron makes it a good choice for classification problems. Classification is the process of choosing an object class based on its features. The set of classes is known prior to the learning. In our case, these classes are the quadrants of the Cartesian Coordinates System. Each perceptron can produce two outputs. This means that we can recognize two quadrants using a single perceptron. Since we have four quadrants (classes), we need two perceptrons that will assign one of the four classes to any object (a point).

Alright, you now know what neurons are and how neural networks are built. But how do they learn to solve various problems? Let's shed some light on this.

Remember when I said that before a neuron produces an output, the inputs vector is multiplied by the weights vector? This is a crucial thing to keep in mind. The whole learning idea is all about changing the weight of each input. This is how neural networks learn. Initially, we provide random values for all the weights and then the example flow usually looks like the following:

1. We provide an input to a neural network.
2. The inputs vector is multiplied by the weights vector and the network produces an output.
3. We compare the output of the network with the expected output.
4. We calculate an error and update weights in the network based on that error.

This process is repeated over and over again until the calculated error value gets small enough that we accept this. At this point, we say that the network is trained.

There are many ways to calculate the error rate based on which we update the weights. In more advanced nets, the procedure is quite complicated. However, in our example, we are using only two perceptrons, and therefore the algorithm is very simple. We will update the weights using this equation:

$$w_i' = w_i + \alpha(y' - y)x_i$$

We can read it as follows: the new weight value is equal to the old value plus a difference between the expected and actual output multiplied by the input value and the learning rate, *alpha*. The learning rate is a constant value that denotes how aggressively the weights will be updated. It shouldn't be too big as the weights might be changed too much every time. It also shouldn't be too low as the learning process may take a very long time. The difference between the expected and actual output is important as it will increase the weight value if the actual output is smaller than expected, and decrease the weight value otherwise.

Now that you know a bit of theory, let's think about our particular case and create a model that will suit our requirements.

Designing a model

Alright, after this very quick introduction to neural networks, we are ready to put the theory into practice. Our task is a simple classification problem. We want to assign every point to one of four classes (quadrants). As mentioned earlier, in order to recognize four classes, we need two perceptrons. Each of these two perceptrons will produce only one of the two possible outputs – 1 or 0, which maps to a certain class. If the output is 1, we can say that the given perceptron has activated. In order to better understand the idea behind our solution, let's break this down into two simpler problems:

- The first problem is to recognize, based on point coordinates, to which half of the Cartesian Coordinates System it belongs – either the upper half or the lower half. We have only two classes here – upper and lower, so we need only one perceptron for that. We could prepare the training dataset in such a way that, after training, the perceptron would activate (in other words, return 1) if the point belongs to the upper half, and wouldn't activate (in other words, return 0) otherwise. We could map the returned value to one of our classes and, based on that, our intelligent program would be capable of recognizing the upper and lower halves of the coordinates system.

- The second problem is very similar to the first one, with the only difference being that we want to recognize the right and left half of the coordinates system. This time, we would prepare the training set so that the perceptron would activate if a given point belongs to the right half, and wouldn't activate otherwise. Again, based on the returned value, we could map it to one of our classes and our second intelligent program would be able to recognize the right and left halves of the Cartesian system.

At this point, the solution to our original problem seems quite simple, doesn't it? All we need to do is to combine these two solutions and create a program that makes use of two perceptrons and, based on the returned values from each of them, map the result to one of our four classes. As shown in *Figure 11.1*, the top-right quadrant is marked I, the top-left one is marked II, the bottom-left one is marked III, and the bottom-right quadrant is marked IV. We can make use of our two perceptrons to predict the quadrant. Let's name them. The first one, which recognizes the upper and lower halves, will be called **P1**, and the other one **P2**. Now, let's go through an example to see how we can predict a quadrant based on the results of P1 and P2.

Given the point A(12, -4), we must tell which quadrant it belongs to. Firstly, we provide its coordinates to P1. For P1, only the Y-coordinate is important and, based on that, it does not activate, meaning that the point A belongs to the lower half of the Cartesian system. Then, we provide the same coordinates to P2. For P2, only the X-coordinate is important and, based on that, it does activate, meaning that point A belongs to the right half. So, point A belongs to the lower half according to P1, and to the right half according to P2. This implies that point A is placed in the bottom-right quadrant of the Cartesian system, quadrant IV, which is true. And this is the algorithm that we are going to use in our project! To better understand it, have a look at the next table:

	P1	P2
Activated (1)	Upper	Right
Not activated (0)	Lower	Left

Table 11.1 – Visualization of P1 and P2 results

So, as you can see, there are precisely four possible outcomes that directly imply the quadrant of the Cartesian Coordinates System that any point belongs to. Basically, this is how we are going to implement our solution. We will create two perceptrons that will work as presented in the following diagram:

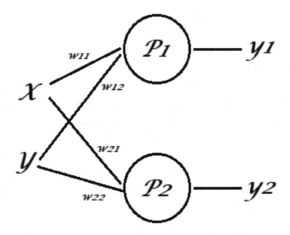

Figure 11.3 – Simple intelligent model consisting of two perceptrons

As you can see, our model will have two inputs and two outputs – one for each neuron. Based on these two results, we will determine the quadrant of a given point. If both neurons were to activate, this means the first quadrant; if only the first one were to activate, this means the second one; if none of them were to activate, this means the third; and if only the second neuron were to activate, this means it's the fourth quadrant.

At this point, you have the necessary theoretical background relating to neural networks and you know precisely how we are going to implement our solution. You are now ready to get your hands dirty and finally start coding in Bosque. Let's do it!

Implementing the intelligent model

The implementation of this project will basically require all the knowledge from the previous chapters. We will make use of custom types, entities, functions, collections, iterations, and multiple entrypoint functions. If you have not covered these topics yet, I strongly suggest you take a step back and learn the required concepts first. However, if you are familiar with them, it is finally time to utilize all the learned concepts. Having said that, let's not waste more time and write some code.

Creating the basic functionality

First things first, let's define an entity called `Perceptron`, which will represent our perceptrons:

```
entity Perceptron {
    field weights: List<Float64>;
    field alpha: Float64 = 1.0f;
}
```

Every perceptron is going to have the weights vector (represented by `List<Float64>`) and the learning rate alpha equal to 1.0. The alpha value has been picked arbitrarily and works the best in our particular case.

Another thing we need is the activation function. As mentioned in the previous section, in perceptrons, we use the threshold function, which returns only two results – 1.0 and 0.0, depending on whether the argument is greater than zero. The definition may look like this:

```
function activation(s: Float64): Float64 {
    return if (Float64::compare(s, 0.0f) == 1) 1.0f else 0.0f;
}
```

Please note that in order to compare floating-point numbers in Bosque, you need to use the `Float64::compare` method. This returns three possible results, -1, 0, and 1, depending on whether the first number is less than, equal to, or greater than (respectively) the second number. In this case, we want to check whether s is greater than 0.

The last element that is required to fully cover perceptron functionality is the ability for it to multiply the inputs vector and the weights vector. In fact, we have already written a function that solves this problem in *Chapter 10, Iterative Processing and Recursion*, in the *Multiplying vectors* section. Let's recall what it looked like:

```
function multiplyVectors(
    vector1: List<Float64>,
    vector2: List<Float64>
): Float64 {
  return Float64::sum(
        vector1.mapIndex<Float64>(
            fn(el, i) => Float64::product(
```

```
                    List<Float64>@{ el, vector2.get(i) }
            )
        )
    );
}
```

At this point, we have all the necessary pieces to try and test whether we are able to perform basic operations on an example perceptron. Let's write a simple program that creates a perceptron, provides some inputs, and then generates an output:

```
entrypoint function main(): Float64 {
    let p = Perceptron@{ List<Float64>@{ 2.0f, 3.0f } };
    let inputs = List<Float64>@{ 2.0f, 4.0f };
    let dotProduct = multiplyVectors( inputs, p.weights );
    let output = activation(dotProduct);
    return output;
}
```

So, as you can see, we are instantiating the Perceptron entity and providing some random weights to its weights vector. Then, we are creating a random inputs vector and using the `multiplyVectors` function to calculate the dot product of the two vectors. Finally, we are passing the dot product to our `activation` function and returning it. If you try and compile this program, you will see the following output:

```
1.0f
```

This means that with given weights and inputs, it has activated. Alright, we can go further and create a function that will make our perceptron learn.

Writing the training algorithm

In order to train the perceptron, we need to perform certain operations *iteratively* until our training set is fully processed. At each step of iteration, we have to take the training sample, create an input vector from it, and multiply this and the current weights vector. Then, we need to pass the result to the activation function and use the output to update the weights. These steps must be repeated for all of the training samples.

Please note what I said – we need to do something at every **step** of **iteration**. Do you know what Bosque feature we can use here? Of course, we can make use of the NSIterate namespace and its steps<T>() function. Let's create a train function with the given three parameters: a perceptron of the Perceptron type, the training set of the List<[Float64, Float64, Float64, Float64]> type, and the perceptron number of the Int type. This function will return a new, trained perceptron. Have a look at the following fragment:

```
function train(
    perceptron: Perceptron,
    trainData: List<[Float64, Float64, Float64, Float64]>,
    pNum: Int
): Perceptron {
    return NSIterate::steps<Perceptron>(
        perceptron,
        trainData.size(),
        fn(perc) => {
            // Do the training step
        }
    );
}
```

So, as mentioned earlier, we are defining a function with three parameters. The return type is Perceptron, as we will receive a new, trained perceptron after training. Don't worry about the missing fragment - we'll get back to it in a second. Let's have a quick stop here and understand why the trainData argument is of the List<[Float64, Float64, Float64, Float64]> type. This signature means that we are expecting a list of tuples where each of the tuples will consist of four floating-point numbers. The first two are going to be the X- and Y-coordinates of a point that the perceptron is learning to classify; this is probably understandable. You may be wondering what these last two floats are. The answer is quite simple if you think about it.

In order for the perceptron to learn, we must make it process a sample input and compare the actual result with the expected one. This looks the same for humans – we are learning by looking at examples and comparing our results with expected ones and, if our result is wrong, we try to adjust our knowledge. In our case, we want to show the perceptron some coordinates and the result we are expecting – activation or no activation (1 or 0). Based on this, it will adjust its weights if the result was incorrect. So, the third and fourth floats are the results we are expecting to get from a neuron (P1 and P2, respectively) after processing the coordinates.

In order to make it more readable, let's define a custom type called `Sample` and update the `train` function signature:

```
typedef Sample = [Float64, Float64, Float64, Float64];
```

The updated `train` function signature will look like this:

```
function train(
    perceptron: Perceptron,
    trainData: List<Sample>,
    pNum: Int
): Perceptron {
    ...
}
```

Notice the highlighted part. Now it's clear that we are expecting a list of training samples as the second argument. Having explained this, let's now go further and add the rest of the `train` function code. The missing PCode body will look like the following:

```
fn(perc) => {
    let {
        weights = w, currentSample = i, alpha = a
    } = perc.{ weights, currentSample, alpha };

    let [x, y, target1, target2] = trainData.get(i);
    let target = if (pNum == 1) target1 else target2;
    let sum = multiplyVectors(List<Float64>@{x, y}, w);
    let output = activation(sum);

    let w1 = w.get(0) + a * (target - output) * x;
    let w2 = w.get(1) + a * (target - output) * y;

    return perc.update(
        weights = List<Float64>@{w1, w2},
        currentSample = i + 1
    );
}
```

The training is happening iteratively and, at each step, we are changing the perceptron – the weights are being updated. After the last step, the `steps<Perceptron>()` function will return a fully trained perceptron because it will perform `trainData.size()` steps. Now, let's break down the PCode function body.

Firstly, we are extracting and renaming (for better readability) a few fields from the `perc` argument, which is the current state of `perceptron` passed as an argument to the `train` function. Notice that we are accessing the `currentSample` field, which wasn't added initially. Let's now add it:

```
entity Perceptron {
    field weights: List<Float64>;
    field alpha: Float64 = 1;
    field currentSample: Int = 0;
}
```

This field is required to keep track of the current iteration number for the current perceptron. Thanks to this field, we know which sample to access from the training set in its current iteration.

In the next line, we are extracting a point's coordinates and the target value (expected result – 1 or 0). Then, we are calculating a dot product of the inputs vector (created as `List<Float64>`) and the weights vector and storing it in the `sum` variable. After that, the dot product is passed to the `activation` function and the result is stored in the `output` variable.

At this point, the program is processing an ith sample using the current perceptron weights values and the result of the activation function is stored in a variable. Now, we are ready to actually make it learn. All we have to do is make use of the delta rule, described in the *Brief introduction to neural networks* section, and update the perceptron's weights. In our particular case, the perceptron is going to have only two weights. This is an important piece of information because, thanks to that assumption, we don't have to use an iteration through all the weights. We can just write two lines of code updating each of the two weights. This is exactly what these two lines of code are doing in the `train` function:

```
let w1 = w.get(0) + a * (target - output) * x;
let w2 = w.get(1) + a * (target - output) * y;
```

Each weight is updated using the same formula. To the old value, we are adding the result of multiplication of the alpha value (learning rate), the difference between the expected and the actual result, and the input value that influenced this weight. The new values are stored in the w1 and w2 variables.

The last line of the PCode function is responsible for returning a new, changed perceptron for the next iteration. It makes use of the bulk update operation and sets new (just calculated) weights values as well as incrementing the currentSample counter.

Let's have a quick stop here again and see how we can use the train function to train a sample perceptron. Firstly, we need to create a training set, which is a list of the List<Sample> type. Then, we need to replace the created perceptron with a trained one. The rest is the same as before. The complete example of its use is presented here:

```
entrypoint function main(): Float64 {
    var p = Perceptron@{ List<Float64>@{ 2.0f, 3.0f } };

    let trainSet = List<Sample>@{
        [5.0f, -5.0f, 0.0f, 1.0f],
        [-5.0f, -5.0f, 0.0f, 0.0f],
        [-5.0f, 5.0f, 1.0f, 0.0f],
        [5.0f, 5.0f, 1.0f, 1.0f],
        [4.0f, 0.0f, 1.0f, 1.0f],
        [9.0f, 9.0f, 1.0f, 1.0f],
        [9.0f, -3.0f, 0.0f, 1.0f],
        [5.0f, -6.0f, 0.0f, 1.0f],
        [5.0f, -10.0f, 0.0f, 1.0f],
        [6.0f, 8.0f, 1.0f, 1.0f],
        [-6.0f, 3.0f, 1.0f, 0.0f],
        [-7.0f, 6.0f, 1.0f, 0.0f],
        [-7.0f, -1.0f, 0.0f, 0.0f],
        [-6.0f, -6.0f, 0.0f, 0.0f]
    };
    p = train(p, trainSet, 1);
    let inputs = List<Int>@{ -2.0f, 4 };
    let dotProduct = multiplyVectors( inputs, p.weights );
    let output = activation(dotProduct);
    return output;
}
```

Notice the highlighted part. We had to change `let` to `var` and create a `trainSet` list. The perceptron with random weights is passed to the `train` function, along with the `trainSet` list, and a new, trained perceptron is returned. We have also changed the inputs vector to see whether the result will differ from the previous one. In the `trainSet` list, we have created 14 samples with some coordinates and the expected results. Although we are only training a single neuron here, we set both expected results properly so that we don't have to fix it later once we add the second neuron. The third parameter in the `train` function is set to 1, which means that for now, only the first expected result from each tuple is going to be picked. As you can see, we are expecting 1 if the *X*-coordinate is positive, and 0 otherwise. If you compile and run this program, you should see the following result:

```
1.000000
```

If you got the same result, this means that your perceptron works fine... for a single hardcoded point coordinate! At least this is what we can tell with all certainty. We don't yet know whether the training was successful, for two reasons.

Firstly, the truth is that in real life, 14 training samples is far too few to properly train an intelligent model. Normally, we would need hundreds and thousands of samples to achieve that. However, our current problem is quite simple, and 14 samples should suffice. Nonetheless, if you want to use more data, feel free to do so. You can type them manually or you can generate them using a simple script. One way of doing so is presented in the next example – using JavaScript:

```javascript
function randomInt(min, max) {
        min = Math.ceil(min);
        max = Math.floor(max);
        return Math.floor(Math.random() * (max - min + 1)) +
        min;
}
for (let i = 0; i < 100; i++) {
        const x = randomInt(-100, 100);
        const y = randomInt(-100, 100);
        const eo1 = y >= 0 ? 1 : 0;
        const eo2 = x >= 0 ? 1 : 0;
        console.log(JSON.stringify([`${x}.0f`, `${y}.0f`,
        `${eo1}.0f`, `${eo2}.0f`]) + ',');
}
```

This code outputs 100 rows with random points and expected outputs set so that it fits our example. All you need to do is to run it and copy and paste the generated output into your Bosque program. You can also use another approach, or you can skip generating more data – the 14 samples presented above should be enough in our particular case. If you decide to use this script to generate more data, keep in mind that it uses pseudo-random numbers that may not be equally distributed. It may cause your training set to contain only points from one or two quadrants, and that would directly cause our perceptron not to train properly. In such an instance, run the script a couple of times until a *better* training set is generated.

The second and most important thing is that we haven't tested our model properly. Checking a single point coordinate is not enough to tell whether the training was a success. We need more test data to be sure. We will take care of that in the *Defining two entrypoint functions* section. As for now, be aware that if you got the same result as has been shown, this means that you are doing everything correctly and can proceed with the project. If the result is different, this is probably caused by a *bad* training set and you should generate a new one.

Wrapping the classification feature

At this point, we do have a pretty good working artificial neuron. However, using it is rather inconvenient. We have to create a new inputs vector and use the `multiplyVectors` and `activation` functions every time we want to classify something. This will get even more ugly when we create the second perceptron – we will have to repeat the code twice. The best practice is to always wrap the constantly repeating code in a function so that it will be easier to maintain. So, let's go ahead and wrap the repeating piece of code in a `classify` function. This is what it can look like:

```
function classify(
    x: Float64, y: Float64, perceptron: Perceptron
): Float64 {
    let sum = multiplyVectors(
        List<Float64>@{ x, y }, perceptron.weights
    );
    return activation(sum);
}
```

So, as you can see, it accepts three arguments. The first two are *X*- and *Y*-coordinates of a point. The last one is a perceptron from which we are taking the weights vector for multiplication. The return type is the same as the `activation` function – `Float64`. In the body of our helper function, we are performing the vector multiplication and passing the dot product to the `activation` function whose result is returned from our wrapper function.

Now, we are ready to create two perceptrons that will solve our initial problem. But before we do that, let's make one more improvement. Currently, we only see 0s and 1s depending on whether a neuron has activated. Based on that, we have to think which quadrant a point belongs to. In order to make it more human-readable, let's define another helper function, called `getQuadrant`, which will return a string saying which quadrant it is. Such a function may look like this:

```
function eq(a: Float64, b: Float64): Bool {
    return Float64::compare(a, b) == 0;
}
function getQuadrant(
    p1Out: Float64, p2Out: Float64
): String {
    let o1, o2 = p1Out, p2Out;
    return if(eq(o1, 1.0f) && eq(o2, 1.0f)) "Quarter 1"
        elif(eq(o1, 1.0f) && eq(o2, 0.0f)) "Quarter 2"
        elif(eq(o1, 0.0f) && eq(o2, 0.0f)) "Quarter 3"
        elif(eq(o1, 0.0f) && eq(o2, 1.0f)) "Quarter 4"
        else "Unknown";
}
```

Basically, this is *Figure 11.3* represented in Bosque code. We are returning a string indicating which quadrant of the Cartesian system is depending on the P1 and P2 results. In Bosque, if you are returning an `if` statement, you must always follow it with an `else` block. Otherwise, an error will be thrown. This is why we have this last `else` block added, which will never be met because there are only four possible scenarios. Also, because comparing `Float64` types is a bit inconvenient (takes a lot of space), we defined a helper function, `eq`, which returns `true` if numbers are equal and `false` otherwise.

Alright, now we are indeed ready to test the whole functionality with two perceptrons. Let's not waste any time and get going.

Firstly, we need a training set and two perceptrons with random weights. The training set must be prepared for two neurons now since they must return different values for the same coordinates. The code will look like the following:

```
let trainSet = List<Sample>@{
        [5.0f, -5.0f, 0.0f, 1.0f],
        [-5.0f, -5.0f, 0.0f, 0.0f],
        [-5.0f, 5.0f, 1.0f, 0.0f],
        [5.0f, 5.0f, 1.0f, 1.0f],
        [4.0f, 0.0f, 1.0f, 1.0f],
        [9.0f, 9.0f, 1.0f, 1.0f],
        [9.0f, -3.0f, 0.0f, 1.0f],
        [5.0f, -6.0f, 0.0f, 1.0f],
        [5.0f, -10.0f, 0.0f, 1.0f],
        [6.0f, 8.0f, 1.0f, 1.0f],
        [-6.0f, 3.0f, 1.0f, 0.0f],
        [-7.0f, 6.0f, 1.0f, 0.0f],
        [-7.0f, -1.0f, 0.0f, 0.0f],
        [-6.0f, -6.0f, 0.0f, 0.0f]
    };

var p1 = Perceptron@{ weights = List<Float64>@{1.0f, 3.0f} };
var p2 = Perceptron@{ weights = List<Float64>@{2.0f, 4.0f} };
```

Nothing new here. There are only two things that you need to pay attention to. The first is that in the training set, we are providing two expected results in each sample now. The first one expects a neuron to be activated for positive Y-coordinates (P1), and the second for positive X-coordinates (P2). The second thing is the highlighted part. In fact, it is optional, and you don't need to write it. Bosque will match the fields in the same order as provided. I provided the field name just for clarity here.

The next thing to do is to train our perceptrons with proper expected results. This is how we do it:

```
p1 = train(p1, trainSet, 1);
p2 = train(p2, trainSet, 2);
```

After that, we need to define some coordinates and run the classifiers like this:

```
var x = -2.0f;
var y = 4.0f;
let p1Out = classify(x, y, p1);
let p2Out = classify(x, y, p2);
```

The last thing to do is to pass the p1Out and p2Out variables to our getQuadrant helper in order to get the string representation of a quadrant. We could assign the answer to a variable, but we can also return the result directly from the main entrypoint function like this:

```
return String::concat("Answer: ", getQuadrant(p1Out, p2Out));
```

Remember to change the return type to String in order for that to work.

Once you try to compile this program and run it, you should see the following result:

```
"Answer: Quadrant II"
```

If you see this text on your screen, this means that you have successfully implemented the core functionality, which solves the initial problem of predicting the quadrants of the Cartesian system based on a point's coordinates. The last thing that is left to do is to create two entrypoint functions to fulfill all the project requirements.

Defining two entrypoint functions

Back in the *Defining project requirements* section (at the very end), I said that we will need two programs. One of them will train and test our perceptrons and return the trained parameters (weights). The other one will make use of those trained values and predict the quadrant. You may be wondering why that is required. It would be simpler to have all of this in one program. Well, you are right, but the biggest downside of such an approach is that we would have to run the training and testing every time we want to process a new point. In our particular case, it wouldn't be that big of a problem because our training set is rather tiny. However, if we had to process millions of training samples in order to train a single perceptron, the amount of time required to complete the training would be enormous. Moreover, it would not make any sense to repeat the training multiple times once we have well-trained neurons. For these reasons, we will split the logic into two entrypoint functions and compile two programs out of it. Let's see how we could achieve this.

The first entrypoint will not require any arguments. It will only run training, then testing, and then return the trained weights. The second program, on the other hand, will receive a bunch of arguments – six, to be more precise. The first four will be the weights of our two perceptrons that will be returned by the first program. The last two are going to be the X- and Y-coordinates of a point that we want to process. That way, we will be able to process any amount of new data without the need to repeat the training – the trained parameters (weights) will be provided as arguments. Having said that, let's dive into the refactor.

So, let's start with the first entrypoint, which is supposed to only perform training and testing and return the weights after that. In order to do that, let's create a new entrypoint function called `preTrain` with a return type of `List<Float64>` (a list of weight values):

```
entrypoint function preTrain(): List<Float64> {

    let trainSet = List<Sample>@{
        [5.0f, -5.0f, 0.0f, 1.0f],
        [-5.0f, -5.0f, 0.0f, 0.0f],
        [-5.0f, 5.0f, 1.0f, 0.0f],
        [5.0f, 5.0f, 1.0f, 1.0f],
        [4.0f, 0.0f, 1.0f, 1.0f],
        [9.0f, 9.0f, 1.0f, 1.0f],
        [9.0f, -3.0f, 0.0f, 1.0f],
        [5.0f, -6.0f, 0.0f, 1.0f],
        [5.0f, -10.0f, 0.0f, 1.0f],
        [6.0f, 8.0f, 1.0f, 1.0f],
        [-6.0f, 3.0f, 1.0f, 0.0f],
        [-7.0f, 6.0f, 1.0f, 0.0f],
        [-7.0f, -1.0f, 0.0f, 0.0f],
        [-6.0f, -6.0f, 0.0f, 0.0f]
    };

    var p1 = Perceptron@{weights = List<Float64>@{1.0f, 3.0f}};
    var p2 = Perceptron@{weights = List<Float64>@{2.0f, 4.0f}};
    p1 = train(p1, trainSet, 1);
```

```
    p2 = train(p2, trainSet, 2);
    let trainedWeights = List<Float64>::concat(
        p1.weights, p2.weights
    );
    return  trainedWeights;
}
```

So, as you can see, we are only defining the training set and the perceptrons themselves. After training, we are returning a list of trained weight values. In fact, you could rename the `main` function that you have created for testing purposes earlier and replace its body with the new one. Or, you can just remove the `main` function and implement only `preTrain`. The next thing that we must do is perform the testing phase. In order to do that, we need to declare another function that will create a testing set and validate the trained weights. The algorithm will go like this:

1.   Initialize two perceptrons with the trained weights.

2.   Create the test set containing multiple test samples with the expected output.

3.   For each sample:

a. Get the point coordinates and target outputs.

b. Create the inputs vector.

c. Run the `classify` function for each of the two perceptrons.

d. Compare the actual output with the expected one and if it's not the same, count the invalid output.

Pretty straightforward, right? Basically, we want to simply iterate over the test set and count all the cases where the output produced was invalid. Remember that it's a testing phase – we don't modify any weights. All we are doing is testing whether the trained weights have proper values. So, let's move on and define the `testModel` function. Have a look at the following code:

```
function testModel(
    p1w1: Float64, p1w2: Float64,
    p2w1: Float64, p2w2: Float64
): String {
    var p1 = Perceptron@{ List<Float64>@{ p1w1, p1w2 } };
    var p2 = Perceptron@{ List<Float64>@{ p2w1, p2w2 } };

    let testSet = List<Sample>@{
```

```
                [58.0f, 8.0f, 1.0f, 1.0f], [81.0f, 29.0f, 1.0f, 1.0f],
                [24.0f, -15.0f, 0.0f, 1.0f], [88.0f, 4.0f, 1.0f, 1.0f],
                [-61.0f, 80.0f, 1.0f, 0.0f], [51.0f, -99.0f, 0.0f,
    1.0f],
                [59.0f, -21.0f, 0.0f, 1.0f], [-59.0f, -47.0f, 0.0f,
    0.0f],
                [-15.0f, -8.0f, 0.0f, 0.0f], [77.0f, -53.0f, 0.0f,
    1.0f],
                [-72.0f, -76.0f, 0.0f, 0.0f], [-91.0f, 71.0f, 1.0f,
    0.0f],
                [67.0f, 55.0f, 1.0f, 1.0f], [97.0f, -17.0f, 0.0f,
    1.0f],
                [-6.0f, -67.0f, 0.0f, 0.0f]
        };


    _debug("Performing validation of the model...");


    // Validate test samples against actual outputs


    return "Done.";
}
```

So, as you can see, this function accepts four parameters – two weights of each perceptron. Next, the test set is created. In this example, only 15 samples are provided as the test set – let's be honest, that's not many. In fact, you can use the same script that's been used to generate the training set to generate more samples in the test set. I strongly recommend you do so. You should generate at least 100 samples or more, just to see whether the training was really successful.

You have probably noticed that the main part is missing – let's add it. Put the following code under the comment that says // Validate test samples against actual outputs:

```
let invalid = NSIterate::reduce<Int>(
    0,
    ListOf::range(0, testSet.size()),
    fn(acc, i) => {
        let [x, y, target1, target2] = testSet.get(i);
        let inputs = List<Int>@{ x, y };
```

```
            let p1Out = classify(inputs, p1);
            let p2Out = classify(inputs, p2);

            if (p1Out != target1 || p2Out != target2) {
                _debug(List<String | Float64>@{
                    "---- Invalid output! ----",
                    "Expected: ", target1, target2,
                    "Got: ", p1Out, p2Out,
                    "For input: ", x, y
                });
                return acc + 1;
            }
        return acc;
    }
);
_debug(List<String | Int>@{
    "Test ended. Number of invalid outputs:", invalid,
    "; Total samples: ", testSet.size()
});
```

The most important thing is the iteration itself. As you can see, we are using the
`NSIterate::reduce<T>()` function. The reason is that, thanks to this, we can count
the number of invalid cases and print it out. We are also using the `ListOf::range()`
method to generate a list of integers that are used as indexes. In the PCode function, we
are extracting the required parameters and running the classifier for each of the neurons.
Then, the check is performed – if any of the output values are incorrect, a message is
printed and the number of invalid cases is increased by 1. Otherwise, we are not changing
the counter. Notice a trick that I used to print a message. Since, in the current version
of Bosque, you cannot convert a number to a string, it's inconvenient to print readable
messages with `_debug()`. In order to work around this, we can create a list containing
`String` or `Float64` values and then just print it.

Alright, let's see how we can use this function. In the `preTrain` function, just before the `return` keyword, let's place the following code:

```
NSMain::testModel(
    trainedWeights.get(0),
    trainedWeights.get(1),
    trainedWeights.get(2),
    trainedWeights.get(3)
);
```

To improve the readability of the output, you can also add this line before `return`:

```
_debug("Model trained and tested - see output above for
details. Calculated weights:");
```

Let's compile this program. In order to do this, we have to use two additional flags for the ExeGen tool described in *Chapter 2, Configuring the Bosque Environment*. First of all, we have changed the default name of an entrypoint. We don't have a `main` function anymore – we have the `preTrain` function. So, to tell ExeGen what entrypoint to look for, we must use the `-e` flag. At the same time, we want to change the output executable name because our project will consist of two executables. We must use the `-o` flag for that. Assuming you named your file `ai-classifier.bsq`, the command to run looks like the following:

```
$ exegen ai-classifier.bsq -e "NSMain::preTrain" -o "train.exe"
```

This will result in generating a `train.exe` file. If you run this program, in an ideal case, you should see the following output:

```
"Performing validation of the model..."
{"Test ended. Number of invalid outputs:", 0, "; Total samples:
", 15}
"Model trained and tested - see output above for details.
Calculated weights:"
{1.000000, 3.000000, 7.000000, -1.000000}
```

However, it is likely that the training set you generated wasn't perfect and therefore the training also wasn't fully successful. In the result, some of the test samples may fail. In that case, you may see an output similar to this one:

```
"Performing validation of the model..."
{"---- Invalid output! ----", "Expected: ", 0.000000, 1.000000,
```

```
"Got: ", 1.000000, 1.000000, "For input: ", 97.000000,
-17.000000}
{"---- Invalid output! ----", "Expected: ", 0.000000, 0.000000,
"Got: ", 0.000000, 1.000000, "For input: ", -6.000000,
-67.000000}
{"Test ended. Number of invalid outputs:", 2, "; Total samples:
", 15}
"Model trained and tested - see output above for details.
Calculated weights:"
{1.000000, 3.000000, 7.000000, -1.000000}
```

As long as the number of invalid outputs in our project is not greater than 10-20% of the test set size, this is acceptable. If this number is greater, I'd suggest you rerun the training with a different training set.

In the last line of the output, we can see the trained weights of P1 and P2 that we will have to pass as arguments to the second program that we are about to create. If your result differs, don't worry; if your training sets differ, the output will also differ. If testing has gone well, let's move on and create the second entrypoint function.

As previously mentioned, the second entrypoint function should accept six arguments – four weights and two coordinates. It should also return a string denoting a quadrant of the Cartesian Coordinates System. But, most importantly, it should not run training at all. It should make use of the weights provided and calculate the output right away. Have a look at the implementation:

```
entrypoint function run(
    p1w1: String,
    p1w2: String,
    p2w1: String,
    p2w2: String,
    x: String,
    y: String
): String {
    var p1 = Perceptron@{
        weights = List<Float64>@{
            Float64::parse(p1w1), Float64::parse(p1w2)
        }
    };
    var p2 = Perceptron@{
```

```
        weights = List<Float64>@{
            Float64::parse(p2w1), Float64::parse(p2w2)
        }
    };
    let p1Out = classify(x, y, p1);
    let p2Out = classify(x, y, p2);
    return getQuadrant(p1Out, p2Out);
}
```

So, we have created a new entrypoint in the same file, called run. This accepts all the required parameters described above and returns a string. In the body of this function, we are simply creating two new perceptrons and providing them with the weights values taken from parameters. Then, we are processing the x and y parameters using each of the perceptrons and returning the result of the getQuadrant function.

Please note that we are accepting six strings as the arguments. You may be wondering why we are doing this. This is because, in the current version of Bosque, you can't use Float64 as the parameter type of an entrypoint function – it causes unexpected errors. This is why we need to accept the String type and then convert it to Float64 using the Float64::parse method.

This time, in order to compile this program, we need to provide different values for the -e and -o flags:

```
$ exegen ai-classifier.bsq -e "NSMain::run" -o "classify.exe"
```

This command will generate a classify.exe executable from the same ai-classifier.bsq file.

And now it is time to test the whole project that you just built. Without further ado, let's jump right into the next section.

Testing the program

In this section, we will run our project and see whether the returned values are correct. If you carefully followed all of the previous instructions, you should not be worried. If you encounter any unexpected errors or the output is incorrect, please make sure that you have followed all the previous steps and that you have identical code as shown in the examples.

Alright, it's time to test things out. Firstly, you need to make sure that you have two executables. If you are running Windows OS, you should have `train.exe` and `classify.exe` files. On Linux and macOS, these files should be called `train.out` and `classify.out`. If you have confirmed that you have these files, it's time to run them.

The first thing to do is to train our model and get the trained parameters. On Windows, you can do it like this:

```
$ .\train.exe
```

On Linux and macOS, the command looks like this:

```
$ ./train.out
```

As the outcome, you should see the result of testing and, in the last line of the output, you should see the trained weights. In my case, the values are as follows:

```
{1.000000, 3.000000, 7.000000, -1.000000}
```

The second step is to run the classifier and see whether it works well. Let's say that we want to classify a point, `B(12, 10)`. We know that it belongs to quadrant I. Let's see whether our program will return the same. On Windows, run the following command:

```
$ .\classify.exe 1 3 7 -1 12 10
```

On Linux and macOS, the command looks like this:

```
$ ./classify.out 1 3 7 -1 12 10
```

If your model has trained well, this is what you should get as the result:

```
"Quadrant 1"
```

It seems like the program works well! Let's see whether it classifies all the quadrants correctly. Go ahead and try to run the classifier for the following points:

- `C(-3.9, 43)`
- `D(-9, -5.4)`
- `E(15.5, -8.3)`

These are the expected results:

- "Quadrant 2"
- "Quadrant 3"
- "Quadrant 4"

If you see these results on your screen, you should be proud of yourself. You have successfully implemented the artificial model that solves the initial problem after learning the rules. Quite impressive! Now go ahead and play with it to see whether it works well for other, random inputs.

Although you succeeded in building the artificial classifier, there is room for improvement in the code we just wrote. Let's see what can be changed for the better.

Improving the code

First things first, let's focus on the types. Just by looking at the code, it's not quite clear what we mean every time we use `List<Float64>`. Sometimes, it means the "inputs vector," and sometimes the "weights vector." It would be much more readable if we had a custom type definition that would speak for itself. Let's create two additional types:

```
typedef WeightsVector = List<Float64>;
typedef InputsVector = List<Float64>;
```

As you can see, they are both the same, but they serve for better readability. Let's apply this change in the code. The weights vector is used in the `Perceptron` entity, the `train` function, and both entrypoint functions. Look at the following examples to see how they change.

In the `Perceptron` entity, we must change the `field weights` definition to look like this:

```
field weights: WeightsVector;
```

Here, we have replaced the `List<Int>` type with the `WeightsVector` one.

Another change has to happen in the `train` function. In the last line of the PCode function, we are updating the weights field in the current perceptron state. This is what the new version of the line should look like:

```
return perc.update(weights = WeightsVector@{ w1, w2 },
currentSample = i + 1);
```

The change is pretty similar to the previous one. We have replaced the `List<Int>` type with the `WeightsVector` type.

The last change in the code is needed in our entrypoint functions and the `testModel` function. In the `preTrain` function, we can change the way we are creating the two perceptrons. The new version should look like this:

```
var p1 = Perceptron@{ WeightsVector@{ 1.0f, 3.0f } };
var p2 = Perceptron@{ WeightsVector@{ 2.0f, 4.0f } };
```

An analogous change should be made in the `run` and `testModel` functions:

```
var p1 = Perceptron@{ WeightsVector@{ p1w1, p1w2 } };
var p2 = Perceptron@{ WeightsVector@{ p2w1, p2w2 } };
```

So, as you can see, we got rid of the `weights =` part, and replaced the `List<Float64>` type with the `WeightsVector` one.

Now it is clear where we are dealing with the weights vector. Let's apply a similar change regarding the inputs vector. The only function that will require modification is the `train` function. However, we can also refactor the `classify` function so that it will receive the `InputsVector` argument instead of separate coordinates. Look at the following examples to see how they change.

In the `train` function, we can change the line where we are calculating the dot product of inputs and weights vectors. The new version should look like this:

```
let sum = multiplyVectors(InputsVector@{ x, y }, w);
```

Here we have replaced the `List<Int>` type with the `InputsVector` one.

As for the `classify` function, we will change the arguments a little bit, as described earlier. The new version should look like this:

```
function classify(inputs: InputsVector, perceptron:
Perceptron): Int {
    let sum = multiplyVectors(inputs, perceptron.weights);
    return activation(sum);
}
```

So, as you can see, the `x` and `y` parameters have disappeared and have been replaced by a single `inputs` parameter of the `InputsVector` type, which is directly passed to the `multiplyVectors` helper.

Don't forget to change the `run` entrypoint and the `testModel` function accordingly. The parts where we are calculating the `p1Out` and `p2Out` values should now look like this:

```
let inputs = InputsVector@{Float64::parse(x),
Float64::parse(y)};
let p1Out = classify(inputs, p1);
let p2Out = classify(inputs, p2);
```

Now we are creating an `inputs` vector and passing it as a whole to the `classify` function.

The last thing that could be improved is the type of data returned from the `getQuadrant` function. Currently, we are returning just a string. Remember what problems may arise from such an approach? This was discussed in *Chapter 3, Bosque Key Features*, when we were talking about typed strings. I think it's a good idea to make use of this feature here. Let's define a regular expression that will describe the result we want to get:

```
typedef Quadrant = /^Quadrant [1-4]|Unknown$/;
```

We want it to be a string starting with `Quadrant`, followed by a number from 1 to 4 or the `Unknown` word.

Now, let's change the `getQuadrant` function accordingly:

```
function getQuadrant(p1Out: Float64, p2Out: Float64):
SafeString<Quadrant> {
    let o1, o2 = p1Out, p2Out;
    return if(eq(o1, 1.0f) && eq(o2, 1.0f)) Quadrant'Quadrant 1'
           elif(eq(o1, 1.0f) && eq(o2, 0.0f)) Quadrant'Quadrant 2'
           elif(eq(o1, 0.0f) && eq(o2, 0.0f)) Quadrant'Quadrant 3'
           elif(eq(o1, 0.0f) && eq(o2, 1.0f)) Quadrant'Quadrant 4'
           else Quadrant'Unknown';
}
```

So, now we are returning a `SafeString<Quadrant>` type, which makes it clear that we are dealing with quadrants and not some random strings. Remember to change the `run` function accordingly. Since the `getQuadrant` function returns a `SafeString<Quadrant>` type, we need to convert it to a string here:

```
return getQuadrant(p1Out, p2Out).string();
```

We can do that by chaining the `.string()` call at the end of the line.

And that concludes this section. You have improved your code a lot. Now it looks much better and all the logic is clear and readable just by looking at the code without the need to perform a deep analysis. Before summing up the whole chapter, let's quickly see how you can enhance this project even more.

Enhancing ideas and suggestions

Just to stimulate your imagination and creativity, I'll provide you with some ideas for enhancing the project you just built.

One of them would be to try to wrap your two executables into some kind of a script that would receive a point's coordinates as arguments and run the training, grab the calculated weights automatically, and pass them to the classifier along with the parameters. The calculated weights could be saved in an external file, which could be used to prevent unnecessary training runs.

Another idea is to wrap the `train.exe` executable into a script that would expect two files as arguments – the training and test sets. Then, it could open those files and pass the training data as arguments to the `preTrain` function, which would allow you to change the training set without the need to recompile the program; it also applies to the `testModel` function.

There are probably many more ways to play with the project. I strongly recommend you try them out to get more familiar with Bosque possibilities and ways to use it in different environments. I'll leave this as an exercise for you. In the meantime, let's summarize the knowledge you gained during this chapter.

Summary

At the outset, let me say that you should be proud of yourself. You have learned a ton of things in this chapter. Congratulations! Let me go through the topics that we covered one by one.

In the first section, we have defined the project requirements. We chose to build an AI program that will learn how to recognize Cartesian Coordinates System quadrants just by looking at any point's coordinates. As a result, you built a program that could be used to classify any objects that can be represented by two numbers and classified into four classes.

Next, you learned about neural networks. You acquired some theory required to build an intelligent model in Bosque. You know what neural networks are, how they work, and what are they built of. You also learned about neurons and a special kind of neuron – a perceptron. At the end of this section, you designed the model that solves our problem.

After that, you finally started coding. Step by step, you built a fully working intelligent program that is able to learn and classify points on the Cartesian system. After testing, you introduced a few changes that made your code look a lot better and more user-friendly.

Last but not least, you learned about possible ways of enhancing the project even further by wrapping the executables into some external scripts that would allow you to achieve even more exciting results.

That was exciting, wasn't it? Please reread some of the topics discussed in this chapter if you feel that you need to. If everything is clear, let's jump into the next chapter, where you will learn more about namespaces, concepts, and entities in Bosque.

Questions

1. What does a neural network consist of?

2. What is a perceptron?

3. What activation function does a perceptron use?

4. What is the name of a rule that we used to update the weights values?

5. What flag for the ExeGen tool do we use to provide a custom output filename?

6. In Bosque, can we have multiple entrypoint functions in one program?

Further reading

Here is a list of useful resources that will allow you to better understand this chapter's contents:

- Goodfellow, I., Bengio, Y., and Courville, A. (2016). *Deep Learning*. MIT Press.

- The online version of the *Deep Learning* book: `https://www.deeplearningbook.org/`

- Rosenblatt, Frank (1958), *The Perceptron: A Probabilistic Model for Information Storage and Organization in the Brain*, Cornell Aeronautical Laboratory

- Gallant, S. I. (1990). *Perceptron-Based Learning Algorithms*. IEEE Transactions on Neural Networks, vol. 1, no. 2, pp. 179–191

12
Namespaces, Concepts, and Entities

Divide and conquer is among the most essential paradigms in software design and one of the most frequently used strategies for dealing with complex problems. For this reason, numerous programming languages adopt this paradigm through different approaches. We could highlight modular programming, object-oriented programming, or the packaging of code in reusable libraries. However, always with the same objective in mind, it allows the programmer to solve a single small problem at a time.

Although Bosque does not currently support reusable code libraries, it is within the immediate roadmap, and we can see evidence of this in the implementations as namespaces, concepts, and entities.

Consequently, in this chapter, we will explore the tools that Bosque has prepared to develop more comprehensive solutions, through the following topics:

- Using namespaces to organize code
- Understanding concepts and entities
- Exploring fields and methods

- Using inheritance
- Using static methods
- Understanding parametric polymorphism

At the end of this chapter, we will be ready to take a step forward in adopting the Bosque programming language, preparing ourselves to apply everything that we have learned in larger, structured, and modular projects.

Technical requirements

The following are the requirements for the chapter:

- A successful installation of Bosque is required (this process has been explained in full in the *Technical requirements* section of *Chapter 2, Configuring the Bosque Environment*).
- A text editor of your choice.

Using namespaces to organize code

While we write code, it is anticipated that, with the increase in the number of lines of code written, we may lose track of all the names and identifiers already used in the code and this might lead to mistakes such as overwriting values or referencing incorrect identifiers. To solve this problem, programming languages have been implementing namespaces for a number of years.

When we talk about namespaces, we are referring to abstract containers that allow us to group identifiers and variables, creating a useful association in terms of avoiding possible duplicate name errors. This allows us to be able to better expose the intent of specific pieces of code.

Additionally, namespaces are useful when building libraries since, as a result of having code that is not visible to the programmer, it might not be easy to avoid duplicating identifiers.

To declare a namespace in Bosque, we will use the `namespace` keyword accompanied by an identifier at the beginning of our script, as follows:

```
namespace MyNamespace;
```

Remembering *Chapter 4, Entrypoint Function*, the Bosque compiler will search, by default, for the entrypoint function called `main()` within the `NSMain` namespace. If we decide to use a different namespace for our script, we must manually specify the entrypoint function using the `--entrypoint` parameter.

Along with namespaces, Bosque also offers us the possibility of using entities and concepts to be able to encapsulate our functions and variables. Let's dive in!

Understanding concepts and entities

Concepts and entities are part of the nominal system of types that Bosque offers. They help us to transfer our experience in object-oriented programming to our Bosque programs. Both of these constructs have been already mentioned in *Chapter 5, Types and Operators*. Let's quickly recall what they are before we jump into more detail.

Concepts

Concepts are entirely abstract types that we will use to model some generic and non-instantiable objects, reminding us of the abstract classes that we will find in other languages.

To declare a concept, we will use the `concept` statement followed by an identifier as follows:

```
concept Animal {
}
```

Within the block enclosed by the braces, we can define some functions that could be overwritten later and some properties that will be inherited by the entities that will implement this concept.

Let's see what a `concept` statement would look like with `field` and `method`:

```
concept Animal {
    field name: String = "Unknown";
    abstract makeSound(): String;
}
```

We are allowed to implement a method instead of just declaring them, but we will see this case later in this chapter in the *Using inheritance* and *Using static methods* sections.

Entities

Entities allow types to be defined that can eventually be instantiated, and that can implement concepts if necessary. To declare an entity, we will use the `entity` statement. Let's see an example:

```
entity Dog {
    field name: String;
    method makeSound(): String {
    return "woof";
    }
}
```

In this piece of code, we see the `Dog` entity's declaration, which has a `name` property and a `makeSound()` method that will return the text `woof`.

To consult its properties or call the `makeSound()` method, it will be necessary to instantiate the entity, which we can do as follows:

```
let bob = Dog@{name = "Bob"};
bob.makeSound(); // woof
```

As we can see in the code, we instantiate `Dog` entity, assigning it the string "Bob" as the value for the `field` name and saving the instance in a variable whose identifier is `bob`, to later call the `makeSound()` method, obtaining `woof` as output.

In the snippets shown previously, you may have noticed that we have used fields to represent properties and methods to write functions. These could easily be confused with variables and functions used in the previous chapters.

In the next section, we will learn how to differentiate between them and understand how to use them.

Exploring fields and methods

Fields and methods allow us to provide properties and actions to our objects. The use of specialized terms instead of variables and functions will enable us to identify that they are only accessible through the instance of an object. They have a limited scope, and their life cycle is determined by the instance's life cycle.

We can declare a field in the same way as we do with variables. The following are a few examples:

```
entity Baz {
field a: Int = 5;          // With type and value
field b: Int;              // With type
field c;                   // Just the field name
}
```

The fields can include a type or a value as you deem necessary. It is important to remember that they are mutable, so their value can be altered later.

On the other hand, methods behave very similarly to functions and are usually declared in the same way. Let's see an example:

```
entity Foo {
    method sayHello()(name: String): String() {
        return "Hello " + name;
    }
}
```

As we can see in the code snippet, we can declare a method using the same structure as a function through the `method` statement.

Methods are able to receive parameters and return values. Additionally, they could query for the fields or variables within the scope of the entity that contains them.

But what happens with the methods defined within a concept? Well, these are inherited by the entity that implements them, which can be adopted or overwritten, as we will see next.

Using inheritance

The concept of inheritance is present in Bosque through the implementation of concepts in entities, transferring all the properties and actions expressed as fields and methods to the entity. Finally, they will be available in an instance. To implement a concept in an entity, we will use the `provides` keyword.

To understand it better, let's see an example:

```
concept Animal {
    field name: String = "Unknown";
    abstract makeSound(): String;
    method sleep(): String {
        return "zzz";
    }
}

entity Dog provides Animal {
    // Do something
}
```

In the previous snippet, we see that the Dog entity implements the Animal concept. This implies that Dog will have inherited the name field and the makeSound() and sleep() methods, which we can refer to through the instance, as seen in the following code snippet:

```
let bob = Dog@{name = "Bob"};
bob.sleep(); // zzz
```

As we can see when instantiating the Dog entity, we are able to call the methods and ask for the value of the inherited fields without problems.

But what about the makeSound() method? If we were to try to call it, we would get an error, method not implemented. This is because this method has only been declared, and we must implement it in our entities before calling it.

To implement a declared method, we have to use the override statement, which will also help us if we wanted to write the operation of a declared method and implemented it in a concept.

Let's see an example:

```
concept Animal {
    field name: String = "Unknown";
    abstract makeSound(): String;
}

entity Dog provides Animal {
```

```
        override makeSound(): String {
                return "Woof";
        }
}
```

```
let bob = Dog@{name = "Bob"};
bob.makeSound();          // Woof
```

In this example, we see that the Dog entity, in addition to implementing the Animal concept, implements the makeSound() method through overriding, whose result we see when calling the makeSound() method through the bob instance.

Now, let's look at a more classic inheritance application, as we usually use it in object-oriented programming, where inheritance allows us to avoid code repetition by having similar objects that can share properties or methods.

In the following example, we will implement a concept to abstract an animal and three entities – Dog, Cat, and Bird, which, being animals, share properties and some actions, but can also have their own actions and particular properties.

First, we will define a concept in order to be able to represent the idea of an animal, which has generic methods such as sleep(), eat(), and makeSound():

```
concept Animal {
        field name: String = "Unknown";
        method eat(): String {
                // Eat
                return "yummy"
        }
        method sleep(): String {
                // Sleep
                return "zzz"
        };
        abstract makeSound(): String;
}
```

Then we create an entity destined to represent a specific type of animal – a dog:

```
entity Dog provides Animal {
     override makeSound(): String {
          return "Woof";
     }
}
```

As we can observe, the makeSound() method has been overwritten to return the specific sound of a dog. This is because, when using the provides keyword, the Dog entity inherits all the fields and methods declared in the Animal concept, so if we want to implement a method with particular functionality, we must overwrite the inherited method.

In the same way, we create an entity to represent the cats, and we will overwrite the makeSound() method to return the sound of a cat:

```
entity Cat provides Animal {
     override makeSound(): String {
               return "Meow";
     }
}
```

And finally, we also implement a Bird entity in which we can implement the fly() method to represent an action that only birds can perform:

```
entity Bird provides Animal {
     override makeSound(): String {
          return "Tweet";
     }

     method fly(): String {
          return "Flying … ";
     }
}
```

To summarize, we see that all animals share actions including sleep, eat, and walk, so it is unnecessary to implement them repeatedly in each of the entities, but implement them in the Animal concept instead.

On the other hand, we can also observe that even though all animals have the same method called makeSound(), each animal implements this differently since they emit different sounds. To do that, we use method overwriting.

Finally, we see that we have implemented an additional method in the Bird entity since birds are the only ones that can fly in that group.

However, is it always necessary to instantiate objects to be able to use their method? Not really. That's why we will look at static methods next.

Using static methods

By definition, a static method is one that could be used without the need to implement the object that contains it. This gives us the option of using entities as containers of grouped methods under certain criteria that the programmer deems appropriate; for example, to create an entity that houses useful methods of unit conversion.

To mark a method as static in Bosque, we will use the static statement instead of the static method, as follows:

```
entity UnitConverter {
    static poundsToKilograms()(pounds: Float64): Float64 {
        return pounds * 0.453592;
    }
    static milesToKilometers(miles: Float64): Float64 {
        return miles * 1.60934;
    }
}
```

As we can see in the previous example, the poundsToKilograms and milesToKilometers functions would not have to depend on an instance because the programmer would not be interested in doing something specific with the instance, but only needs to use the functionality offered by the method.

In this scenario, requiring the implementation of an instance for the UnitConverter entity would mean an extra unnecessary step, and this is where the static methods do their job.

To use a static method, it is necessary to use a double colon, ::, as follows:

```
UnitConverter::poundsToKilograms(100);        //  453.592
UnitConverter::milesToKilometers (10);        //  16.0934
```

Next, we will see how Bosque implements parametric polymorphism.

Understanding parametric polymorphism

Parametric polymorphism is a way in which programming languages have implemented polymorphism while keeping full-static safety. This happens through generics, so that a function does not depend on the type of its parameters.

By definition, parametric polymorphism allows us to have one implementation supporting many different types. Let's see an example.

The following snippet shows us a function that receives two integers and returns the sum of them:

```
sum(a: Int, b: Int): Int {
return a + b;
}
```

But what if we also want to support the sum of two values of the `Float64` type? We would have to implement a new method designed for `Float64` values, as shown in the following snippet:

```
sum(a: Float64, b: Float64): Float64 {
return a + b;
}
```

But writing an additional method with the same functionality is not the smartest thing to do. We could apply parametric polymorphism and write a single function that works for both `Float64` and `Int` arguments through generics as follows:

```
function sum<T>(a: T, b: T): T {
return a + b;
}
```

As we can see, now, the `sum` function does not expect a unique type, but allows parameters of any type. So, if we want to use integers, we should use the following command:

```
var output: Int = sum<Int>(5, 7);      // 12
```

And if we want to add floating-point numbers, we should write the following command:

```
var output: Float64 = sum<Float64>(5.5, 7.2);          // 12.700000
```

The use of parametric polymorphism is not limited to primitive types, but we could use entities and have polymorphism closer to how we know it in object-oriented programming.

Summary

In this chapter, we have understood how the Bosque nominal type system allows us to have tools to reuse our previously acquired knowledge about object-oriented programming to build our programs.

We have also learned how to build concepts and entities to represent objects and how concepts such as inheritance or static methods can be adopted within our Bosque scripts.

Additionally, we have prepared for the future, familiarizing ourselves with the namespaces that will allow us in the future to structure more complex libraries or projects using Bosque.

We can say that we are now ready to create code and solve problems using Bosque in the next and final chapter. We will learn to test our code to build quality and fail-safe software.

Questions

1. What's the difference between a function and a method in Bosque?
2. What is the `override` keyword used for?
3. Does Bosque support the POO paradigm?
4. What is a static method?

Section 4:
Exploring Advanced Features

In this part, we explain in detail the features presented earlier in the book as well as introducing the Bosque testing tool. After reading this section, you will understand how Bosque code is structured and know how to ensure that your programs are reliable using SymTest.

This section comprises the following chapters:

- *Chapter 12, Namespaces, Concepts, and Entities*
- *Chapter 13, Testing in Bosque*
- *Chapter 14, Project: Path Optimizer*

13
Testing in Bosque

So far, you have learned a lot of useful and practical things regarding the Bosque language. You know the idea of the language as well as the syntax and constructs that have been implemented in Bosque. Put simply, you know the language well enough to write programs or even a larger projects. But as we know, writing the business logic is only one part of the development process. Other parts include, for example, writing documentation and... tests! And that is what we will focus on in this chapter. You will learn about the concept of symbolic testing and will learn how to ensure the code's quality using Bosque features and the SymTest tool. Before you jump into this chapter's content, be aware that the SymTest tool is at a very early stage of development, and we can't expect much from it. In its current state, it allows only for pretty basic testing, but you will learn about its possibilities and what it is designed for.

Here is the list of topics that we are going to cover:

- Discovering symbolic execution
- Introducing SymTest – the Bosque symbolic testing tool
- Practicing symbolic testing
- Working with sanity checks in Bosque

By the end of this chapter, you will have sufficient knowledge for you to use pre- and postconditions, as well as the SymTest tool and invariants in Bosque.

Technical requirements

In order to better understand the contents of this chapter, it is recommended that you already know the following topics:

- Bosque syntax

- Basics of invariants and pre- and postcondition use in Bosque

You can also get acquainted with the examples shared on GitHub at `https://github.com/PacktPublishing/Learn-Bosque-Programming/tree/main/Chapter13`.

Discovering symbolic execution

Let's start this chapter with a little bit of theory. In order to learn how to symbolically test your code in Bosque, you need to know what symbolic execution is. In fact, this concept is not so new. It was introduced in the 1970s, so it's about 50 years old. Symbolic execution is a program analysis technique that can be used to determine what inputs influence the control flow and in what way. It can also generate test inputs that may cause errors in your application to help diagnose any potential problems. It's a very powerful algorithm that in some way changes the way we think about tests.

Normally, when we write unit tests, we provide some example inputs and make assertions in order to ensure that the result of a function is as expected. Using the symbolic testing technique, we are able to discover inputs that will cause every path of a function to execute. If any of the paths will eventually lead to an error being thrown, the symbolic testing algorithm will find out what specific input leads to this place. This way, you are discovering the failing inputs rather than providing them yourself in your test cases. So as you can see, it is somewhat the opposite of unit testing. This doesn't mean, however, that symbolic testing is better, or should be used instead of the more common classical unit testing. Rather, it's a technique that extends and complements what we do on a daily basis.

Symbolic testing is still the subject of intensive research. The first document was published in 1976, and since then, there have been dozens of others. Since the Bosque project itself is currently also in the R&D phase, it feels like a perfect candidate to incorporate symbolic testing into its development. Of course, as useful as the symbolic execution algorithm is, it also does have certain limitations.

One of these is that it does not scale easily to very big programs. As I said before, during symbolic execution, the algorithm explores the program paths and checks what inputs are causing it to be executed. It's not hard to imagine that while it might work quite well in small programs, in the bigger ones that have complicated control flow, it can be a challenge to use it in this way—this leads to a phenomenon called **path explosion**. Another limitation is that symbolic executors cannot deal with arrays, since an array is a collection of many values, and during processing, the executor would have to treat the whole array as one value or each of its elements as a separate value. The second approach is problematic because in order to dynamically calculate an element value, we would need to know what the index value is at a specific call. There are more limitations, such as pointer handling or interactions with the environment (for example, dealing with a program that uses system commands that are out of the symbolic execution tool scope). One example of such an interaction is performing I/O operations. It is hard to deal with this challenge in terms of symbolic testing because usually these operations are delegated to the system and executed as system calls. This is out of the symbolic execution scope, and therefore it can't be controlled. There are a few ways to handle this issue, but all of them have their disadvantages. Let's quickly discuss them so that you know why symbolic testing is still under intensive research.

In order to overcome the challenge of symbolically testing a program that performs I/O, you can use one of many approaches. The first is to simply execute the system calls directly. The problem with this is that it permanently affects the system state, so it's really hard to properly test everything—imagine unit testing a function that saves or reads the file from some location without mocking the system calls. Another approach is to model the environment, which you can think of as the equivalent of mocks in classical unit testing. The problem with this solution is that you have to implement many models that may be quite complex. Another approach is to virtualize the entire system state during testing. While this may solve some of the previous problems, it is not so optimal, as it may use lots of memory.

So, as you can see, the research is indeed necessary because there are still areas that are quite problematic. Nonetheless, even with these limitations, symbolic testing is an interesting technique worth learning.

With that said, let's see how we can use a symbolic testing tool in practice with Bosque.

Introducing SymTest – the Bosque symbolic testing tool

If you have installed Bosque on your system, you will also have installed SymTest. It's a command-line program designed to symbolically test the Bosque source code. A deep analysis of how it works internally is out of the scope of this book. However, there are a couple of facts that are worth pointing out. Under the hood, SymTest uses something called **Z3 Theorem Prover**. It is a **Satisfiability Modulo Theories (SMT)** solver created by Microsoft. *SMT problem* is a mathematical logic term that refers to a decision problem for logical formulas. In fact, the definition is a lot more complicated and touches on many topics in the field of math. For the sake of this chapter, it is enough to know that it is a kind of mathematical logic problem that can be expressed using a set of formulas. This kind of problem needs to be solved using a symbolic analysis of a computer program, and that's why SymTest uses an SMT solver. In Bosque, these problems are expressed using an SMT-LIB2 script, which is generated on the fly and processed by the Z3 prover. All of this work is happening in the background, and you, as a developer, do not need to worry about it too much. This concludes this short introduction to the theory behind the SymTest tool. Now let's learn how to use it.

Before we start using this tool, I think it's a good idea to get familiar with its usage guidance first. As mentioned earlier, SymTest is a command-line tool. As such, it has a few parameters that we are going to introduce in a moment. But first, it's worth pointing out that—unlike the ExeGen tool described in *Chapter 2, Configuring Bosque Environment*—we do not have an alias command that we can use from any place in our system. The tool needs to be called directly using the node command. So, for example, if you want to run it on a file that is created in the same directory that Bosque is installed in on your system, you can do it like this:

```
$ node ./impl/bin/runtimes/symtest/symtest.js myfile.bsq
```

However, this way of using this tool is not so convenient. In order to make your life easier, it's a good idea to create an alias manually so that you can use it from any location in your system.

Creating an alias for the SymTest command

In order to create a custom alias, you need to perform a few steps depending on your operating system. We'll start with the easier one.

MacOS and Linux

If you are using macOS or Linux OS, you are lucky, as there is very little to do here. The first thing that you need to do is to open the terminal and run the following command:

```
$ cd
```

It will change your current working directory to your home folder. You should be there by default if you started a new terminal app, but it's always good practice to make sure you know where you are running your commands from. Once you are in the home directory, you need to open the `.bashrc` file and edit it. You can edit it in any text processor you wish, really. I prefer to use VIM, so my command would look like this:

```
$ vim .bashrc
```

If you also want to use VIM, you can use the same command; otherwise, please use an appropriate one. There are a variety of command-line text editors available (like, for example, Nano), but you can also open this file in any GUI editor. Once you have this file opened, you have to add this line at the end:

```
alias symtest="node /[...]/impl/bin/runtimes/symtest/symtest.
js"
```

Please note that you should replace [...] with the **absolute path** to your Bosque installation directory.

Now save the `.bashrc` file, and in your terminal, type this command:

```
$ source ~/.bashrc
```

This command will initialize your alias. From now on, you should be able to use the `symtest` command from any place in your system. You can now jump to the *Testing the SymTest alias* section in order to test it.

Windows

As for the Windows OS, there is a little bit more work to do. In fact, there is more than one way to create the `symtest` command alias—we will choose the easiest one. It's not perfect, but it's the quickest and the most straightforward way. We will create a folder that will be added to your `Path` environment variable, inside which you will be able to create `.bat` files that will serve as aliases. In fact, they will be regular programs rather than actual aliases, but eventually they will allow us to use the `symtest` command across the whole system, and that's exactly what we want to achieve. Alright, let's get things done.

The first thing to do is to create the directory that will contain our `.bat` files. You can choose any location—wherever you feel is appropriate. If you don't have any preferences, then you can create it directly on your `C:\` drive. Let's name it `aliases` so that the path will look like this:

```
C:\aliases
```

Now, you have to add this path to the `Path` environment variable. If you don't know what it is, it's enough for you to know that environment variables are system-wide values that can be read from any place in your entire operating system. There are many environment variables that are important and reserved for some specific tasks. You can also create your own custom environment variables. The `Path` variable is responsible for providing a list of paths that contain executable binaries. It is used to find a program to run when you are using the command line. For example, when you try to run a command that the system does not recognize, it will look up every directory specified in the `Path` list for a program with the same name as your command. In our case, if you try to use the `symtest` command, the system will not recognize it, and so it will start the `Path` lookup. But the command will not be found, so you'll see an error. Let's make the system find it and edit the `Path` value. In order to do this, you need to open the **Control Panel** and open the **System** settings. On the left-hand side of the window, you will find a couple of options. Click the **Advanced system settings** option, as highlighted in the following screenshot:

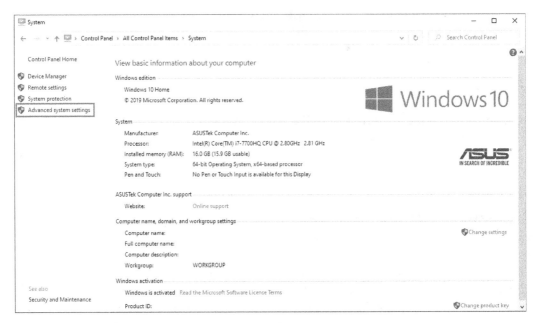

Figure 13.1 – System settings window

Now, in the **System properties** window that just appeared, navigate to the **Advanced** tab. At the bottom, under the **Startup and Recovery** section, click the **Environment Variables…** button highlighted in the next screenshot:

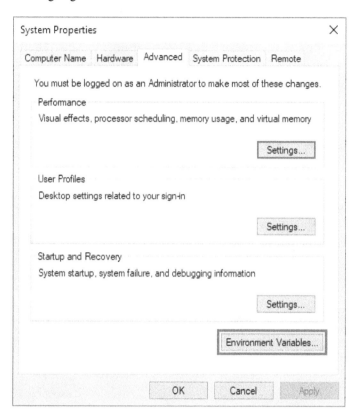

Figure 13.2 – System Properties window

In the **Environment Variables** window, there are two lists of variables. The first one is the list of variables defined for the current user. Only this user has access to them. The second list contains variables defined for the whole system and all users. You may see duplicated variables that are defined in both lists—this is nothing to worry about, it's OK. We are interested in the **Path** variable—find it in the first list and click on it. If it isn't in the first list, you can either create a new variable named `Path` using the **New...** button or you can find it in the **System variables** list. If you are not sure where to click, have a look at the next screenshot:

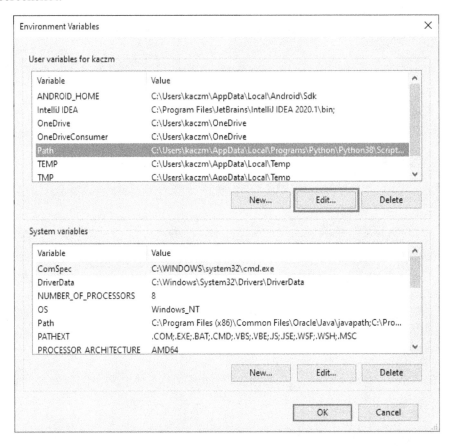

Figure 13.3 – Environment Variables window

Once you have clicked on the **Path** variable, click on the **Edit...** button under the list—the **Edit environment variable** window should open with similar content to the following screenshot:

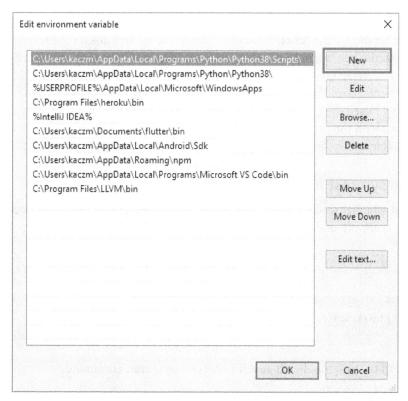

Figure 13.4 – Edit environment variable window

On the right-hand side of the window, find and click the **New** button as marked on the image. Once the new cursor shows up, fill the new row with the following content:

```
C:\aliases
```

If your directory with alias scripts is created in a different location, make sure that you provide the correct one here. Now you can close all the opened windows by clicking **OK** on each of them in order to save the changes.

Alright, you have prepared the system configuration, so now it's time to create your first alias. Inside the alias (or whatever you have named it) directory, create a new file called symtest.bat. It's important for it to have the .bat extension because otherwise it won't work. Put the following content into this file:

```
@echo off
echo.
node C:\[...]\BosqueLanguage\impl\bin\runtimes\symtest\symtest.
js %*
```

Now save the file. We won't dive deep into details of what this code does; it's enough to know that first we disable the functionality that shows the commands on the screen as they are being executed. Then, we output a blank line and after that we run the Bosque SymTest tool. Note the %* characters at the end of the node command. They are a placeholder for all of the arguments passed to the symtest command—they will be passed to the node command. Also, I used the [...] placeholder in the path pointing to the symtest.js script. Replace it with the path that you installed the Bosque language in. From now on, you should be able to use the symtest command from any place in your system.

Testing the symtest alias

It's time to test whether it works. Go ahead and create a simple program in Bosque. It can be something as simple as this:

```
namespace NSMain;

entrypoint function main(arg: Int): Int {
        return arg * 2;
}
```

Save the file and try to symbolically test it using our new alias command:

```
$ symtest main.bsq
```

You should see an output similar to this one:

```
Symbolic testing of Bosque sources in files:
main.bsq
...
Transpiling Bosque assembly to bytecode with entrypoint of
NSMain::main...
Running z3 on SMT encoding...
Detected possible errors!
Rerun with '-m' flag to attempt to generate failing inputs.
```

Don't worry about the possible errors part—the program is expected to fail symbolic testing. We'll get to that in a second in the *Practicing symbolic testing* section. But first, let's focus on the -m flag and the rest of the parameters that you can pass to the symtest command. If you received a different output or some unexpected commands, please make sure that you followed all the required steps described earlier. In the meantime, let's learn how to use the SymTest tool.

Command line parameters and flags

The SymTest tool accepts a few flags that allow you to slightly affect the behavior of the program. Let's have a look at them one by one:

- `-e, --entrypoint [entrypoint]`: If your program contains multiple `entrypoint` functions, you can use this flag to specify which one you want to analyze. By default, the `"NSMain::main"` will be used. An example usage may look like this:

  ```
  $ symtest main.bsq -e "NSMain::run"
  ```

- `-m, --model`: If the analysis of your programs uncovers possible errors in your code, you may want to know what the inputs that cause your program to fail are. If that's the case, you can use the `-m` flag, which will make the SymTest tool generate failing inputs and print them on the console. An example usage may look like this:

  ```
  $ symtest main.bsq -m
  ```

- `-v, --verify`: This flag is a switch between the symbolic tester and the verifier. When used, the verifier will be run instead of the symbolic tester. Unfortunately, at the time of writing, it hasn't been fully implemented yet and throws unexpected errors, and therefore I do not recommend using it. However, if you are reading this at a time when it works properly, you can use it like this:

  ```
  $ symtest main.bsq -v
  ```

- `-o, --output [file]`: You can use this option to get the SMT model saved into a file. After symbolic analysis, the model will be outputted into a chosen file, which you will be able to use afterward. It's an option for more advanced users that wish to perform some manual work with the Z3 Theorem Prover mentioned earlier. An example usage may look like this:

  ```
  $ symtest main.bsq -o model.out
  ```

These are all of the parameters that are supported by the SymTest tool at the time of writing. Remember that you can use multiple flags at once. For example, if you want to generate failing inputs and output a model into a file, you can use both `-m` and `-o` flags.

> **Important note**
>
> At the time of writing, there are some missing features in this tool, and therefore some of the examples presented in this chapter may not work properly. There are existing PRs on the official GitHub repository that fix some of these errors, but keep in mind that it may not work for you if the PRs are not merged yet.

At this point, you know what the SymTest tool is, what it can be used for, and how to customize its behavior. This knowledge is quite useful, as it allows you to explore a whole new area of testing scenarios. Now it's time to turn this knowledge into practice. Let's see how you can use symbolic testing in Bosque.

Practicing symbolic testing

Firstly, let's get back to our simple example that we wrote to test whether the `symtest` command works. As a reminder, this is what it looked like:

```
namespace NSMain;


entrypoint function main(arg: Int): Int {


        return arg * 2;
}
```

When you ran the symbolic testing, you saw information about the possible errors that were detected. It is time to check these errors and see whether there is anything we can do about them. In order to make the SymTest tool generate some failing inputs, you need to pass the -m flag:

```
$ symtest main.bsq -m
```

After running this command, you should see an output similar to this one:

```
Symbolic testing of Bosque sources in files:
main.bsq
...
Transpiling Bosque assembly to bytecode with entrypoint of
NSMain::main...
Running z3 on SMT encoding...
Detected possible errors!
Attempting to extract inputs...
arg = 4503599627370496
```

Note the `Attempting to extract inputs...` part. Right beneath that, there is this line:

```
arg = 4503599627370496
```

It refers to the `arg` argument declared to the `entrypoint` function `main`. SymTest detected that if we pass the number `4503599627370496` as an argument to our program, it will fail. Let's see if this is true:

```
$ ./a.exe 4503599627370496
Bad argument for arg -- expected (small) Int got
4503599627370496
```

If you got the same error, it's fine. It looks like our simple program will fail when a big number is passed as an argument. You may be wondering what is wrong with this number. In Bosque, there are two constant fields defined in the `Int` entity—`Int::min_value` and `Int::max_value`. Their values are `-9007199254740991` and `9007199254740991` respectively. The number that SymTest returned as possible error is half of it. This is because we are returning a doubled value of the argument passed to the `main` function. After multiplying it by 2, we will get a number bigger than the `Int::max_value`. Did you think about that when you were writing it? This is why symbolic testing is so useful.

Alright, we have found one failing input, but how do we deal with it? Well, there are two ways. The first way is to use `BigInt` instead of `Int`. It is a core type created to handle big numbers. However, this entity is not fully implemented yet, and you can't really use it. The second option is to use the `requires release` precondition, which will prevent it from passing too big an argument. This is how we could do it:

```
entrypoint function main(arg: Int): Int
        requires release (arg < Int::max_value / 2);{

        return arg * 2;
}
```

This way, we are ensuring that the `arg` value must be less than half of the maximum `Int` value. Let's run the symbolic testing again to see if we have fully resolved this issue:

```
$ symtest main.bsq -m
Symbolic testing of Bosque sources in files:
main.bsq
...
Transpiling Bosque assembly to bytecode with entrypoint of
NSMain::main...
Running z3 on SMT encoding...
```

```
Detected possible errors!
Attempting to extract inputs...
arg = (- 4503599627370496)
```

Something is still not right. The error has changed—now we are handling very big numbers correctly, but what about very small numbers? They need to be properly handled too. Let's fix this by modifying the `requires release` condition:

```
entrypoint function main(arg: Int): Int
        requires release (arg < Int::max_value / 2) && (arg >
Int::min_value / 2);
  {


        return arg * 2;
}
```

Now rerun the SymTest tool. It should finally say that it didn't find any errors. If you run it with the -m flag, you will see a warning like this:

```
Cannot generate model '-m' as errors were not found?
```

After you remove the -m flag, this is the output you should see:

```
$ symtest main.bsq
Symbolic testing of Bosque sources in files:
main.bsq
...
Transpiling Bosque assembly to bytecode with entrypoint of
NSMain::main...
Running z3 on SMT encoding...
Verified up to bound -- no errors found!
```

This means that our program is finally error proof. It is a very convenient way of ensuring the software quality. Let's see how we can improve our code using built-in features by looking at some more examples.

Working with sanity checks in Bosque

We have already partially covered this topic in *Chapter 3, Bosque Key Features*. We talked about the `invariant` keyword, and the `requires`, `requires release`, and `ensures` conditions. We also mentioned the assertions and checks. Let's see how we can use them in practice along with the SymTest tool.

Before we get started let's consider an example program. It's not going to be rocket science. For the sake of this chapter we will build a simple Bin2Dec converter. It will take the provided binary number and return its decimal representation. We will limit the binary representation to four bits and will require every bit to be passed as a separate argument. It may look a bit inconvenient and it's true but it will make you understand the SymTest tool better.

At this point you already know the Bosque syntax and most of the rules so I won't dive deep into the implementation. Have a look at the following code:

```
namespace NSMain;

function power(base: Int, exp: Int): Int {
    return if (exp == 0) 1 else base * power(base, exp - 1);
}

entity Context {
    field position: Int = 0;
    field bin: List<Int>;
    field acc: Int = 0;
}

entrypoint function main(p1: Int, p2: Int, p3: Int, p4: Int):
Int {
    let b = List<Int>@{p1, p2, p3, p4};
    let ctx = Context@{bin = b.reverse()};
    let resCtx = NSIterate::steps<Context>(
        ctx,
        ctx.bin.size(),
        fn(ctx) => {
            let dec = power(2, ctx.position) * ctx.bin.get(ctx.
position);
            return ctx.update(acc = ctx.acc + dec, position =
```

```
ctx.position + 1);
      }
  );
   return resCtx.acc;
}
```

Here we are defining a helper function named power that performs the mathematical operation in the recursive way. Then, we are defining a helper Context entity that will hold essential data required for conversion (you've seen similar entities across this book a few times already so I hope you know how it works by now). Eventually, we are constructing our main function that accepts four Int arguments and using NSIterate::steps<T>() function simply converts the bits to their decimal representation. The way it works is simple:

1. Create a list of bits provided in arguments

2. For every bit, calculate 2 to the power of current bit position and multiply it by the current bit

3. Update the accumulated value and current position

That way we get the result and return it as return `resCtx.acc`.

Alright, if you try to compile this program and run it, it will work without any errors. Go ahead and try this out. Assuming you named your file bin2dec.bsq, in order to compile this you need to run:

```
$ exegen bin2dec.bsq
```

Now run this program and see the result:

```
$ ./a.exe 1 1 0 1
13
```

The result is correct because 1101 in binary is equal to decimal 13. Now let's run the SymTest tool to see if there are any possible errors:

```
$ symtest bin2dec.bsq
```

You should see that there were errors detected. Re-run this command with the -m flag to see them. You should see something similar to this one:

```
Symbolic testing of Bosque sources in files:
```

```
bin2dec.bsq

...

Transpiling Bosque assembly to bytecode with entrypoint of
NSMain::main...

Running z3 on SMT encoding...

Detected possible errors!

Attempting to extract inputs...

p1 = 10

p2 = 12

p3 = 14

p4 = 9007199254740992
```

It looks like there are some failing inputs in the main entrypoint. As you can see, we have a problem with Int bounds again. Let's define a function that checks the boundaries and apply it in the requires release check. This is how the function could look like:

```
function inBitBounds(...values: List<Int>): Bool {
    return values.allOf(
        fn(v) => v == 0 || v == 1
    );
}
```

Notice that actually we can narrow down the possible values to only two – 0 and 1 – because these are the only possible values for numbers in binary system. That way we fixed two problems – integer boundaries and validity of the bits. You can use this function as following:

```
entrypoint function main(p1: Int, p2: Int, p3: Int, p4: Int):
Int
    requires release inBitBounds(p1, p2, p3, p4);
{
    let b = List<Int>@{p1, p2, p3, p4};
    let ctx = Context@{bin = b.reverse()};
    let resCtx = NSIterate::steps<Context>(
        ctx,
        ctx.bin.size(),
        fn(ctx) => {
            let dec = power(2, ctx.position) * ctx.bin.get(ctx.
position);
```

```
            return ctx.update(acc = ctx.acc + dec, position =
ctx.position + 1);
        }
    );
    return resCtx.acc;
}
```

Notice the highlighted part. Here we are defining the `requires release` precondition. It is checked always – in debug mode as well as in the optimized builds. We are using our helper function to check if all of the parameters have a proper value.

Another thing worth doing is ensuring that the result we produce from the main function is not greater than 15 because this is the maximum decimal value that you can store in binary representation. This is how we can do that:

```
entrypoint function main(p1: Int, p2: Int, p3: Int, p4: Int):
Int
    requires release inBitBounds(p1, p2, p3, p4);
    ensures $return <= 15;
{
    // The code has not changed at all
}
```

Thanks to that, we will make sure that this function returns valid result and nothing else.

One more thing that can be improved is to ensure that our position field in the `Context` entity has always a valid value and the bin list has the length of 4. We can do that using the invariant keyword like this:

```
entity Context {
    field position: Int = 0;
    field bin: List<Int>;
    field acc: Int = 0;
    invariant $position <= $bin.size();
    invariant $bin.size() == 4;
}
```

Invariants are checked before an instance of that entity is created. It means that thanks to that, there is no any moment in time that an instance with invalid values (violating invariants) exists. It is a very convenient way of checking various conditions.

> **Important note**
>
> As mentioned earlier, in the current state, the tool is missing some of its features, and therefore the next command will not execute properly unless you comment out the `invariant` check in the `Context` entity like this:
>
> ```
> // invariant $position <= $bin.size();
> // invariant $bin.size() == 4;
> ```
>
> If you leave it in, SymTest will fail with an unexpected error.

Alright, after all these modifications, let's see if anything has changed in the result of symbolic tests:

```
$ symtest bin2dec.bsq
```

If you have followed all of the changes carefully, you should see the `Verified up to bound -- no errors found!` message, which means that there are no more errors detected.

I strongly recommend that you play with the SymTest tool and the built-in features that allow us to ensure high software quality. In the meantime, let's sum up what we have learned so far.

Summary

In this chapter, you learned a few new things about testing software and how Bosque utilizes these techniques in order to allow you to create high-reliability software. Let's go through the topics that we covered one by one.

Firstly, you learned about the concept of symbolic execution and how it can augment classical unit testing. You know that it is not a new thing, but it's still under intensive research, which means that there are still a lot of things to discover in this area.

Then, you learned about the SymTest tool. It is a command-line tool that allows you to symbolically test Bosque source code. You learned how to create an alias, which makes it a lot easier to use this tool. You also learned how you can customize its behavior using flags, but also learned that this tool is currently quite limited and allows for rather basic testing—you can't use it for more advanced programs as it will fail to analyze it. Nonetheless, you learned about its possibilities and you have an idea of what it aims to do.

After that, you practiced symbolic testing using the SymTest tool. You saw that even for very simple programs there may be inputs that will cause your program to fail, and you learned how to deal with them using the built-in `requires release` precondition.

Last but not least, you have created a simple number converter in order to symbolically test it. You identified possible errors thanks to the SymTest tool and fixed the issues so that the code is secure and error proof.

In the next chapter, we will build an application that finds the shortest path between two cities.

Alright, it is time for the last set of questions, where you will be able to use all of the knowledge that you have gained in this book so far. It will help you to better remember the concepts you have learned. Let's not waste any more time and jump right into it.

Questions

4.   What is symbolic testing?

5.   What is the SymTest tool?

6.   What is the Z3 Theorem Prover?

7.   What are pre- and postconditions in Bosque? What keywords do we use to apply them?

8.   What are invariants?

Further reading

Here is a list of useful resources that will enhance your knowledge about the topics covered in this chapter:

* Programming Z3: `http://theory.stanford.edu/~nikolaj/programmingz3.html`

* King, J.C. 1976. '*Symbolic execution and program testing*'. *Communications of the ACM.* 19(7) (July 1976), 385–394. DOI: `https://doi.org/10.1145/360248.360252`.

* Khurshid S., PĂsĂreanu C.S., Visser W. (2003). '*Generalized Symbolic Execution for Model Checking and Testing*'. In: Garavel H., Hatcliff J, (eds) *Tools and Algorithms for the Construction and Analysis of Systems.* (TACAS). Lecture in *Notes in Computer Science*, vol 2619. Berlin, Heidelberg: Springer. DOI: `https://doi.org/10.1007/3-540-36577-X_40`.

14
Project: Path Optimizer

During the last few years, we have witnessed the emergence of new companies that have changed the way we take taxis, shop online, and drive our cars.

Many of these innovations have resulted from engineering teams' effort to build efficient algorithms to calculate the optimal routes to move from one geographical point to another at an optimal cost.

For this reason, we will learn how to solve an optimal path problem using Bosque to provide to our readers another practical Bosque application to solve real-world problems through the following topics:

- Defining requirements
- Implementation of the program
- Building and running

At the end of this chapter, we will have learned how to implement one of the best-known algorithms for finding optimal routes using Bosque, which we will be able to use on practical real-life projects.

Technical requirements

You need an installation of Bosque (the complete process of installation was explained in *Chapter 2, Configuring the Bosque Environment*).

You'll also need a text editor of your choice.

Defining requirements

As we have seen in previous practical chapters, we will start by defining the problem and the objectives that we will achieve during this project's development.

In this chapter, we'll build a program that allows us to calculate the optimal route to get from point A to point B, considering that each of the possible paths chosen could directly impact the calculation of time or cost.

To simplify the problem and to facilitate the design of an adequate algorithm, we are going to simplify the problem. See the diagram on the left side of the following figure. Now imagine you can move from point A to point B using any path, without any problems:

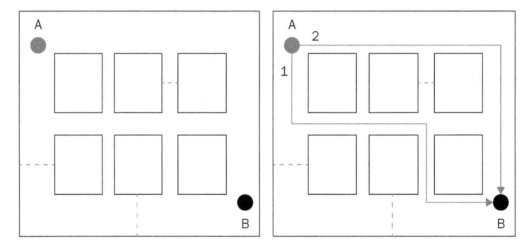

Figure 14.1 – Paths from A to B

On the right side of *Figure 14.1*, you can see that you can choose several paths. However, if you consider the obstacles (marked by the dotted lines), our options are reduced but still, you could choose paths 1 or 2.

If we want to bring our representation closer to a real scenario, we must consider that a specific path involves different traffic levels, traffic lights, the state of the road, or available lanes. So we will need a way to represent how these variables impact the cost and time of choosing a specific route.

As we can see in the following figure, we will use weighted weights to summarize the impact of all the variables on time and cost when choosing each of the route sections:

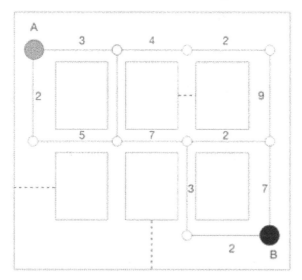

Figure 14.2 – Path segments between A and B

We could try to find a shorter path from the previous image, starting from segments with minor weights. But we have to remember that an optimal path could start from a high number too, and later on find lower weights, which in sum could result in a route with lower costs, so this initial reasoning could be misleading.

For this reason, the best way to calculate the optimal route is to try to explore every possible path, discarding the paths whose sum of weights give us higher numbers than previously explored paths. This reasoning is referred to as *Dijkstra's shortest paths algorithm*.

At this point, we have deduced that to calculate the optimal route, we must apply the Dijkstra's algorithm, which receives the following arguments: an available path matrix, the weight of each segment, the starting node, and the destination node.

We can define our to-do list as follows:

1. Storing our problem data in an orderly structure
2. Implementing Dijkstra's algorithm to get the optimal route
3. Processing our data using the written algorithm and returning a human-readable format

Now that we have our list of tasks, in the next section, we will see our program's implementation.

Implementation of the program

In this section, we will implement the program in Bosque to calculate the optimal route following the tasks defined in the previous section.

Storing our problem data in an orderly structure

In order to correctly represent our practical case, we will represent our graph through an adjacency matrix stored in a two-dimensional array, as we can see in the next figure:

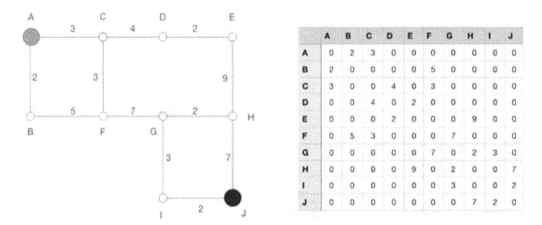

	A	B	C	D	E	F	G	H	I	J
A	0	2	3	0	0	0	0	0	0	0
B	2	0	0	0	0	5	0	0	0	0
C	3	0	0	4	0	3	0	0	0	0
D	0	0	4	0	2	0	0	0	0	0
E	0	0	0	2	0	0	0	9	0	0
F	0	5	3	0	0	0	7	0	0	0
G	0	0	0	0	0	7	0	2	3	0
H	0	0	0	0	9	0	2	0	0	7
I	0	0	0	0	0	0	3	0	0	2
J	0	0	0	0	0	0	0	7	2	0

Figure 14.3 – Adjacency matrix

In this adjacency matrix, we represent the section's weight between two points on the graph. When there is no connection between two points or the same place, it is assigned zero to denote that they are not possible routes.

Now that we have a data matrix, we can implement it in Bosque using Int value lists, as we can see in the following code:

```
var graph: List<List<Int>> = List<List<Int>>@{
        List<Int>@{0, 2, 3, 0, 0, 0, 0, 0, 0, 0},
        List<Int>@{2, 0, 0, 0, 0, 5, 0, 0, 0, 0},
        List<Int>@{3, 0, 0, 4, 0, 3, 0, 0, 0, 0},
        List<Int>@{0, 0, 4, 0, 2, 0, 0, 0, 0, 0},
        List<Int>@{0, 0, 0, 2, 0, 0, 0, 9, 0, 0},
        List<Int>@{0, 5, 3, 0, 0, 0, 7, 0, 0, 0},
        List<Int>@{0, 0, 0, 0, 0, 7, 0, 2, 3, 0},
        List<Int>@{0, 0, 0, 0, 9, 0, 2, 0, 0, 7},
        List<Int>@{0, 0, 0, 0, 0, 0, 3, 0, 0, 2},
```

```
                List<Int>@{0, 0, 0, 0, 0, 0, 0, 7, 2, 0}
    };
```

This matrix will allow us to represent an iterable structure in order to be able to implement our algorithm more easily.

To have ordered code, we will store this information within an entity that represents our graph and contains our case's variables.

Let's see the implementation of our `PathContext` entity:

```
entity PathContext {
    field graph: List<List<Int>> = List<List<Int>>@{
        List<Int>@{0, 2, 3, 0, 0, 0, 0, 0, 0, 0},
        // ...
        List<Int>@{0, 0, 0, 0, 0, 0, 0, 7, 2, 0}
    };

    field v: Int = 0;
    field unvisited: List<Bool> = List<Bool>@{
        true, true, true, true, true,
        true, true, true, true, true
    };
    field psc: PathStepContext = PathStepContext@{
        distances = List<Int>@{
            0, Int::max_value, Int::max_value,
            Int::max_value, Int::max_value,
            Int::max_value, Int::max_value,
            Int::max_value, Int::max_value,
            Int::max_value
        }
    };
}
```

In this code, we see two new elements: the `unvisited` list, which will allow us to record the points we have already passed through, and the `psc` field, which stores each of the steps in the algorithm that we will use to calculate the optimal route.

Now that we have the necessary information to represent our problem data, we will implement the algorithm.

Implementing Dijkstra's algorithm to get the optimal route

Dijkstra's algorithm is one of the best-known algorithms for calculating optimal routes based on external variables that condition each of the route segments, and this is why we will use it to solve our problem.

Let's see the pseudocode of Dijkstra's algorithm:

1. Mark all nodes as `unvisited`.

2. Mark the initial node as `current`. For the current node, set the tentative distance to zero, and set it to infinity for all other nodes. In our case, infinity is going to be the maximum possible value.

3. Calculate the accumulated weights from the current node to its unvisited neighbors, compare them, and assign the smallest value as a possible optimal path.

4. Once all of the unvisited neighbors are calculated, we will mark the current node as visited and will never check it again.

5. Otherwise, select the unvisited node that is marked with the smallest path, set it as the new `current` node, and go back to *step 3*.

Each repetition of this list of tasks is considered a step of the algorithm. As you may have noticed, it is essential to be able to store the tentative distances, so we are going to implement an entity that allows us to keep the information related to the execution context of each step:

```
entity PathStepContext {
    field distances: List<Int>;
    field i: Int = 0;
}
```

Additionally, in order to simplify our algorithm, we are going to create two useful functions that allow us to encapsulate code that we will use frequently. They are as follows:

- `findIndexOfMin`: This will allow us to calculate which element has the minimum tentative distance:

```
function findIndexOfMin(
    dists: List<Int>, unvisited: List<Bool>
): Int {

    let unvisitedDistances = unvisited.mapIndex<Int>(
```

```
        fn(curr, i) => if (curr == true) dists.get(i)
else Int::max_value
    );
```

```
    return unvisitedDistances.lastIndexOf(
        unvisitedDistances.min()
    );
}
```

- findNeighbours: This function will allow us to obtain the neighboring neighbors for each node of the graph:

```
function findNeighbours(
    arr: List<Int>
): List<Int> {
    return arr
        .mapIndex<Int>(fn(c, i) => if(c != 0) i else -1)
        .filter(fn(i) => i != -1); // filter out
non-neighbours
}
```

Now that we have implemented the entities that allow us to encapsulate the data associated with each algorithm's context and the practical functions, we can focus on writing our main algorithm.

First, let's see how the algorithm works graphically:

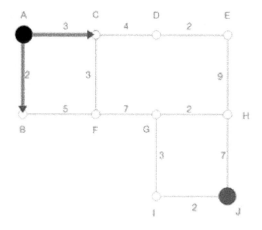

Figure 14.4 – Graphical representation of the algorithm

After determining our starting point, we add the distance from our starting point to the current node (in this case, 0). Now we are going to calculate the distance between each of its neighbors. Let's start with B, 0 + 2 = 2, then we take point C, and we calculate the distance 0 + 3 = 3. Finally, we compare these values and decide that the next step is the unvisited node with the lowest distance value, in this case, B:

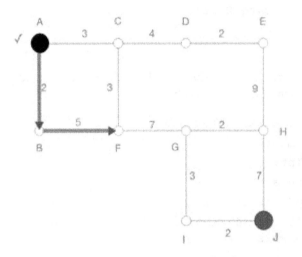

Figure 14.5 – Minimum unvisited node, B

Now we have a new current node from where we will repeat the previous procedure. We will calculate the sum of the distance from A to B and from B to F. In this case, 2 + 5 = 7, so we compare that value with the minimum value C (3) and choose the lowest value, 3, which takes us back to node C. We leave node B marked as visited:

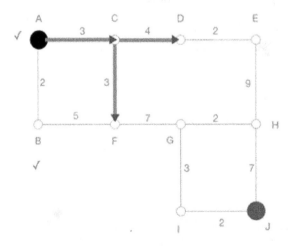

Figure 14.6 – Node B marked

At this point, we must repeat the procedure constantly until we mark the destination node as visited or reach the termination conditions outlined in the pseudocode of our algorithm.

Now that we have a better idea of how the algorithm works, let's see what this implementation would be like in Bosque:

```
var pc = PathContext@{};
pc = NSIterate::steps<PathContext>(
    pc,
    pc.graph.size(),
        let neighbours = findNeighbours(pc.graph.get(current));
        let psctx = NSIterate::steps<PathStepContext>(
            pc.psc.update(i = 0),
            neighbours.size(),
            fn(psc) => {
                let n = neighbours.get(psc.i);
                let notVisited = pc.unvisited.get(n) == true;
                let distToN = psc.distances.get(current) +
pc.graph.get(current).get(n);
                let dists = psc.distances.mapIndex<Int>(fn(d,
i)=>{
                    return if (notVisited && distToN <= psc.
distances.get(n) && i == n) distToN else d;
                });
                return psc.update(i = psc.i + 1, distances =
dists);
            }
        );
        return pc.update(
            v = pc.v + 1,
            unvisited = pc.unvisited.mapIndex<Bool>(fn(curr, i)
=> if(i == current) false else curr),
            psc = psctx
        );
    }
);
```

In this code, we can observe the use of NSIterate to solve the iteration of our graph and represent the steps of our algorithm.

We also calculate the neighbors and update the current node according to the new conditions in each step. Finally, we make the necessary comparisons to calculate the new values for the next step and update the viewed nodes and the estimated distances in order to prepare our data for the next step.

Processing our data using the written algorithm and returning a human-readable format

To return an understandable result for humans, we will return a list of distances that contains the minimum distance between the initial node and all the other nodes where we can quickly identify the minimum cost or time to reach the destination node.

We could return a list of floats or just print our values using _debug as follows:

```
_debug("Shortests paths from vertex 0:");
_debug(pc.psc.distances);
```

Finally, we can insert our code in a generic entrypoint function to allow the execution of our program, as follows:

```
entrypoint function main(): String {

    // our algorithm goes here …

    _debug("Shortests paths from vertex 0:");
    _debug(pc.psc.distances);
    return "Done.";
}
```

Now that we have understood how to use Bosque to implement our code to find the cost of the optimal route, we will see how to run our program.

Demo and running our program

Because we have a common entry point, we can do a compilation without extra arguments. For this, we will use the following command:

```
exegen script.bsq -o output
```

When executing the previous command, we will generate the binary called `output` that contains the executable version of our program; then, when executing our program we will obtain something similar to the following:

```
Shortests paths from vertex 0:
{0, 2, 3, 7, 9, 6, 13, 15, 16, 18}
Done
```

This means that the distance from the initial node to the final node (vertex 5) is 9 because at index 5, there is number 9. Indexes here denote vertex numbers.

Summary

In this chapter, we have learned how to solve an optimal path search problem using Bosque. We have been able to review concepts that we have previously learned throughout this book.

During the project's development, we have learned how to implement Dijkstra's algorithm using Bosque, which will help us build future real-life projects implementing many other well-known algorithms.

At the end of this chapter, we have consolidated our learning about the language, and we are ready to understand any code written in Bosque and create our solutions.

It is time to take one last step in our journey and learn how the Bosque language is implemented, how it works, how to contribute and what's next. All of these things are presented to you in the next two appendices. In *Appendix A: Advanced Topics*, you will learn how programming languages are built and dive deep into Bosque project structure. You will also learn how to contribute in order to improve the language by yourself. In *Appendix B: What's Next in Bosque*, you will discover the project roadmap and learn what to expect in the future of Bosque development. Go ahead and jump right into it!

Questions

1. What is an adjacency matrix?
2. What is Dijkstra's algorithm for?
3. What is a graph?

Further reading

- Cormen, Thomas H.; Leiserson, Charles E.; Rivest, Ronald L.; Stein, Clifford (2001). *Section 24.3: Dijkstra's algorithm*. Introduction to Algorithms (Second ed.). MIT Press and McGraw–Hill. pp. 595–601

- Knuth, D.E. (1977). *A Generalization of Dijkstra's Algorithm*. Information Processing Letters

Appendix A
Advanced Topics

In this appendix, we will show what the Bosque project structure looks like, describe its internals, and show you how you can contribute to the project. Since the project is still under heavy development, lacking certain implementations, and with bugs and feature requests still present, everyone is welcome to improve the language with their own contributions. This appendix is rather introductory so you won't have much to do here. Instead, you will learn where to find the source code, understand its overall structure, and see how to make your own changes and suggestions.

Here is a list of topics that we are going to cover:

- Discovering the Bosque source code and the project structure
- Learning how to report bugs and feature requests
- Learning how to contribute

At the end of this appendix, you will know what the process of designing a new programming language looks like. You will also be familiar with the code structure of the Bosque project and will be able to report bugs and feature requests, as well as being able to contribute.

Technical requirements

In order to better understand the contents of this appendix, it is recommended to have knowledge on the following topics:

- All of the contents of this book covered thus far
- Basic knowledge about creating programming languages
- An understanding of the basics of Git and GitHub

Discovering the Bosque source code and the project structure

If you want to be able to contribute to the Bosque project, or just want to know how it works internally, you should get familiar with the project structure. In this section, we will briefly discover the structure of the code to teach you how Bosque is built and where to look for various files. Of course, we will not analyze every file and every line of code, as this would require even more lines of text and this is beyond the scope of this book. We'll quickly go through the structure just to get some orientation. Firstly, let's understand what is needed to create a programming language.

Understanding the design of a programming language

There are a couple of things to think about when creating a programming language. Just to be clear – there is no perfect recipe for this. There are always many ways to achieve the same thing – regardless of what this thing is. What I want to say is that usually developers follow some patterns when it comes to creating a programming language (and this applies not only in programming, actually). So let me quickly list some of the steps that you probably should take if you ever want to create another programming language.

The first thing to decide is whether the language will be compiled or interpreted. The difference is that compiled languages are harder to design and implement because you need to come up with a way to transform the code written in your new language to machine code – you need to create a compiler. Interpreted languages are easier because you only need some runtime that will interpret your code and execute it. You can make use of another programming language and will not have to think about compilation at all. In other words, you need to create an interpreter. Both approaches have their own advantages and disadvantages – you need to decide which one will better meet your needs. But that's not all that you need to think about.

Another thing to take into consideration is how your language will actually look and what the syntax rules will be. In every language (not only programming ones) there is a set of rules that define how to use it – the grammar. You need to think about the syntax, what is legal and what is not. Put simply, you need to decide how your language is going to be interpreted and understood. This is the moment where it's a good idea to create an **Abstract Syntax Tree (AST)**. The AST is a result of parsing the source code. It is a tree representation of the source code where each node represents some language construct. It is something that is very useful both for humans and machines. The former are able to visualize the grammar and better understand the code. The latter are able to easily process such structures. Let's mention one more thing that you need to have covered – the parser.

Parsing is the process of consuming the code and validating the syntax. Once you figure out the syntax of your programming language, you will have to create a parser that will validate the code that is written according to the grammar and generate the AST. It sounds easy but is not – you have to take into consideration many cases and decide whether this is a legal syntax or not.

Last but not least, we cannot forget about semantics. The syntax describes how the language is constructed – in other words, it answers the question, does it look like valid code? Are all of the keywords, braces, and operators properly placed? Semantics, however, answers a different question: what does this code mean? Can these parentheses be placed after this name? For example, in your new language, this syntax may be valid:

```
float speed = 10.5;
speed++;
```

The language constructs could be used properly, but semantically it may be incorrect, because you might have decided that only integer values can be incremented using the ++ operator. And that's the difference between syntax and semantics – and both things are very important.

There are many more things to say really, but I just wanted you to have a general picture of what we are talking about. Having said that, let's see how the Bosque project is structured.

Looking at the Bosque source code

As already mentioned a couple of times before, Bosque is an open source project. All of the code is publicly available on GitHub at https://github.com/microsoft/BosqueLanguage. If you haven't already, go ahead and clone the repository so that you can easily browse the files. In order to do that, you can run this command:

```
$ git clone https://github.com/microsoft/BosqueLanguage.git
```

As for the repository in general, there are four branches: `master`, `bmc_preview`, `road_to_1_0`, and `v1`. All of the relevant work is happening on the `master` branch right now. As for the name of this branch – do not get confused with the latest trends in the open source community as many projects have changed the name `master` to `main`. Although currently in this repository it's named `master`, there is a chance that it will get renamed to `main`. You may also want to follow the changes made on the `road_to_1_0` branch because, as of this writing, it will probably be updated soon and merged into `master` at some point. Now let's have a look at the files' structure.

At the root of the project, there are three directories worth mentioning: `bosque-language-tools`, `docs`, and `impl`. If you've read *Chapter 2, Configuring Bosque Environment*, you probably remember the first one. Inside this directory, there are files responsible for the VS Code plugin. You need to copy this one to your VS Code extensions folder in order to install it. The second one – `docs` – contains a few `README.md` files nested in the sub-folders. Here you can find the language documentation as well as some extra stuff such as integration with Docker and public papers about Bosque.

> **Important note**
>
> As of this writing, the Bosque language documentation available at GitHub is not fully up to date. Also, some other docs found in the repo may be a little bit outdated.

The last and most important directory is the `impl` one. Here you can find the Bosque source code. Let's have a quick look at its content.

The impl directory

Inside this folder, there are files responsible for transpiling the source code and the source itself. As you probably remember, Bosque is written entirely in TypeScript. This is why you need to run the build process before you will be able to use it. It's been described in *Chapter 2, Configuring Bosque Environment*.

At this point, you may also be wondering if it's planned to bootstrap Bosque with Bosque itself so that we wouldn't have to install all of these additional dependencies. In case you don't know what bootstrapping is – it is the concept of creating a compiler written in the language that it's meant to compile. An initial version of the compiler is created using a different language. Then, successively, a full version of the compiler is produced using the initial language. That way, we can have a compiler for Java written in Java, or a compiler for C written in C. However, as of this writing, it is not known whether Bosque has such plans or not. It will probably take a while since at this point the changes in syntax are still possible so I don't think we should expect to see any form of bootstrapping before the syntax is finished.

Without further ado, let's jump into the src folder, which is the most interesting one.

In the src directory, there are quite a few folders that contain .ts and .bsq files inside. As of this writing, this is how it looks:

Figure AA.1 – Source code directory structure

The first one – ast – contains files that are responsible for creating and analyzing the AST. You can find files such as body.ts and parser.ts that are responsible for representing every language construct and validating the syntax. If you want to know how exactly the Bosque syntax is validated – this is the directory to look in for an answer.

The next one, called compiler, contains a whole bunch of files with the mir_ prefix. This prefix stands for **Microsoft Intermediate Representation** if you are curious (I was!). These files are responsible for generating something called **MIR Assembly**, which is a structure that contains the whole program cut into atomic operations that are represented by TypeScript objects. This structure is then processed by the ExeGen tool, which uses it to generate the executable binary.

The core directory is full of .bsq files that are core language constructs and types. There are three subdirectories with almost identical files inside – cpp, symbolic, and verify. The second and third ones are used for running symbolic tests and verifying the language itself. The cpp one contains files that are also used by the ExeGen tool for generating the executable binary. These files are pretty much like header files in C++.

The runtimes directory is also very important as it contains the code responsible for tools such as ExeGen or SymTest that you got familiar with in earlier chapters. It also contains the vscmd folder where you can find files responsible for the proper working of the VS Code plugin for Bosque syntax. In my opinion, the most interesting thing here is the exegen folder as it contains the source code of the tool that generates an executable binary out of the aforementioned MIR Assembly. This is where the TypeScript representation is transformed into C++ files and gets compiled using the compiler of your choice (Clang by default).

Inside the `test` directory, you will find test files that are run during the language tests. Their usability is pretty straightforward I think.

In the `tooling` directory, you can find files responsible for generating the C++ code for the ExeGen tool as well as SMT code for the SymTest tool – in the `aot` and `bmc` folders respectively.

The last one – `type_checker` – contains files that are responsible for validating the types in your Bosque code. While the syntax per se may be valid (when checked by the parser), there still can be problems with types. And this is what the `TypeChecker` is for. If you are looking for a place where the types are checked and validated – you just found it.

And this is all there is to say about the source code structure. Let's summarize it.

Summarizing the Bosque structure

At first, the structure may look complicated and not clear. However, after a second look, it starts to make sense. All of the key components are separated from each other so that you can easily find what you are looking for. We did not look at the source code itself as it would require a lot of time to understand it. However, I strongly recommend you have a look at it – just to see how it's done. You may notice that the code is not the clearest thing in the world and you need to pay a higher level of concentration to understand it, but there is nothing we can do about this. Bosque was started as a research project at Microsoft Research and then, after some time, was published on GitHub, so we can't blame the authors for not caring about readability too much – it wasn't their main goal.

Alright, you have some understanding of the project structure and you know how to navigate through the source code. Now let's see how you can report bugs and feature requests, as well as contribute to the project yourself.

Learning how to report bugs and feature requests

As mentioned before, all of the code base is shared on GitHub. If you are familiar with it, you probably know that you can open *issues* in order to ask any questions. As of this writing, the `Discussions` feature (newly added in May, 2020) is not enabled, so all of the conversations are held in the `Issues` tab.

So in case of any concern, you should go to the GitHub repository and open a new issue. Depending on your case, you can choose from a few pre-prepared issue templates. They help improve the quality of questions asked. Have a look at the following screenshot:

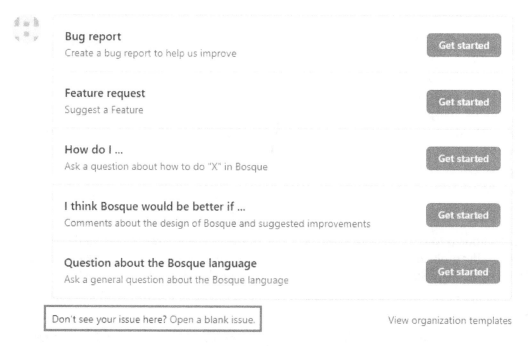

Figure AA.2 – Pre-prepared issue templates

So as you can see, you can pick one of the five templates that will help you ask a good question. If you don't see a template that would fit your needs, you can click the link below the list of templates as marked in the screenshot.

Basically, if you find any bug you should choose the **Bug report** template. However, since the language is new, you probably should double-check if the error you encounter is actually a bug in the language, or just the result of you using the wrong syntax. If you are not sure, you can choose the **How do I…** template to ask a question about the thing you are trying to achieve. If you feel that there are some missing features, you should go with the **Feature request** one. Or if you think that the design of Bosque needs to be discussed, you can choose the **I think Bosque would be better if…** template. The last one – **Question about the Bosque language** – is used to ask general questions about the language. In most cases, the last template should be used when no other option fits your concern.

Alright, you know how to report new issues but how do you actually make a change to the code? The answer is with **Pull Requests (PRs)**. Let's see how you can do it.

Learning how to contribute

Since the code is made public, you can browse it on your own and make changes on your local machine depending on your needs. There may come a time when a change that you made locally is good enough to be included in the main repo. In order to submit your changes, first you need to create a fork of the main Bosque repository. After that, you can make changes in the code and push them to the remote repository that you now own (it's your fork). If you want to merge your changes into the main repo, you have to create a new PR from your fork. After that, your changes will get reviewed and if they're good, the change will be accepted and merged into the main code base. The procedure is quite straightforward and I suppose you already know how to do it. If not, please refer to the official documentation about this at `https://docs.github.com/en/free-pro-team@latest/github/collaborating-with-issues-and-pull-requests/creating-a-pull-request-from-a-fork`.

Every PR is different and it is hard to give definitive guidelines on how to create a perfect one. However, there are some general rules that I'll share with you.

The first one is to keep PRs small and concrete. Try to limit the changes so that they solve one specific problem that you want to address. Avoid making changes in many files if that is not necessary because it will be hard to analyze your changes and decide whether they should be accepted or not.

Another piece of advice is to properly describe the reason for this PR and the changes that it introduces. It helps a lot since the description may give pointers on which changes are essential and why they are even necessary. A good description may even lead to the eventual closure of your PR as it will turn out to be unnecessary, or it is decided that the bug you are trying to fix should be fixed in another way. Don't be worried if that happens – you helped in addressing the root issue and it is much appreciated! An example of a good PR description may look like the one that I opened in order to fix a bug in the SymTest tool:

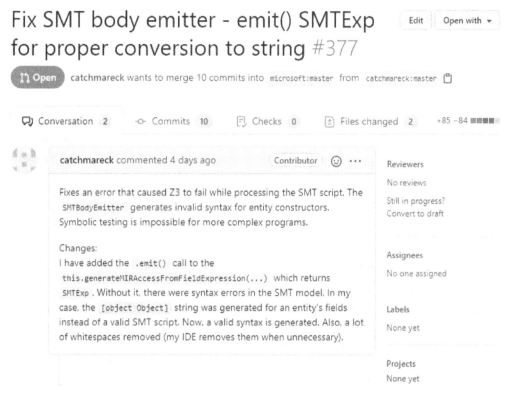

Figure AA.3 – Example PR description

So as you can see, I have explained what I intend to fix and then have described the changes that I made in relation to it.

The last piece of advice that I want to share with you is to properly title the PR. Try to keep it short and concise. At the same time, it should summarize the changes that you made so that it will be easy to know what you are suggesting to change.

Alright, that concludes the advanced topics that were introduced in this appendix. Let's summarize what you've learned.

Summary

I must admit, you have learned a lot of practical things in this appendix. Let's quickly go through the topics that we discussed.

The most important and interesting topic that you discovered is the process of designing a new programming language and the source code of Bosque. You have foundational knowledge of how to create a new programming language and how the Bosque language is designed, as well as its code structure. Thanks to this, you are now able to suggest your own changes.

Then, you learned how to report bugs and submit feature requests using GitHub Issues. You know what templates to use to ask certain questions.

You have also learned how to contribute to the Bosque project via PRs. You know what the general guidelines are for how to create a good PR so that it could easily be verified and accepted. This is essential knowledge if you want to see your changes in the main repository.

Now it's time for you to turn the theory you've learned here into practice, start playing with Bosque, and contribute. Who knows, maybe one day it will become a globally used programming language similar to other Microsoft languages such as TypeScript or C#. It would be nice to have your name in the contributors list, don't you think?

Questions

1. What is the difference between compiled and interpreted programming languages?
2. How does the parser differ from the type checker?
3. What is MIR Assembly in the Bosque project?

Further reading

Here is a list of useful resources that will enhance your knowledge about the topics discussed in this appendix:

- *How to Build a Programming Language, Part I*: `https://www.kidscodecs.com/build-a-programming-language-1/`

- *How to Build a Programming Language, Part II*: `https://www.kidscodecs.com/designing-programming-language-part-ii/`

- *I wrote a programming language. Here's how you can, too.*: https://www.freecodecamp.org/news/the-programming-language-pipeline-91d3f449c919/

- *Abstract syntax tree*: https://en.wikipedia.org/wiki/Abstract_syntax_tree

- *Working with forks*: https://docs.github.com/en/free-pro-team@latest/github/collaborating-with-issues-and-pull-requests/working-with-forks

- *Creating a pull request from a fork*: https://docs.github.com/en/free-pro-team@latest/github/collaborating-with-issues-and-pull-requests/creating-a-pull-request-from-a-fork

Appendix B
What's Next in Bosque?

Although Bosque is still an experiment, thanks to the creator's effort and the contributors' work, it has been possible to bring the language to the point where we can use it for real projects. However, today we are still limited due to several important features not yet implemented.

That is why *Appendix B* has been written – to invite you to explore the language's roadmap and discover what features will arrive in the first 1.x versions, through the following topics:

- Exploring the Bosque language roadmap
- What we should expect in the next versions

At the end of this appendix, you will be prepared for the arrival of new features, and will have enough information to be able to decide whether Bosque is the appropriate language for your next project.

Exploring the Bosque language roadmap

Currently, in the Bosque project, a branch has been created named `road_to_1_0`, which aims to host the contributions required to complete the first 1.x version of the language. For this, a roadmap has been drawn up containing the features that are expected to be included in this version, which we will review next.

Let's first look at some of the big changes and improvements coming:

- One of the most important improvements to come is a new verification module, so that type verification allows errors to be detected more clearly, enriching the reports.

- On the other hand, in order to enhance Bosque, the possibility of allowing a clean integration with Node.js has been proposed so that it is possible to have a parseable JSON object as a signature, channeling calls from JavaScript through an N-API module to a set of endpoints exposed using API types from a set of Bosque code files.

- Constant improvements are expected in the compilation process, such as the implementation of inlining in the IR or the common subexpression elimination.

- Some improvements to the GC are planned also.

Let's see some of the novelties that we can expect in the definition of the language and its syntax:

- In the same way as we currently have typed strings, we will have typed numbers to allow us to write more expressive code, for example: `let weight = 5.0_Pounds`.

- Improvements in the tuples and records to allow us to use tuples or records as key types.

- The implementation of literal template types is also expected.

- Improvements in type inference.

Finally, there is a series of unimplemented items marked as TODO, of which we can highlight the following:

- The project operation

- Virtual updates and virtual invariants

- Synthesis blocks

What we should expect in the next versions

As with any language in the middle of the development and experimentation process, some characteristics outlined in this book may eventually change in favor of further improvements to the language, so it is crucial to be attentive to the announcements of changes in the official repository of the project at `https://github.com/ microsoft/BosqueLanguage`.

Let's see some big proposals for the next versions that are not yet confirmed, but that have been mentioned in the project repository discussion threads:

- It is expected that there may be more official documentation, as currently this is scarce and forces the developer to explore the code to understand some of the language implementations.

- Eventually, it will be possible to package and import third-party libraries so that we can use more pre-designed solutions when building our applications.

- It is theorized that Bosque scripts can be transpiled into C code, which would open up a range of possibilities; for example, the ability to build N-APIs to interact with Node.js.

- The possibility of allowing transpilations of Bosque code to TypeScript has also been discussed.

- It is hoped to be able to have a package manager, although there are still many problems to be solved with this in order to make it a useful and efficient tool.

Summary

As you may have noticed, the Bosque project is continually changing. Many improvements are planned in the following versions. In this chapter, we reviewed the roadmap of the first version 1.x of Bosque. We have also dedicated some lines to taking a step toward the future and exploring the things we expect to see in the following versions of the language.

Packt.com

Subscribe to our online digital library for full access to over 7,000 books and videos, as well as industry leading tools to help you plan your personal development and advance your career. For more information, please visit our website.

Why subscribe?

- Spend less time learning and more time coding with practical eBooks and Videos from over 4,000 industry professionals

- Improve your learning with Skill Plans built especially for you

- Get a free eBook or video every month

- Fully searchable for easy access to vital information

- Copy and paste, print, and bookmark content

Did you know that Packt offers eBook versions of every book published, with PDF and ePub files available? You can upgrade to the eBook version at packt.com and as a print book customer, you are entitled to a discount on the eBook copy. Get in touch with us at customercare@packtpub.com for more details.

At www.packt.com, you can also read a collection of free technical articles, sign up for a range of free newsletters, and receive exclusive discounts and offers on Packt books and eBooks.

Other Books You May Enjoy

If you enjoyed this book, you may be interested in these other books by Packt:

Hands-On Functional Programming with TypeScript

Remo H. Jansen

ISBN: 9781788831437

- Understand the pros and cons of functional programming
- Delve into the principles, patterns, and best practices of functional and reactive programming
- Use lazy evaluation to improve the performance of applications
- Explore functional optics with Ramda
- Gain insights into category theory functional data structures such as Functors and Monads
- Use functions as values, so that they can be passed as arguments to other functions

Mastering JavaScript Functional Programming - Second Edition

Federico Kereki

ISBN: 9781839213069

- Simplify JavaScript coding using function composition, pipelining, chaining, and transducing
- Use declarative coding as opposed to imperative coding to write clean JavaScript code
- Create more reliable code with closures and immutable data
- Apply practical solutions to complex programming problems using recursion
- Improve your functional code using data types, type checking, and immutability
- Understand advanced functional programming concepts such as lenses and prisms for data access

Packt is searching for authors like you

If you're interested in becoming an author for Packt, please visit `authors.packtpub.com` and apply today. We have worked with thousands of developers and tech professionals, just like you, to help them share their insight with the global tech community. You can make a general application, apply for a specific hot topic that we are recruiting an author for, or submit your own idea.

Leave a review - let other readers know what you think

Please share your thoughts on this book with others by leaving a review on the site that you bought it from. If you purchased the book from Amazon, please leave us an honest review on this book's Amazon page. This is vital so that other potential readers can see and use your unbiased opinion to make purchasing decisions, we can understand what our customers think about our products, and our authors can see your feedback on the title that they have worked with Packt to create. It will only take a few minutes of your time, but is valuable to other potential customers, our authors, and Packt. Thank you!

Index

www.ingramcontent.com/pod-product-compliance
Lightning Source LLC
Chambersburg PA
CBHW062059050326
40690CB00016B/3148